Understanding early childhood

Understanding early childhood

Issues and controversies

Helen Penn

Open University Press

Open University Press
McGraw-Hill Education
McGraw-Hill House
Shoppenhangers Road
Maidenhead
Berkshire
England
SL6 2QL

email: enquiries@openup.co.uk
world wide web: www.openup.co.uk

and Two Penn Plaza, New York, NY 10121-2289, USA

First published 2005

A catalogue record of this book is available from the British Library

ISBN 0 335 21134 8 (pb)   0 335 21135 6 (hb)

Library of Congress Cataloging-in-Publication Data
CIP data applied for

Typeset by RefineCatch Limited, Bungay, Suffolk
Printed in the UK by Bell & Bain Ltd, Glasgow

Contents

Acknowledgements

Priscilla Alderson is Professor of Childhood Studies, Social Science Research Unit, Institute of Education, London University

Val Thurtle is Senior Lecturer in Community Health Care, Faculty of Health and Social Care, South Bank University.

Preface

When one considers how many facts – habits, beliefs – we take for granted in thinking or saying anything at all, how many notions, ethical, political, social, personal, go to the making of the outlook of a single person, however simple and unreflective, we begin to realize how very small a part of the total our sciences – not merely natural sciences, which work by generalizing at a high level of abstraction, but the humane, 'impressionistic' studies, history, biography, sociology, introspective psychology, the methods of the novelists, of the writers of memoirs, of students of affairs from every angle – are able to take in. And this is not a matter for surprise or regret; if we were aware of all that in principle we could be aware of we should swiftly be out of our minds.[1]

I have written this book as a result of teaching courses on child development to undergraduates taking early childhood courses at the University of East London. I am very grateful to my students for being so patient as I explored my ideas – and prejudices – with them. The students I have taught have been mostly mature entrants, non-traditional students many of whom come from ethnic minority backgrounds. This year several students are in their fifties. Many of the students hold down jobs. They are nursery nurses or special needs assistants or childminders. They work in schools, day nurseries, family centres, neighbourhood nurseries, playgroups, or in out-of-school clubs or special schools. Some have unrelated jobs as security guards, or sales assistants, in order to finance their studies. Some have set themselves the goal of becoming teachers, and the early childhood degree offers them a route into teaching. They all have had a great deal of practical experience to draw on, but for many, there is a yawning gap between their experience and the academic expectations of a university. All the time they are concerned about relevance, the relevance of what they study to what they do.

Moreover, in bringing up children all sorts of experiences matter, and 'scientific' understandings of childhood are only part of the story. As Isaiah Berlin's quote above suggests, there are many facets of human experience which might be relevant in understanding everyday life. As he also said (in his very long-winded way), if understanding is confined to scientific generalizations, it misses what is most important about everyday life.

> It [scientific understanding] must necessarily leave out of account that vast number of small, constantly altering, evanescent colours,

scents, sounds and psychical equivalents of these, the half-noticed, half-inferred, half gazed-at, half unconsciously absorbed minutiae of behaviour and thought and feeling which are at once too numerous, too complex, and too indiscriminable from one another to be identified, named, ordered, reordered, set forth in neutral scientific language. . . . [Yet] the more sensitively and sharply aware of them we are the more understanding and insight we are rightly said to possess.[2]

In this book I try to steer between two positions. I try to challenge some of the simplistic nostrums of policy and practice. I argue against the all-pervasive idea of 'ages and stages' or 'developmentally appropriate practice' that underwrites so much policy and practice in early years. At the same time, I recognize some of the important insights that have been gained by psychologists who study children directly. But I argue that child development is not enough. There is so much that it does not explain, and indeed cannot. Child development is problematical. It claims to be a science, but its scientific record is contradictory. It has not enabled us to make useful predictions about bringing up children, although it may have helped in treating highly specific disorders in children.

In this account of early childhood, I aim to take a wider perspective and show what other disciplines and topics might also be relevant in studying children. In particular, children live in many different contexts, now and in the past. I have become convinced – as have many others – that child development, in so far as it exists at all as an underpinning discipline for working with children, is too narrow and confining. For example, it simply does not have the scope or methodologies to take account of the majority of the world's children who live in poor countries. It cannot analyse the circumstances of their lives that are created by political and economic systems; and it ignores the relevance of these contexts. This distortion presents us with ethical as well as theoretical problems. It is important to know how children live in other countries, or how they lived at other times. People's expectations of children and childhood have been, and continue to be, very diverse, and the differences are worth exploring.

Every so often someone (re)discovers the brain and genetics. Perhaps these 'hard sciences' can help us make predictions where child development fails. Ideas about brain development and genetics have been used again and again over the past century in order to explain children's behaviour. We are told that true understanding is just around the next corner. Brain research has been promoted in the field of early childhood in an extraordinarily propagandist manner. The claims of some psychologists are breathtaking. *'We've learned more in the last 30 years about what babies and young children know than we did in the preceding 2,500 years.'*[3]

Genetics too is used to explain behaviour. We are on the verge, so the popular press declaims, of identifying all kinds of rogue genes that will explain good or bad behaviour, explain why we are fat, why we are thin, why we are brainy or why we commit crimes. Students of early childhood need to know the basis of these claims, if only to refute them.

This book, then, takes a broad perspective about the contexts in which children grow and change. It explores some of the ideas, micro and macro, which may be of relevance in thinking about children and childhood and in working with young children. It has also left a lot out. It contains very little economic analysis. Yet inside and outside of the family, ideas about what children are worth, how that worth is rated against other expenditure, and what kinds of proofs of worth are necessary, are crucial in any arguments made for more, or better, provision for children. The position of those who care for and educate young children, the support they offer in the home or out of it, also has a value within the economy. An economy of children and childcare would make a substantial book in its own right.

Nor have I included philosophy. The history and study of ideas is a basic curricular subject in every French child's education. Philosophy was the predecessor of psychology and of so many of the sciences. Logic and ethics are central to philosophical enquiry. Being able to think logically and discuss the ethical implications of what you do and say are at the heart of wisdom. In the Early Childhood Development Studies Degree course at the University of East London we did at least glance at (a cartoon of) Descartes. His famous statement, 'I think therefore I am', has echoed through the centuries, and has certainly influenced how we think about ourselves and our actions.

But as Isaiah Berlin comments, we have to draw the line somewhere or else we would go mad. In the last resort, books have to aim at coherence, even if it is a coherence that is imposed on a very incoherent reality.

Two colleagues have contributed to this book. Priscilla Alderson has written a chapter on the assumptions and impact of the child rights movement. She contrasts this with traditional approaches to child development. Val Thurtle has co-written the chapter on the study of young children from a health perspective. Both of these fields are important for students of early childhood.

This book was written in England and in South Africa. Inevitably, given its starting point, the book dwells more on the situation in the UK than elsewhere. However, I have been at pains to try to be international, and to locate my comments about the circumstances in the UK, Europe or North America in a much wider perspective than may usually be the case. English-speaking countries have notoriously poor provision for young children.[4] But in any case, the situation of children looks very different from the non-industrialized countries of the South.

Finally a word about referencing. This book is not so much an academic textbook as a book intended to stimulate discussion. So I have not put references in the text itself. If readers want to look up sources, all the names of authors mentioned can be found in the References section at the end of the book. In addition I have provided notes for each chapter that give precise details of quotations in the text, and any additional information about sources that cannot be found in the References section.

This book is dedicated to the students on my courses. 'It's a bit hard to follow you', they have sometimes said about my red herrings, my more obscure references, and my polemics. So thank you for keeping my feet on – or near – the ground. All of the students have made useful contributions, and their comments have shaped the book. But I owe special thanks to Veronica Burton, Dallas Davis, Ann Grisham, Karen Horsley, Cyrilla Jervier, Nina Kemp, Edna Usher, Sue Warren and Karen West for their lively and thoughtful comments. I hope they have been as rewarded having me as a teacher as I was by having them as students. I must also thank my colleague Carolyn Silberfeld who has put up with my endless digressions and excuses for tasks not done.

My grandson Mothibi Kekana and his best friend Desteni Malebubana Metsiny (Desi) have been a source of inspiration and a mine of information. They have drawn some of the chapter headings and illustrations. They worked very hard on them. The trade-off was that I played in the swimming pool with them. We both benefited from the deal.

Johannesburg, 2004

Notes

1   Berlin 1997: 15
2   Ibid.: 25
3   Gopnick *et al.* 1999: 3
4   See Bradbury and Jantti 1999.

1 Remembering Childhood

Around the hamlet cottages played many little children, too young to go to school. Every morning they were bundled into a piece of old shawl crossed on the chest and tied in a hard knot at the back, a slice of food was thrust into their hands and they were told to 'go play' whilst their mothers got on with the housework. In winter, their little limbs purple mottled with cold, they would stamp around playing horses or engines. In summer they would make mud pies in the dust, moistening them from their own most intimate water supply. If they fell down or hurt themselves in any way, they did not run indoors for comfort, for they know all they would get would be 'sarves ye right. You should've looked where you wer' a-goin!'

This is an extract from a well-known book by Flora Thompson, called *Lark Rise*. She was writing about her childhood in an Oxfordshire village in the 1880s. The childhood she describes sounds abusive to our modern sensibilities. But she did not think so.

They were like little foals turned out to grass and received about as much attention. They might, and often did, have running noses and chilblains on hands, feet and ear-tips; but they were hardly ever ill enough to have to stay indoors, and grew sturdy and strong, so the system must have suited them. 'Makes 'em hardy' their mothers said, and indeed hardy they became, just as the men and women and older boys and girls of the hamlet were hardy, in body and spirit.[1]

Literature is full of rich accounts of childhood. The Irish writer Frank O'Connor describes his childhood in a way that is so funny and charming, that you seem to catch a glimpse of a magical time when he thought the world should rearrange itself about him.

In the afternoon, at mother's request, father took me for a walk. . . . Father and I had quite different notions of a walk in town. He had no proper interest in trams, ships and horses, and the only thing that seemed to divert him was talking to fellows as old as himself. When I wanted to stop he simply went on, dragging me behind him by the hand; and when he wanted to stop I had no alternative but to do the same. I noticed that it seemed to be a sign that he wanted to stop for a long time he leaned against a wall. The second time I saw him do it, I got wild. He seemed to be settling himself forever. I pulled him by the coat and trousers, but unlike Mother, Father had an extraordinary capacity for amiable inattention. I sized him up and wondered, would I cry, but he seemed too remote to be annoyed even by that. Really, it was like going for a walk with a mountain! I had never met anyone so absorbed in himself as he seemed.[2]

There are also vivid accounts of non-western childhoods. Camara Laye wrote about his life as the child of the local goldsmith in a rural village in French West Africa. He was brought up in a compound always full of people, visitors, relatives and his fathers' apprentices. He describes his first impressions of school.

Once in school we went straight to our seats, boys and girls sitting side by side, our quarrels over; and, as soon as we had sat down, we became all ears and sat absolutely still, so that the teacher used to give his lessons in impressive silence. I should just like to have seen what would have happened if we had so much as stirred in our seats. Our teacher moved like quicksilver; he never remained long in the same place, he was here, there and everywhere. His flow of talk would have bewildered less attentive pupils. But we were remarkably attentive, and we found it no strain to be so. Young though we were, we all regarded our school work as something deadly serious. Everything we learned was strange and unexpected; it was as if we were learning about life on another planet; and we never grew tired of listening . . . an interruption was out of the question; it simply did not occur to us.[3]

Camara Laye admits later in his story that this attentiveness was under-written by corporal punishment. There were frequent beatings from teachers. There was also bullying by older pupils. But in his recollections, he said that learning was so precious to him and to his friends that they learnt despite, not because of, the threat of beatings. The physical punishment was cruel and unnecessary but endurable. 'Our love of knowledge had to be ineradicable to survive such ordeals.'

Some of these reminiscences about early life describe unimaginable childhoods such as that of the orphaned Russian writer Maxim Gorky; or the Serbo-Croat-Jewish writer Danilo Kis, who spent part of his childhood in a concentration camp; or Bessie Head, the South African writer abandoned by her white mother for being black; or the abused black American writer Maya Angelou. Their childhoods were so comfortless, so full of pain, hunger, despair and longing that you wonder how they ever survived and made good. Books about difficult childhoods have topped bestseller lists. Such books are popular perhaps because they are testimony to the resilience of the human spirit; they demonstrate that early experiences are survivable however extreme they may have been. They also illustrate the unpredictability of experience. In general, 'bad' childhoods harm children, and vice versa. But 'in general' is not the same as 'in particular'. On an individual basis it is almost impossible to make predictions about what kind of adult a child will become.

Yet there are lots of stories about childhood, by writers who think in some way their childhood critically shaped them. They trace the development of the person they are now by trying to remember and make sense of the past. Their narratives construct a continuity of self and experience. But are they useful in helping us – people who work with young children – understand a new generation of children? Childhoods are so very diverse and unique that, looking back, adults sometimes seem surprised at the person they have become. Can a gifted writer looking back truly describe the experiences of being a child, especially being a young child?

What is memory really like? Our memory is an essential – perhaps the most important – aspect of our self-identity. It ties our past to our present and enables us to imagine the future. Without it, you are unanchored, like someone with Alzheimer's disease. But where do childhood memories fit in to this construction of self? Is it only important things that we remember, those events that made us feel deeply at the time? Or do later events add a layer to those earliest memories, so that what we remember is an amalgam of many events, what we did, when we did it again, mixed up with what our parents told us we did? The Martinique writer Patrick Chamoiseau writes about this jumble of memory. 'Childhood is a treasure whose geography you never clearly reveal. In it you mix up eras and ages, laughter and the illusion of having laughed, places and sensations that weren't even born there.'[4]

How do you remember: in pictures, or in words, or by ideas or by a mixture of all three? The writer Vladimir Nabokov, in his autobiography *Speak Memory*, describes his memory of the process of consciousness:

> In probing my childhood I see the awakening of consciousness as a series of spaced flashes, with intervals between them gradually diminishing until bright blocks of perception are formed, affording memory a slippery hold.[5]

Children seem to remember things more vividly than do adults, and their memories are more often *eidetic*, that is photographic. But if we remembered everything with such vividness, we could not cope. We have to filter what we see and hear as we grow older. In experiments it is common to find children with photographic memory, but it is rare in adults. We lose it along the way. We learn instead what it is important to pay attention to and what not, which memories it is important to store and which we can forget. Steven Rose in his book *The Making of Memory* suggests that there are several kinds of memory besides eidetic memory. There is *procedural* memory, that is, remembering how to *do* things with our bodies, such as riding a bicycle or swimming. There is *declarative* memory – remembering what things are called, people's names, the titles of books, and so on. There is *episodic* memory, that is remembering the order of sequence of events in one's life. There are also other ways to categorize memories. Rose queries whether the brain deals with memory in different kinds of ways; different kinds of memory setting up different neural pathways. This is discussed further in Chapter 4.

Nonetheless, some psychologists think we do indeed remember most things, at least the important things, and that if we are helped to dig deep enough, we can retrieve those earliest memories. Others have argued that what babies and very young children experience is 'blooming, buzzing confusion'. A baby experiences life as chaotic, fragmented and disordered and she has to learn about the patterns and meanings of the events that happen, and latch onto the things which seem important, like the voice and smell and feel of the person who most often cares for her and feeds her. Even if babies see and hear much more than we once thought they did, and they very quickly begin to make sense of the 'blooming, buzzing confusion', how does such recognition turn itself into memory, especially if young children are con-tinually re-evaluating their experiences to try to make sense of them? Other psychologists would argue that very young children, at least, cannot possibly remember details from their early life, because they would not have had the cognitive capability to identify, classify, sort or retrieve those memories.

We all think we can remember some events from our childhoods. Writers such as Flora Thompson and Frank O'Connor may have very clear childhood memories, but they are also very good at embroidering and reordering their memories to turn them into an entertaining story. Can we use such stories as a source of information about childhood? Do we really learn in a straight-forward way from our own experiences, by analysing our memories of childhood? Can we, as adults, get an inside feel of what childhood is like for a child?

The systematic study of childhood

So far I have argued that there are many different ways of remembering child-hood. Our own and other people's memories of childhood are a powerful, if complicated, source of understanding. Memories are forceful but subjective; we have all lived through childhood but just how much can we generalize from our own childhood or that of someone else? But if not our own memor-ies, what other insights into childhood can we use? Is it possible, through systematic experimentation, to identify universal, age-related traits that all children have in common, and use these as the basis for developing a science of childhood? This, after all, is what psychologists claim to be doing. Can young children themselves describe clearly or accurately what they think and feel, or do we have to observe them and make informed guesses based on what we know about children in general? Psychologists claim that child devel-opment adds to personal expertise and understanding. 'A broad scientific framework can enrich [our] understanding of development, add intellectual excitement to the learning process, and guide the practical applications of our work.'[6]

Child development is the discipline that is commonly supposed to offer a systematic, objective and scientific study of childhood. A familiarity with 'the facts' of child development, so it is often argued, will help practitioners be more skilful and knowledgeable. But there are problems in understanding and interpreting the everyday world of children (or anyone else). These problems can be summarized as follows:

- universality versus particularity;
- continuity versus discontinuity;
- objectivity versus subjectivity;
- competing disciplinary frameworks;
- translating theory into practice.

These themes run through this book, each chapter considering them from a different angle. First, however, we take an overview of the different positions.

Universality versus particularity

What you feel about your own experiences is unique (although it is always good to find someone who seems to share your experiences). The world is also full of surprises. The Greek historian Herodotus in the 5th century BC wrote about the extraordinary twists and turns of life in different places, the sheer oddness and idiosyncrasy of each existence. Man is the victim of fortune, he thought, and human happiness never remains long in the same place. So, can the idea of 'ages and stages' be superimposed on the quirkiness of individual experiences and the luck of the draw?

The notions of 'child development' and 'ages and stages' are odd given the great variety of human life and experience. Biological changes such as rates and patterns of growth, skeletal, muscular and physiological development, can be measured and charted (although even these are not so straightforward as many manuals would have us believe). A doctor or a forensic scientist could give a reasonable estimate of someone's age by looking at their body or their bones. But social changes are another matter. Do living, thinking, feeling people really change in the same identifiable ways and at the same identifiable pace? And if children are changing very fast as they grow, does that mean we should not take their feelings or views seriously until they are older, and the rate of change has slowed down? Does it make a child more or less of a person, depending on which stage of life he or she has reached? If children are 'developing', what are they supposed to be developing into? At what point does a person's developmental stage become of less importance, compared with their rounded persona as an adult? We may talk of a typical 7-year-old, but can we talk of a typical 17-, 27-, 37-, 47- or 57-year-old?

Young children do change a great deal, and they change rapidly. This rapid pace of change means that our assumptions about what a child can or cannot do might quickly become inappropriate. We would not expect a 2-year-old to pronounce perfectly grammatical sentences, but we would expect an 8-year-old not to use babytalk. People, especially people working with young children, may feel in need of some guidelines about what kinds of behaviour to expect. The findings of child development can be used as a basis for such advice. The difficulty is that values and beliefs about bringing children up are not constant; they vary enormously over time and in different places.

For example, the education given to well-to-do children, girls as well as boys, in Tudor times makes amazing reading; a de luxe Renaissance education expected and routinely achieved the most prodigious accomplishments in children. Edward VI (the son of Henry VIII) by the age of 11 was writing, in French, a substantial treatise on papal supremacy – in exquisite italic handwriting. Elizabeth I, Edward's half-sister, was also extremely well educated, spoke several languages fluently and also had perfect handwriting. The historian Diarmaid MacCulloch has suggested that study of educational methods in Tudor times, best described as a system of apprenticeship to scholars, would reveal some extraordinary assumptions about children's ability to learn.

On the basis of these historical variations, another historian, Michael Zuckerman, argues that theories which suggest regular and predictable patterns of development hinder and obscure our understanding of childhood. Psychologists, in his view, spend too much time trying to simplify and to make generalizations from particular lives. They ignore the messy, contradictory realities of everyday life.

We can hardly do the most elementary empirical work, let alone the more theoretical exercise, if we do not address these questions of competing realities, or at least competing claims on reality.[7]

So one set of arguments concerning child development, or the uses it is put to in policy and practice, claim that it oversimplifies. It condenses all kinds of complexities into simple and straightforward patterns. Nicolas Rose has argued that the 'normal' child is in fact a curious mix of statistical averages and historically specific value judgements. The most striking aspect of the 'normal' child is how abnormal he or she is, since there is no such person in reality and never has been. The advantage of defining normality is that it is a device that enables those in control or in charge to define, classify and treat those who do not seem to fit in.

Continuity versus discontinuity

The discussion at the beginning of this chapter was about memory. Is the child we dimly (or clearly) remember in ourselves the same as the person we are now? The eminent psychologist Jerome Bruner, in his book *Acts of Meaning*, argues that we are continually adapting and re-adapting our own personal stories to make sense of them, to make them hang together in a coherent narrative. Children, especially, try to make narrative sense of their experiences. Some children whose life at home and life at school are very different, for reasons of language or religion or social class, try very hard to fit these different experiences together to make sense. We make narrative patterns out of our experiences vertically (over time) and horizontally (over place). No wonder, in the highly mobile, very diverse societies of the developed world we have some difficulty in establishing a solid sense of self. The sociologist Ulrich Beck has described contemporary society as 'risk society'. Traditional boundaries and constraints have broken down, and people's life trajectories are not tied to those of their parents. Each individual young person 'must therefore learn, on pain of permanent disadvantage, to conceive of himself or herself as the centre of action, as the planning office with respect to his/her own biography, abilities, orientations, relationships and so on.'[8]

Children, then, are actively creating their own (dis)continuities. So does it make sense, in the face of this complex, creative process, to adopt ages and stages as a framework for understanding children? The psychologist Piaget hypothesized that there are logical stages in learning to think. He put forward the ideas of 'accommodation' (getting used to new ideas) and 'assimilation' (making these ideas part of thinking) as a way of understanding the changes from one stage of thinking to another. His concept of stages of thinking has been widely extended to explain the development and progression of many other kinds of behaviour. Piaget made a very good job of trying to define thinking processes, although his work is now dated. But defining the stages of any kind of learning or behaviour in a watertight way, and then explaining how children progress from one stage to another, is extremely tricky. Just how tricky is explored in Chapter 3.

Objectivity versus subjectivity

Another theme is the idea of 'objectivity'. Could a more scientific approach, using the rigorous experimental methods of the 'hard' sciences such as physics, help us understand children better? Are precise measurements and observations and clever experiments more 'accurate' than our own 'common-sense' memories and understandings? Most textbooks argue that such methodologies provide a degree of objectivity. They can and should be used to analyse behaviour. Such methods, they claim, enable researchers to stand aside from their own assumptions and prejudices in order to minutely record the events and experiences of childhood. These questions about scientific methodologies are discussed in Chapter 2.

Some of the fears about making people in general, and children in particular, the object of scientific scrutiny concern manipulation and disregard of feelings. Observations and experiments concerning children may be carried out in a very kindly way, but they raise questions about the autonomy of the child. Can you observe what a child does without enquiring into what he or she feels and thinks? And can you guess what he or she feels or thinks if they do not choose to or cannot tell you? Is it even important to know about feelings when investigating behavioural change or highly specific aspects of cognitive development? Can you ignore your own feelings if you are the experimenter or observer, observing children behave or perform in certain ways? An adult taking part in a research project – or even being observed by an inspector in a classroom – might be very critical of the person who is judging her behaviour. Are children oblivious to it?

Many experiments using children as subjects are conducted 'objectively'. The investigator may be very kind to the children taking part in the experiment, but the feelings and thoughts of the children themselves are regarded as being unreliable, hard to establish, or irrelevant. The investigator also rules out his own feelings as any part of the experiment. What matters most in a scientifically conducted experiment is how carefully the experiment has been set up, how meticulously the procedures have been followed, how much data there is, and how accurately the data is being measured. Much of the information about child development comes from experimental data. At least one critic, Erica Burman, says that the overwhelming majority of psychological research on very young children is concerned with methodology rather than with actual events, precisely because it is so difficult to measure very young children's behaviour.

Observation is the most familiar method for carers and teachers trying to familiarize themselves with children's capabilities and preferences. It is, perhaps, a way of getting around the fact that young children are often not very articulate about what they are doing. To make sense of their behaviour you have to watch them for some time, to tease out their intentions and estimate their capabilities. But observation is a method that also has its pitfalls. It is difficult as a practitioner to observe a child in a nursery or other childcare setting without prior expectations about what the child should be doing. In English nurseries much observation is designed to assess children's performance, for instance in the key areas of the foundation stage of education, that is, seeking proof that the regime of the nursery is working. In addition, observation may be perceived by children as surveillance. Corsaro has suggested that one way to observe children – at least as a researcher if not as a teacher – is to take the role of 'least adult'. This means trying to be a friend of the children involved, to act as a very large boy or girl in the peer group. Not surprisingly, it is a method that has not caught on.

Scientists consider that it is important to have data that is collected in as neutral and as reliable a way as possible. Other scientists or researchers can then check the results by repeating the experiment, and they should get exactly the same results when they do. There are many debates about scientific methodologies. The metaphor of science as an unstoppable march towards more detailed information and more accurate prediction of the world in all its aspects has been vigorously questioned. Scientists have been described as belonging to an exclusive club, where all the members share the same paradigms and discourses; that is, they have ideas and assumptions in common, they check them out only with one another, and are very unsympathetic to anyone outside the club who introduces new paradigms or discourses. Science, too, has its fads and fancies, its blind alleys, its grand theories that get superseded by other grand theories, its overenthusiastic and intrusive methods.

Scientific methodology has its roots in physics, chemistry and mathematics. No one denies that the progress of mankind in many ways is dependent on the progress of science, but there have also been plenty of mistakes on the way. There have been mistakes in understanding the factual evidence and, as importantly, mistakes in ethics; the problems about applying new evidence and facts. The genetic manipulation discussed in Chapter 5 is a case in point. Can scientific methods, and the positivist assumptions behind them (that is, that science will eventually reveal all), be transferred easily and directly to the human sciences, especially to the study of childhood?

In the field of early childhood there are certainly ups and downs, and reversals of 'scientific understanding' about childhood. Christina Hardyment has written about the history of advice manuals for parents on bringing up children. Many of these claim to draw on the latest 'scientific evidence' yet the advice they give invariably reflects the time at which they were written. It is possible to argue that in the field of child development, the theories of childhood tell you more about the theorist and his time and place than they do about childhood itself, since the behaviour of very young children is essentially ambiguous and unknowable. We inevitably impose our own constructions and interpretations on what we observe. How detached can you be in collecting evidence? This quotation from the psychologist Nicolas Tucker illustrates both the limitations and the ambitions of psychologists.

> The psychologist is usually working only within his own culture and time. With his nose pressed hard up against the evidence in this way, it is not surprising that broader trends in child development may escape his view, even if he could think of ways to measure them. . . . Nevertheless, accurate, intelligent observation of children is still the basis for a great deal that is known about them, and is particularly valuable if it produces ideas that can later be tested in more controlled situations. . . . Psychology is still far and away the best tool we have for understanding children.[9]

So how do we understand childhood, especially early childhood? What actually happens in these first few years? We know enormous changes take place, but how do we account for them? Who influences what? How can we investigate and explain these changes? Can we use them to inform practice in caring for and educating young children?

The arguments about how to apply science to the study of young children are essentially about the problems in measuring the complexity, diversity, unpredictability and irregularity of everyday events; events which are being not only observed but actively experienced by those being observed. The educationalist Carol Fitz-Gibbon said of education that, 'in all but the most simple systems, there is complexity beyond the reach of most theories and predictions'.[10] She argued that such complexity can only ever be gradually and partially unpicked, but we should start on the job by using rigorous investigative scientific methodologies. The sustainability of this argument is explored in Chapter 2.

Competing disciplinary frameworks

A third theme to appear in this book concerns disciplinary frameworks. Which ones are most appropriate for the study of young children? Child development may be regarded as a crucial topic for those studying to become teachers or carers of young children, because it focuses exclusively on children. But there are other important sciences too – biology, physiology, genetics and neurosciences. There are also social sciences such as sociology, anthropology and history. Which sciences are most useful in understanding childhood? Where do we draw the line? Is the 'scientific' methodology different depending on which subject you study?

Each discipline operates within a particular set of paradigms or discourses (or ideas or assumptions) about what constitutes its foci and its boundaries. Erica Burman, in her book *Deconstructing Developmental Psychology*, closely examines the paradigms of developmental psychology, that is the particular ideas or assumptions held by the scientific club of developmental psychologists. She argues that the studies of infancy are dominated by discussions of methodology, because it is so difficult to attribute intentionality to infant behaviour. In order to achieve results, these methodologies concentrate on what is measurable. They tend to suppress 'the indeterminate, ambiguous non-instrumental features of infant behaviour'.[11] For example, studies which show how babies repeat and echo their mother's facial expressions may leave out a great deal of data which is simply uninterpretable. Babies wrinkle their noses, flick their eyes or open and shut their mouths for no very obvious reasons. Erica Burman goes on to argue that the notion of the child at the heart of developmental psychology is one of dependency and inadequacy. A child may be very attractive – especially to its parents – but at bottom we fear that it is an aggressive and primitive being who needs to be shaped and educated.

Much research nowadays is interdisciplinary. There are many books – like this one – which argue that we have to try to map the edges and the overlaps between a series of disciplines in order to better understand childhood. Martin Richards argues that any theory of development should be 'epigenetic', that is, it should try to combine a range of understandings about development from the genetic to individual reflections on personal experience *and try to work out the connections between them*. He, too, argues that human activity is immensely complex. Any attempt to understand and explain it must take account of the effects of feedback and readjustment to feedback at many levels, genetic, physiological, psychological and social. '[Epigenetic theories] begin with a notion of a system in which there are multiple interconnections and which is hierarchically organized into multiple levels from societies through individuals to cells and their chemical constituents. Mutual influence is to be found at all levels.'[12] Nevertheless, he still thinks it is worth trying to find a psychological theory of everything.

Richards argues that whilst development processes continue across time, and like 'Time's Arrow' are unidirectional (you only get older and not younger), starting and end points are usually arbitrarily fixed. For instance, should you take a person's genetic inheritance into account in trying to understand their development? And if genetics is important, how far back do you try to trace the genes? Is the genetic information actually any use? The most well-known genes are 'faulty' genes that cause major disruption; genes that cause serious dysfunctioning such as Huntington's chorea can be traced across generations. However, as the genome project (see Chapter 4) shows, genes which show a clear association between behaviour and genetic make-up are unusual. In general, the hope of linking particular behaviours to particular genes is a vain one.

So where do you start? Genetic inheritance is still important, because it is one set of – always interrelated – factors which shape us. Similarly, where do we stop? Do people go on developing until they die? (Or perhaps even carry on after death, as the poet Dante suggested, moving through circles of purgatory until they reach heaven.) Many psychologists now talk of lifespan development rather than child development. How do we set the framework and draw the limits of what we call child development? When does a child stop being a child? It certainly varies from place to place. Even in the UK we contradict ourselves. A child may not vote; you are only old enough to vote at 18. But you can marry at 16, and be tried and imprisoned – like the children who killed James Bulger – before you are a teenager.

Richards ends his article by claiming that new and promising avenues of research lie in focusing on 'the diversity of cultures and of individual experiences of children. This work raises exciting new challenges which demand a new perspective.'[13] The sociology of childhood is a relatively new area of study which focuses on what it means to be a child in an adult-dominated and orientated society. It takes children's own views of their situation as an important source of evidence. Richards considers that this avenue of investigation will offer useful insights in understanding the phenomena of childhood, especially when linked with other disciplinary areas of study.

Translating theory into practice

There are many textbooks or handbooks for practitioners working with young children that try to distil a range of empirical and theoretical findings about child development into a set of handy prescriptions. The most well-known of these handbooks, *Developmentally Appropriate Practice*, is used all over the world. It is produced by the National Association for the Education of Young Children (NAEYC) in the USA. It is discussed in more detail in Chapter 9. There are many other practice handbooks. They reinterpret a range of evidence, mostly from child development, but also from genetics and the neurosciences, to inform practice with young children.

Often the evidence they use does not justify the extrapolation to everyday practice with young children. A leading example of this eager overuse of highly specific and limited findings is work on neurology. Even the most enthusiastic of neuroscientists admits there is no general theory of brain functioning. There are many diverse, highly complex and sometimes contradictory findings about different parts of the brain. But we are a long way from understanding how they add up or can explain or predict behaviour. Yet practitioners have been led to believe that these findings have great significance for practice. For instance, it has been claimed that reading books to a child before the age of 2 years stimulates neuron development and enhances the child's subsequent progress; yet there is *no direct evidence* which would support such a claim. The misuses of findings from the neurosciences and genetics are discussed in Chapter 4.

Popular magazines such as the UK *Nursery World* carry frequent articles that refer to child development. Consider this article, for instance, part of a series.

> Test your understanding of child development by following the pro-gress of Jasmine over the following months. Each column will note specific milestones and allow comparison of Jasmine, a healthy full-time baby, with developmental norms by way of demonstrating how individual growth rates vary among 'average' babies. Each column will include questions about important points in the development of a healthy infant.[14]

Hidden in this extract are a number of common assumptions: that normality can be measured as acceptable deviation from a statistical average; mental development is the same as physical development; and develop-ment can be compartmentalized into stages with identifiable signposts or markers.

Nicolas Rose has also suggested that in practice the function of psychology has been to sort out the sheep from the goats. It defines what is and what is not acceptable behaviour, and identifies those who deviate from it. In Rose's view, developmental psychology has been regarded as a popular and useful subject because it has enabled institutions – especially educational and childcare institutions – to compartmentalize children so as to manage and organize them better. There is some truth in this, although practitioners themselves might express it in a different way. They are more likely to say that knowing what to expect enables them to help, encourage and shape young children's behaviour and learning. How ideas translate into and shape practice, explicitly or implicitly, is another major theme of this book.

Students' memories of childhood

Individual childhoods are so specific and unique, and yet so much part of their time and place. Any explanations of child development must allow for this diversity and complexity of experience, as well as teasing out what children might have in common at different times and in different places. The many different circumstances of childhood in other countries, especially in countries of the developing world, are considered in Chapter 5. But even in a rich country like the UK, children's experiences are likely to be very different from one another. As a recent UNICEF report suggests, there are enormous differences between the experiences of children from rich and poor families.

In urban areas many nationalities come together, and many languages are spoken. Population mobility is much greater in urban areas – children move around much more with their families. There are also many refugee families, whose children are likely to have a very bad time. As Suzanne Hood has pointed out, refugee children have considerable difficulty in accessing even standard services such as education, let alone more specialized services.

I asked a group of early childhood students to explore their memories of childhood. What were the events that had stuck in their minds? How influential did they feel those early experiences had been on the way they thought and acted now? Below are some extracts from their replies.

> I was born in England but my parents originate from Pakistan. For the first three years of my life I was brought up in West Yorkshire. We lived in a small terraced two-bedroom house. The climate up there was very cold and it was an extremely hilly area. The town was exceedingly quiet and the people there had more of a quiet lifestyle. . . . At the age of 3 we moved into a three-bedroom house in London. . . . Everyone seemed very busy. It was very noisy. My religion, which is Islam, was practised by my mum but not as much by my dad. From a young age we were sent to the mosque to read the Quran, which Muslims hold to be a divine revelation. We also dressed in a certain way by wearing a headcovering called the *hijab* and not wearing revealing clothes. My parents set down the limits and told us what was right and wrong. As I got older I started to practise my religion more. My parents did not force it upon me; it was just something I felt I wanted to do. I thought if I was going to practise my religion I might as well do it properly.

> I remember my plastic doll, because I used to put it in my back and tie it with a wrapper. Myself and my sister, we used to play together, and we gave ourselves funny names like 'mum and dad' and 'fish-seller' and so on. We used to do cooking play, we went into grandmum's kitchen and pinched some of her cooking ingredients, then we went outside into the bush and plucked some vegetables for soup. Sometimes we ate the soup, sometimes not. I also remember feeding my grandmum's goat. Goats always like people who feed them. We had a cat. My grandmum used to say that a cat's back never touches the

ground. I always wanted to experiment. I will hold the cat's four legs, then I will try to get his back to touch the ground. But those cats are very clever. Their back never touched the floor, truly.

My father worked on the railway until I was 2 years old then he got a new job at Ford's. This meant we had to move so my dad could travel to work and my mother was near some of her own relations. My childhood was probably not that much different to many others yet still very distinctive to me. As a child I can always remember getting on well with my sibling yet that does not mean we did not argue, as I believe all children argue with their brothers and sisters. . . . My mother believed that a house was to be lived in and so we were always allowed to do pretty much what we wanted. She also believed that a child should not be sat in a corner in case it got dirty so we always made mud pies and dug up the garden.

I only have one brother, who is older than me. As children we would continuously argue over little things. Since I was born up to the age of about 3 or 4 years old, I remember living with my parents, grand-parents, brother, aunt, uncle and two cousins. I never got on really well with my youngest cousin because I can remember constantly arguing with her; even the smallest things that she would do really annoyed me. My cousins were staying with us because their parents went out to work, while my mum was at home taking care of them as well as my brother and myself. My cousins got a lot of attention from my grandmother but she did not pay attention to me. I always got the feeling she did not like me because she never showed any affection towards me. She was always taking good care of my brother and my cousins but she never took any interest in anything I did. I never really got on with my grandmother as a child, even to this day I do not get on with her. The reason for this is partly because my parents would tell me a story about the way she treated me as a child. When I was a baby, I would be lying on the floor, crying and instead of pick-ing me up, my grandmother would push me out of the way by using her leg. I think the reason for this was partly because there were too many girls in my grandmother's family.

Coming from a Sikh family, I found that I did not have a strict upbringing although both of my parents were from religious, strict upbringings. As a child I can remember playing with my neighbours children who were from Jamaica. This never affected my family in any way. My parents would often invite our opposite neighbour, who was an English family, for dinner; they would come to our birthday parties and any religious events. My parents would often go to the temple and pray and would also take part in helping the temple, to make food and to take it in turns to read the holy book. Although religion was not imposed on me as a child, there were times when I had to dress up in a traditional outfit for any religious events that were taking place in our local temple. This was to show respect towards the holy man and the temple and religion.

My three brothers' names were Ray, Gary and Mark. Ray and Mark were children from my mother's first marriage and Gary was from my father's first marriage. My three brothers shared a bedroom. Two in bunk beds, and Ray, the eldest of my brothers, slept in a separate bed. I spent most of my time playing inside as I wasn't allowed to play outside until the age of 8. I attended the WPA nursery. The one thing I remember most about the nursery is the glass of orange squash and the pink wafer biscuits we used to be given at break time. My favourite toy was Noah's ark. As a result my parents took us all to Windsor Safari Park when I was 4 years old. I really enjoyed it. The animals were not in cages but were roaming free in the park. It was like walking through the African jungle.

It was my nan who I have most memories of. She was a very warm and caring person; she lived down our road so she was someone I saw a lot. Every day in fact, she would take my sisters to school or pick us up. She was always on the go and loved cooking, especially fairy cakes. No one could cook cakes like my nan. . . . My nan always came shopping with us on Saturday morning. We would walk to Green Street and back again. I remember once when we were on our way home a couple asked the way to a place not far from where we were. Nan was explaining to one of them how to get there, mum was busy sorting one of us out (my sisters and I were always arguing) and the other person stole my mum's purse from the top of her bag. My nan was fuming; you should have heard her! She didn't swear that much normally, but she did that day.

Both of my parents worked, my dad worked at Rolls-Royce and my mum is a nurse. We lived in a two-bedroom house with no bathroom but we did have an outside toilet. I used to visit my aunt twice a week to have a bath and a hairwash. . . . All my friends' family worked in the factories, it was not just the men who worked there, you would find that their mums and daughters would be working in the typing pool. It was a close-knit community, as well as whole families working together, all social/fundraising events were to do with the factory, and even at Christmas time you would always have parties or pantomimes to go to. Everybody knew you and all your business. There was also a large military connection with the likes of grandparents who served in the war. . . . When I was young there were no fears of main roads or what sort of people were about. I played out in the middle of the road with my sisters and friends without any fear. Nobody played in the back gardens, it was the norm to play in the street and later on everyone had bikes and would go to the parks; you only came home when it was getting dark.

I was raised in a town called Abeokuta. I grew up in a big compound. Compound according to the dictionary simply means an enclosure round a house or factory. Therefore we have a set of people living in a compound and we are relatives. For example, my grandmums, sisters, stepfather, stepmother, stepsisters, great-great-grandchildren and so on. At my grandmother's there were only 15 children living together as a family. We played together, we ate together from one bowl. We only ate separately when we wanted to eat rice. We also showered in an open bathroom. We slept together on a mat in the big front room. . . .

We respect people that are older than us and we found it easy to live with people. If we want to greet an adult that is older than us, girls should lean down while boys should prostrate with their chest on the floor.

I have lived in a beautiful villa with a swimming pool. Thanks to God, my parents were able to afford to buy me all what a child wishes to have. The one thing my parents did not want to get me and this was a dog. In my religion, dogs are considered to be dirty animals and if they are indoors, angels do not enter. But when my father explained to me, I was convinced and I forgot about having a puppy.

When my sister Zineb was born I really enjoyed having a baby sister, but as she started getting older, I started to regret I had a younger sister. When we were both children, Zineb used to imitate all what I did and this really irritated me. My mother told me to take care of her and take her with me wherever I went. For example, whenever I was invited to a birthday party, my mother used to tell me to let my sister come with me, and if I said no, she would not let me go. . . . I hated it and I used to cry and cry and shout 'Why were you born!' My brother was born when I was 9 years old. My sister used to spend time playing with him so I felt that I started getting my freedom back. I never had any problems with my brother since he was a lot younger than me. Now that he is 10 years old, I feel that I am his mother. I have seen him grow each year and I believe that Hadj will never grow up in my eyes. He will always be the baby I used to take care of and kissed him on the lips.

There are recurrent themes in these accounts: significant adults; sparring with brothers, sisters, other relatives and friends; places and spaces; food; animals and possessions. In these memories the students try to locate themselves, define their freedoms and restrictions. But reading these accounts the overall impression is the extraordinary diversity and vividness of the memories. One of the questions which runs through this book is, can we do such diversity and self-insight justice in our understandings of early childhood? Does knowing about 'ages and stages of development' illuminate what these students thought or felt?

Because most of the research literature in child development records attempts to establish what is common in young children's behaviour, the issue of what is not common has been of less interest. Moreover, young children's autonomy, competence, interdependence and resistance have been continually underestimated or disregarded, since within the paradigm of child development, children are mostly regarded as immature adults, many steps and stages away from the meaningful, decision-making maturity of adulthood.

Summary

Child development, then, although it uniquely focuses on childhood, has lots of yawning gaps as a subject. It is a near-impossible task to separate out what factors may be universal and apply to all children and what factors are local and particular, and then to find foolproof methods of investigating them. It is difficult to reconcile subjectivity and objectivity, what you feel with what you observe in others. Keep in mind the question of why and how child development is relevant to working with children. Discussion about the methodologies and explanatory frameworks used to try to understand young children crop up in every chapter in this book.

The aim of this book is to explore different ways of investigating, writing about and understanding early childhood. It questions simple assumptions about early childhood as 'the foundation' for later life. It does not try to minimize the importance of early childhood, or the insights that have been gained in the field of child development. But it does try to step back and take a broad view of many of the assertions and assumptions about what children are and what they can do. There is an extraordinary wealth of material to draw upon, as some of the examples in this and following chapters suggest.

Main messages from this chapter

1   Read about childhood. Literature has a lot to say about it.
2   Don't deny your own experiences. They are relevant to the way in which you think about childhood.
3   You need to be an all-rounder to understand childhood. Child development is necessary but nowhere near sufficient as a basis for working with children.

What to read next

Read one of the autobiographical stories of childhood mentioned in this chapter.

Notes

1   Thompson 1939: 40
2   O'Connor 1963: 22
3   Laye 1959: 64
4   Chamoiseau 1999: 3
5   Nabokov 2000: 18
6   Cole and Cole 1996: Preface
7   Zuckerman 1993: 239
8   Beck 1992: 135
9   Tucker 1977: 35
10   Fitz-Gibbon 1996: 49
11   Burman 1994: 33
12   Richards 1998: 143
13   Ibid.: 145
14   *Nursery World*, 15 May 2000: 23

2 Researching Reality

The nature of research

When I first began to do research, after many years as a practitioner and policy maker, I thought research was a way of getting more detailed information about a subject, and relaying it to others as objectively as possible. The word 'research' is commonly used in this way. Journalists 'research' articles for the newspaper; students 'research' essays; planners 'research' an application to use a piece of land for building; MPs' assistants 'research' important political questions. Increasingly, the word 'research' is used to mean checking something out on the web. Research in this sense means obtaining a collection of facts that may be useful in order to present a particular point of view.

But research which is part of scientific activity is, unfortunately, not so straightforward. It is a problematic activity. It is tied to understandings about truth and bias, reality and resources. In the social sciences, especially, dealing with complex human activities, 'facts' are elusive. The famous American novelist William Faulkner wrote at the end of his life:

> Truth – that long clean clear simple undeviable unchallengeable straight shining line, on one side of which black is black and on the other white is white, has become an angle, a point of view.[1]

A sense of certainty about what is right is often confused with 'truth'. We cannot invent 'facts' but we can certainly report them wrongly, or interpret them wrongly. Often, people interpret and respond to events unpredictably. Good research has somehow to take account of as many different ways of looking at an event as possible, in order to try to understand it and make accurate predictions for the future. But if an event is complex to understand, then more time and more care are needed to investigate it thoroughly and unravel what is happening. And that usually – but not always – means more resources to carry out the investigation. Sometimes the words 'scholarly research' are used to indicate that a piece of research has been carried out with great care, and all the possible resources and references have been double-checked before coming to a conclusion.

The theories behind research

Facts and research cannot be separated from theory. Theories are the organizing ideas that bring a number of facts together, and suggest which facts are relevant and should be included and which are irrelevant and should be left out. 'Theory' is used in many senses, from a hypothesis or explanation about a limited set of data, to meta-theories or 'meta-narratives' which try to explain a whole range of events.

We also all hold many 'common-sense' theories about why events turn out the way they do. These common-sense theories are sometimes popularized versions of scientific theories. For example, one of the most powerful theories in child development in recent times has been the idea that very young children are exclusively or almost exclusively dependent on their mothers. I have an old poster of a mother rocking a cot, with the caption 'the hand that rocks the cradle rules the world'. This poster expresses the common-sense theory that mothers, above all, shape the way their children learn and behave. This theory, like most common-sense theories, has some truth in it. After the Second World War, when society needed to reorganize and find jobs for men returning from the armed forces and provide for evacuated children and war orphans, it became politically expedient for policy makers to stress how important mothering was. They seized on John Bowlby's theories of attachment and popularized them in many official publications (see Chapter 3).

Many programmes of research were set up to find out if children behaved better or worse, or learnt more or less, depending on the kind of maternal care they received. Much of this research appeared to suggest that children were better off at home with their mothers than in any other form of care. The theory behind these programmes of research was called 'attachment theory' and it gave a scientific voice to many people's worries about the position of women and children after the war. In turn, the theory was popularized through radio broadcasts and popular books and manuals. Many practitioners such as nursery nurses, teachers and social workers, felt, or came to believe, that the research backed up their own deeply felt ideas about what was best for young children. There were even programmes of research to find out why some women defied or denied their maternal instinct and left their children in order to go out to work.

It is only more recently, since the mid-1970s, as society has changed yet again and there has been more insistence on women's rights and equality, that this theory about maternal attachment has been subject to review.

Re-examining the research on mothering and daycare with the benefit of hindsight, much of it now seems to be narrow or biased, particularly in relation to sex or in relation to the variety of family and kinship arrangements across the world. As theories are replaced or modified, the 'facts' change along with them. So research and facts cannot easily be separated from the theories behind them, especially when the theories are implicit. An implicit theory is like a common-sense theory: one that is so widely known and shared that no one considers it necessary to explain or examine it.

Theories are at the heart of practice, planning and research. All thinking involves theories and it is not necessary to use academic texts about theories before using them. A mother may choose to stay at home and bring up her child without reading a single academic text on the matter. But because theories powerfully influence what the 'facts' are and how evidence is collected, analysed and used and understood, it is important to examine them. Theories that are implicit and taken for granted may not only confuse but they may also obscure new insights because they work unnoticed.

In the next chapter I discuss some of the theories, including attachment theory, which have been a powerful influence in early childhood. These theories are explicit theories about child development, and all have large bodies of research behind them. I use the remainder of this chapter to examine other kinds of theories about how knowledge is produced. Scientific researchers also hold theories, implicit as well as explicit, about how best to do their research and obtain the information they are seeking. They hold theories about the nature of reality and how scientists can describe and explain it. This chapter discusses the main types of theorizing about what constitutes facts and reality.

Theories about theorizing: positivism

Positivism is a view of scientific knowledge and research which can be described as follows:

- One view of the truth: indisputable, scientifically established evidence.
- Precise measurement using sophisticated technology.
- Logical, deductive reasoning from the evidence.
- A neutral observer/researcher.
- Detached, decontextualized data.
- Cumulative progress towards a better, more technologically advanced world.

Most of the theorizing in the physical sciences is what is called 'positivist'. It aims to discover general laws about relations between phenomena, particularly cause and effect. Then the discoveries are, if possible, put to practical use. Science is about changing the face of the world. Electronics, space travel and keyhole surgery, to name just a few recent scientific revolutions, have come about through scientific experimentation. Scientific knowledge is gained through experimentation and deductive reasoning. Experiments are designed to measure and explain associations and to test whether a law can be shown to hold good in a range of circumstances or whether it is disproved. As the facts are accumulated, so the body of scientific knowledge grows. A positivist approach is one that considers that only scientifically proven knowledge is 'true' and other kinds of knowledge or beliefs are less reliable.

A scientist gazing through a microscope symbolizes a positivist approach. The scientist is a neutral observer, separate from what he is observing; he does not influence it and it does not influence him. He is trying to examine intensely the tiniest part of a phenomenon isolated from its context, and what he sees is visible 'hard' data, which he can measure precisely, and then manipulate – and in today's world, perhaps make money out of it.

But the distinctions between observer and what is observed, detaching or removing a fraction of an object to put under a microscope, cannot work so well when it is other people who are being observed rather than inanimate objects. How do you detach bits of people and examine them? Can bits of a body – skin, eyes, toes – represent a person? Similarly, can bits of a child's behaviour – visually distinguishing between different shapes, recognizing a rhyme, showing attachment – be detached and investigated separately and out of context?

Positivism – examples from medical science

It may be helpful to think of parallel problems in medical science. In medicine, thinking about objectivity and subjectivity, and the relationship between mind and body, is a continuous and problematic issue. Is a positivist approach, which treats people as objects, and investigates specific bodily problems in isolation, the best one to use to cure illness? Such an approach has certainly produced spectacular results, for example in the field of micro-surgery. The body (or parts of the body) is sometimes treated as if the mind does not exist – what people think and feel and how they behave can be considered irrelevant when a doctor decides on treatment. There are many examples in medicine where various kinds of experimental trials indicate that treatment 'works' but the processes that are involved are not really understood. There is also always significant individual variation in response to the treatment. For example, there have been a number of research projects on pregnancy and delivery of babies which have investigated women's feelings of comfort and discomfort in the process, and the kinds of situations which make them feel better. A positivist, mechanical view would focus on technical issues and tend to see a woman as a (not very efficient) machine for giving birth. Of course one wants doctors to be well informed about diseases of pregnancy like eclampsia, and appropriate medical intervention saves lives, but nor should women be left feeling demoralized and dehumanized by the medicalization of childbirth – as many have been.

Another common example is high blood pressure. Doctors know how to measure high blood pressure and what drugs and treatment will lower it. They have found out about drug treatment through carefully controlled experiments using double-blind trials. These trials mean that patients who volunteer for the trial do not know which they are having, treatment drugs or a placebo, and neither do the doctors themselves know until after the trial has finished. Then the differences in blood pressure between those who received the drug and those who did not are measured. If drugs appear to work well in the trials then they can be used for treatment if there are no adverse effects. Yet despite the careful experimentation, and results which show in general that a drug works, doctors still know very little about what causes high blood pressure in a given individual, what the relationship is between stress and high blood pressure, and why individual patients react very differently to stress and to different kinds of treatment.

Pain is another familiar example of the problem of taking an exclusively positivist approach in medicine. Pain relief drugs have been refined through rigorous experiment and cautious insistence on firm experimental evidence such as double-blind trials. Aspirins, paracetamol, and all their chemical cousins have been carefully tested. Yet pain is a paradox, an intense personal sensation, it provides no direct, reliable evidence for the observer. Positivism's strength in precise observation can be a limitation where pain is being assessed. In order to understand pain better, doctors have to think in non-positivist ways, to accept patients' subjective views about what hurts, and see pain as more than physical, involving the mind as well as the body.

The reason that these medical examples are relevant and interesting is that they illustrate the conceptual and practical difficulties of separating the systems of the body that can be investigated by positivist scientific methods – that is, anatomy, physiology, endocrinology, neurochemistry and so on – with what goes on in the mind.

Positivism – measurement and measuring instruments

Sometimes positivist approaches are called 'quantitative' because they frequently (but not always) rely on large numbers of measurements in order to arrive at a conclusion. The historian Theodor Porter has written a history of quantification called *Trust in Numbers*. He argues that measurement is a kind of artificial language, a means of simplifying communication. Quantification is a means of simplifying and rearranging everyday realities into neutral, abstract terms, so the observer can (try to) be a neutral scientist.

> Quantification is a technology of distance. . . . Most crucially reliance on numbers and quantitative manipulation minimizes the need for intimate knowledge and personal trust.[2]

Paradoxically, in highly specialized sciences such as nuclear physics, the progress of science *is* based on knowledge and trust between experts; whereas newer sciences – such as developmental psychology – may feel obliged to stress quantification and measurement.

> In fields dominated by a relatively secure community, much of what we normally associate with a scientific mentality – such as insistence on objectivity, on the written word, on rigorous quantification – is to a surprising degree missing. Scientific knowledge is most likely to display conspicuously the trappings of science in fields with insecure borders, communities with persistent boundary problems.[3]

As pointed out in the previous chapter, Erica Burman suggests that developmental psychology has been driven by technological measurement. As well as all the observation and testing materials, researchers use increasingly sophisticated machinery. Young children's behaviour is very ambiguous, so it needs to be particularly carefully tracked to try to make sense of it; for example by using frame-by-frame analysis of video footage of young children's responses to particular stimuli which can then be computerized and compared across the sample and the slightest differences calibrated. Scanning machines to measure brain imaging are the latest in very complex technology to try to measure children's responses and assess their capabilities. (See Chapter 4.)

Sophisticated technology can in turn lead to new avenues of investigation. Another historian, Lisa Jardine, in her book *Ingenious Pursuits*, has shown how many of the important technological inventions in the seventeenth century grew out of, and in turn helped to develop, scientific thinking. Measurement and sophisticated measuring instruments are usually part of a positivist viewpoint. Closer and extremely detailed examination of a phenomenon, and very detailed measurements on instruments or measurement scales constructed especially for the purpose of quantifying the information, give more detailed and accurate results. Such technological progress has undoubtedly been essential to the progress of the hard sciences, and has led in turn to important new scientific discoveries. The question is whether it has been a similar spur to progress in the social sciences, or whether, as some writers claim, it has distorted understanding.

Positivism in child development

Much developmental psychology nowadays uses positivist methodologies. Almost all the leading academic journals in the field insist on the use of empirical scientific methods. Many psychologists consider that positivist scientific methods are essential to progress, and progress can only be judged by evidence gathered in this way. Hypotheses about minutiae of behaviour are put forward, these hypotheses are tested on children by measuring their behaviour in detail. If the data supports the hypothesis and the results are statistically significant, then the hypothesis holds good. Even psychologists such as Urie Bronfenbrenner who are known for their holistic approach to understanding young children, couch their arguments as a series of positivistic propositions which can be measured and must be proved or disproved.

Up to the 1980s a scientific approach usually meant laboratory-based investigations of children's learning and behaviour. Children came to a psychology laboratory and were presented with different kinds of stimuli, or asked to perform certain sorts of tasks, and their behaviour or responses were closely measured. More recently, journals have become more tolerant of investigations which take place in 'natural' surroundings such as home or school rather than in the laboratory, but these investigations must still meet standard positivist criteria. Often this is done by using measurement scales, such as the Early Childhood Environment Rating Scale (ECERS), which the investigator can apply in situ.

Positivistic medical and biological assumptions underpin much of the thinking about young children. A lot is known about children's biological growth patterns. There is an entire branch of medical science – paediatrics – which deals with children's growth and what affects it. Children mature biologically in predefined sequences that can be broken down into stages (even that is subject to considerable variation). It is commonly assumed that a child's behaviour also follows such patterns and sequences. Some psychologists consider that advances in fields such as genetics, biochemistry, physiology, neurosciences and evolutionary psychology will illustrate even more clearly how mind, brain and body are linked. These advances hold out the promise of being able to describe normal behaviour more accurately and to measure the deviance from it. These claims are explained further in Chapter 4.

Other psychologists, however, consider that it is a big – and unjustifiable – leap to assume that the development of a child's learning and other behaviours unrolls in parallel sequences to biological development. In this book I argue that it does not. Social and intellectual development appear to be of a different order from biological development, involving social interactions and interpretations of cultural life. Using exclusively positivist methods may not be the best way to investigate these differences.

Positivism is both a *way* of doing things – relying on experimental manipulation, deductive reasoning, quantitative approaches, high-tech measurements and neutral investigators – and a *belief* that by using such methods, we advance unequivocally and cumulatively towards understanding and truth.

Theories about theorizing: social constructionism/ naturalism

The difficulties of using positivist theories and methods in everyday life have led social scientists to try to find alternatives that do more justice to complexity and diversity. Naturalist or social constructionist theories contrast with positivist approaches in the following ways:

- Many views of the truth; knowledge not necessarily cumulative.
- Narratives or stories as a way of making meaning clearer, rather than more precise measurements.
- Differences of approach rather than cumulative knowledge.
- Contextualized data.
- Scepticism about progress.

A contrasting view to positivism is to believe that there is not an unequivocal view or truth, and that a range of views can be valid in different ways. Instead of being 'hard facts', phenomena are seen as more like parts of an ocean affected by winds, tides and currents, shifting lights and opaque depths. The novelist Isaac Bashevis Singer has provided a striking metaphor to describe truth. In his short story *A Crown of Feathers*, he ends by saying, 'Truth is as intricate and hidden as a crown of feathers.'

If you take a social constructionist approach there is no neutral, objective perspective, no scientist looking down the microscope or sitting behind the one-way screen in a laboratory. Instead, the observer/researcher takes the view of a questioning outsider. He also recognizes that he himself might have views and his views might colour what he sees; and that the people he investigates might in turn influence him.

Social constructionists believe the human world is different from the non-human world, and consider that positivist models reduce very complicated things and try to measure the unmeasurable. Instead, social constructionists emphasize the meanings which govern how people live and behave. People construct evidence through their own experience. What people say and think and feel, their reported intentions and motives, and the situations they find themselves in, are relevant to understanding their behaviour. The mind's organization of perceptions and emotions influences behaviour.

The social world cannot be understood in terms of cause and effect, or universal laws, or the stimulus–response models of positivism. Instead of trying to predict responses by external causes, social researchers examine the meanings and motives that guide people's behaviour, gradually seeking to describe and construct accounts of particular societies and the complexities of everyday life.

There are two kinds of naturalist or social construction theories: post-modernism and critical theory.

Postmodernism

Postmodernism is an extreme antipositivist viewpoint. Postmodernists are sceptical about what truth is, what counts as knowledge, and who can determine the validity or worth of any enterprise. Postmodernists consider that there are many different kinds of voices, many kinds of styles, and take care not to value or 'privilege' one set of values over another. Postmodernism has become fashionable. In architecture, for instance, a postmodern building is one that may include many different styles of architecture from different periods in history – Egyptian statues, Greek columns, Victorian windows and 'smart' high-tech security.

Although postmodernism has become an important theory in very diverse fields – philosophy, geography and architecture – it has so far had only a small (but increasing) influence in the field of child development. It implies paying particularly careful attention to the 'other', to someone who is different from yourself, in order to fully appreciate their point of view. There is a group of psychologists who call themselves 'the reconceptualizers'. One of the leaders of this group is Joseph Tobin, who first made his name with the publication of a study comparing nursery children in China, Japan and the USA. He pointed out that nursery workers and policy makers in each country had very different expectations of what children could or should be doing, of what was normal and what was 'off the wall'. Tobin came to the conclusion that

> early childhood educational research should be about the cutting edge of the emerging fields of gender studies, queer studies, post-colonialism and cultural studies. Suddenly the most avant garde of theorists are enthralled with the raw gender and power issues that are the everyday stuff of our work with young children. Shouldn't we be joining in with the exploration of these issues?[4]

Critics of postmodernism argue that the philosophy is too relative, that 'anything goes'. Because postmodernists are so concerned about every voice being heard, they are unable or unwilling to compare viewpoints or approaches or say that one is better than another. Critics such as Ann Oakley claim that 'the whole project of desiring to know in order to understand, predict, control and even change is dismissed.'[5]

When there are abuses of power, or gross unfairness, as is the case with the many millions of children who die unnecessarily in the developing world, postmodernism has difficulty in developing a critique or standpoint from which power or abuse can be judged (see Chapter 5 for a further discussion). As a postmodernist, can you say definitely that a particular situation is wrong? This is where psychology strays over the border into philosophy. The distinguished American philosopher Richard Rorty, in his book *Contingency, Irony and Solidarity*, argues that in any situation there will be different points of view and understandings, but that you have to discuss them and reach a consensus, and consensus is perhaps the best you can hope for.

Critical theory

Critical theory is similar to postmodernism in that it attempts to show how people make different but valid sense of their particular experiences. However, critical theory, which developed from sociology, sees society as a collection of many factions competing for power and resources. Instead of seeing deviants as a minority of outsiders, critical theorists show how large groups of people are constructed as inadequate or disabled through their circumstances, such as poverty, instead of through their own failings. Critical theory verges on postmodernism, but postmodernism does not share its radical politics.

In critical theory, science is sometimes defined as a social practice in which knowledge is produced. Those who produce knowledge also control how and when the knowledge is used – 'knowledge is power'. Scientists are a type of elite who have privileged access to information and may abuse their privileges to gain wealth or power.

This kind of critique may be useful in highlighting some of the limitations of conventional child development theory and practices. For example, critical theorists might argue that attachment theory had a political usefulness in keeping women at home when it was expedient to the economy to have them do so. Similarly, Jerome Kagan, the eminent Harvard psychologist, has argued that many of the targeted early intervention programmes in the USA (which, like the Sure Start programme in the UK, aim to help parents from poor areas to bring up their children better) are ways of avoiding confronting the inequalities of society.

> So many people believe in infant determinism [because] it ignores the power of social class membership. Though a child's social class is the best predictor of future vocation, academic accomplishments and psychiatric health, Americans wish to believe that their society is

open, egalitarian, without rigid class boundaries. To acknowledge the power of class is to question this ethical canon.[6]

Many students write in their essays, when they want to prove a point, 'research says that . . .'. As this section has tried to show, research is not neutral. It, too, has to be weighed up and located. Researchers have different ideas about what to investigate and how to go about it. The integrity of research cannot be taken for granted.

Quantitative and qualitative approaches

These differences amongst the different kinds of theories to acquiring knowledge are sometimes called quantitative and qualitative methods. Quantitative methods are mostly positivistic; qualitative methods are mostly social constructionist or non-positivistic. In practice, there is some overlap, and some borrowing. Table 2.1 suggests how qualitative and quantitative approaches might affect how research interviews are carried out.

Designing research

Michael Cole describes psychologists as having 'a toolkit of techniques' rather as doctors have medicine bags. In his view, the skill of a psychologist, like the skill of a doctor, is in selecting the most appropriate tools to investigate the job with which he or she is faced. Students need to understand what these 'tools' are, and many undergraduate courses on research try to do just that – introduce students to questionnaires, interviews, controlled experiments and so on. It is indeed useful to understand the repertoire of techniques that psychologists use to investigate and illuminate particular events in the lives of young children and how the children respond to them, and there are many textbooks which do so.

To an extent, everyone has to be pragmatic. It makes sense to know about a range of measuring scales, longitudinal studies, questionnaire techniques, experimental designs and statistical methods. All researchers have to select the most convenient tools and to operate within the time and money resources available. Yet as we have suggested, research involves much more than the selection of appropriate techniques of investigation. How can we take a tiny slice of someone else's reality and make sure we have truly represented their opinions or actions? How do we know if what we have discovered is true not only of the person(s) we have been investigating, but more generally? What checks and balances are there to make sure the research really does what it sets out to do?

Table 2.1 Comparison of quantitative and qualitative approaches **31**

Research aspect	Quantitative	Qualitative
Analytic categories treated differently	Categories are isolated and defined as precisely as possible before the research is undertaken. The research tests predetermined hypotheses	Categories are isolated and identified during the research, i.e. hypotheses come from the data
Different methods of data collection	E.g. predetermined series of questions asked in exactly the same way to each person, because of concerns about generalizability and reliability	E.g. in-depth interviews, more like a conversation. Interest in the insights into a person's views of the world
Sample size and design	More is better. Sample size and design are rigid and predecided. Sample constructed to be of the necessary type and size to be able to generalize to a wider population. Possible to take subgroup analysis	Less is more; 15 is an adequate sample size. Sample design is flexible and usually evolves as the research progresses. Aims to work longer and in greater depth with a few key informants, in order to understand how they view the world, what categories and meanings they have. Research concerned with insights, not numbers
Issues about the researcher	Attempts to minimize or even eradicate researcher interference	Recognizes that the research process can never be neutral. The researcher is a crucial part of the research process – an instrument in data collection. The interviewer cannot fulfil qualitative research objectives without using a broad range of own experience/imagination/ intellect. Recognizes the complexity of the relationship between the researcher and the informant and the potential power issues which may affect the interview

The four well-known and overlapping criteria for assessing research are usually summarized as follows:

- *Validity*. Questions about validity concern the accuracy of the research. Questions about validity might be: How carefully and accurately have the data been collected, analysed and reported? How closely do the findings represent the reality that was observed or experienced or recounted? Have the research methods influenced and altered people's observed behaviour or their accounts?
- *Reliability*. Questions about reliability concern the logic and transparency of the research. Is the analysis of the data logical, or does it contain any contradictions? Can other researchers understand how the research has been carried out and check the results? Does the interpretation of the data accord with common sense, or a 'reality check'?
- *Representativeness*. Questions about representativeness concern the typicality of the sample. Is it just an exceptional or unusual group of children who are being investigated or are they typical of all children? How well is the selection of the sample explained and justified?
- *Generalizability*. Questions about generalizability concern the way in which the findings can be generalized to other groups and contexts. For example, the famous Head Start programme in the USA is concerned mainly with very poor black and Latino children. There are doubts about the extent to which the findings from studies about Head Start have any relevance in other countries where the gap between rich and poor is less extreme than in the unequal USA.

All these questions about validity, reliability, representativeness and generalizability can be further explored. Whilst they are a useful rule of thumb for judging research, they beg the wider questions of what is acceptable science, and whether developmental psychology is amenable to the positivistic scientific methods of traditional hard sciences.

Evidence-based policy and practice

> If social science is something different from science, how can we be sure about its difference from fiction?[7]

All government policy is an intervention in the lives of its citizens. Politicians believe that certain courses of action will lead to certain positive results (and to their re-election). In the UK, the government has introduced literacy and numeracy hours in schools, child tax credits, regular inspections, NVQs, Sure

Start – a string of reforms that it believes will bring about 'better' early education and care. How do we know any of these work in the very basic sense that they do more good than harm? Do we take politicians' words for granted? How do we know that any apparent effects of these interventions are not just due to chance? How should the interventions be judged?

Randomized controlled trials

In medicine, because the risk of so many interventions is a life or death risk, it is vital to know how well drugs or operations or any other medical intervention works. The most rigorous method for testing a medical intervention (or cure) is called a randomized controlled trial (RCT). A group of people are *randomly* divided into two smaller groups; one group gets the treatment – for example a tablet containing the new medication – the other group gets a placebo, a tablet which looks like medicine but is harmless. The groups are more or less the same – they have been selected randomly – so if those in the group taking the real medicine become healthier than those taking the placebo, the difference is almost certainly due to the medical intervention. If, however, the groups are still the same after the experiment, and no one group is healthier than the other, then the medicine is ineffective. Usually these RCTs are carried out with very large samples.

Some researchers have tried to use RCTs to measure the effectiveness of childcare. Most of these experiments have been carried out in the USA. One famous RCT, known as the Abecedarian project, was carried out in North Carolina. Two groups of children were randomly selected. One group received full-time childcare and the other received only home visiting. At age 6, the cognitive and social development of the children who received full-time childcare was compared with that of the group that got only home visiting. In this RCT, the children who got full-time childcare did better than those who got only home visiting.[8] The children were followed up into adulthood, to see if there was any long-lasting difference between the groups that could be explained by the initial childcare intervention, but the effects petered out.

Another RCT, carried out by Weikart and his colleagues in Ypsilanti, explored the long-term effects of early education (but not care). Weikart claimed that the groups continued to show a difference into adolescence and beyond. The group that had received the intervention were more likely to be in employment and less likely to be in trouble with the law. Weikart's RCT is the *only* source for all the claims that one dollar spent when a child is young saves seven dollars later on, and he was working in circumstances that are not generalizable outside of the USA.[9]

Systematic reviews

Systematic reviews, another type of RCT, also have drawbacks as a source of evidence. They may draw on very particular samples – like the American studies which only investigated children from multi-problem families. They might use different measures of cognitive and social development. For example, a teacher's rating of school readiness might give you a different result from a measure using an IQ test. Some of the RCTs may include qualitative evidence; others will accept only quantitative evidence.

In medicine, there is now a system of systematic reviews called the Cochrane collaboration. A group of researchers get together using the systematic review technique and compare all the evidence on a particular topic, across different studies. They look at how similar the samples were across studies, whether people were recruited into the study ethically or whether they were tricked into doing it; the length of time of the intervention; the validity of the tests to measure efficacy, and so on.

The Department for Education and Skills (DfES) in England has now funded an attempt to develop a systematic review technique for education. It is based at the Social Science Research Unit at the London Institute of Education and called the Evidence-based Policy and Practice Information Centre (EPPI). So far there are twelve systematic review groups, one of which is on early years. For its first systematic review the early years group examined the research on the integration of care and education across the world. When the group focused on research on integration, it found that many of the studies had flaws. For example, it is not possible to compare integrated settings unless the type of education and the hours of care are stated – otherwise you cannot compare like with like. It was amazing how few of the studies that claimed to be dealing with integration managed to say how long children were looked after – most studies, even some very well-known ones, did not get past the starting point. Then it proved impossible to compare the American studies of very disadvantaged children with studies from other countries where there were far fewer disadvantaged children and where nurseries were much more socially mixed. In the end the review revealed how bad a lot of research is in the field of early years. Research does not have to be quantitative but it does need to be well set out, logical and well reported in order to be worthwhile.

One of the principles of the systematic reviews is that they are transparent and their findings are more readily available.[10] Another principle is that the research findings should be made easily accessible – so each review has a layperson's guide, written by a non-researcher, attached to it. The web has made it possible to access research in a way that was previously impossible. Most research starts out being reported in academic journals. There are so many of them – more than 50 in English covering early childhood – that unless you have access to a good university library, it is not easy to check them out, and even then it is hard work. Now many research findings are web-based, so it is easier to be better informed.

The systematic reviews are an attempt to check out policy making. If policy makers claim that a particular policy is working, then how do we know? What does the evidence look like?

Summary

This chapter has explored some ideas about research. It has looked at some of the assumptions that underpin research. There are lots of ways to investigate a topic and the methods that researchers choose to reflect their theoretical approach. But the methods themselves have also to be well-thought-out and carefully described. The mere fact of doing research is not enough; it has to be good research: valid, reliable, representative and generalizable.

Main messages from this chapter

1   If you do not want to drive your tutor up the wall, do *not* call looking things up on the web 'research'. Research is a complicated process of testing out ideas in a systematic way.
2   Never take research for granted, or think that it is beyond reproach. Never say 'research says'. Researchers use different methods to test out their ideas. Researchers are not always good at reporting what they have done. Find out what their method has been, and see if you agree with it. Be critical in how you describe research.
3   Methodology is (surprisingly) exciting. The methods researchers use can make all the difference to what they want to find out. Good questions can be spoilt by bad methods. Clever ways of investigating are worth knowing about.
4   Keep reading. It is important to be up to date about research.

What to read next

Oakley, A. (2000) *Experiments in Knowing: Gender and Method in the Social Sciences.* Cambridge: Polity Press.

Notes

1   Faulkner 1965: 32
2   Porter 1995: viii
3   Porter 1995: 230
4   Tobin *et al.* 1998: 232
5   Oakley 2000: 41
6   Kagan 1998: 147
7   Oakley 2000: 120
8   Ramey and Campbell 1991
9   Weikart 1996
10   The EPPI reviews are on the web at www.eppi.ioe.ac.uk

3 Not Piaget Again

This chapter takes an overview of theories in child development. A number of recent books and articles have expressed concern about the idea of development itself.

First of all, development is assumed to be holistic in the sense that physical, cognitive, emotional and social development are all interrelated and interact with one another. They undoubtedly do. But these categories are themselves artefacts. They are ways of conceptually carving up the changes that take place as young children grow. These categories are being challenged, not least by psychologists and others working outside of Europe and America.

Secondly, development is taken to imply a steady, predictable progress from babyhood to adulthood, with recognizable milestones on the way. But development is characterized by considerable plasticity. There is an enormous margin of adaptation and adjustment to life experiences. The changes that come with age are more typically uneven and patchy in any individual.

Thirdly, development is assumed to be continual and cumulative. Early experiences lay the ground for later ones. Again this is clearly partly true. There are critical periods – for example in the womb or in early infancy – when good nutrition is extremely important for later development. Language acquisition appears to be critically timed. But early experience may be overemphasized. Good schooling may make an enormous difference; so might a good income for someone who has hitherto been very poor. Just because children – people – are so very adaptable, change is possible in all kinds of ways at all ages. In fact there is an enormous self-help industry which proclaims just that – it is never too late to change.

Fourthly, the pace, extent and recognition of the changes of growth and development depend partly on where you grow up. Development cannot be understood outside of a historical and cultural context. Being poor in Mali, or even in Britain, is a different life experience from being rich in America. Most of the children who have been studied by psychologists live in North America or Europe. So studies in other parts of the world that explore children's development, and, more importantly, the ideas that are used to describe and explain development, are very important to right this imbalance.

'Development' is sometimes taken to mean that children are worth less than adults, and their views and concerns are of less importance. Development is synonymous with being a minor. But children, even very young children, demonstrate enormous competences and strong feelings. Relationships between adults and children are invariably unequal; adults are more powerful. Sociologists of childhood such as Berry Mayall, Alan Prout and Alison James have been arguing that these power relationships require more analysis. Indeed, a major governmental research programme in the UK, led by the Economic and Social Research Council (ESRC), called the ESRC Children from 5 to 15 Programme, has been devoted to exploring them.

All these positions are explored in other chapters in the book, as well as in this chapter. They are summarized here as a backdrop and as a reminder of both what child development aims to do and how it falls short.

On the whole, practitioners and policy makers have extracted from and simplified the diverse field of child development to suit their own needs (and without taking much account of the different research perspectives). Yet child development obviously contains some important insights because it is a branch of psychology that focuses on children. A large section of it is concerned with very young children, because that is where the greatest puzzles are. The transformation of babies into children who have sophisticated repertoires of language and behaviour is an everyday miracle. Tracking the miracle gives rise to all kinds of philosophical and ethical issues. Some of the chapters in this book have tried to discuss those issues, but this chapter is more pragmatic. It gives a very brief description of major theorists or schools or theoretical groupings in child development. It also discusses the work of some researchers who have not produced grand theories, but whose work has been important in refocusing ideas in child development.

In child development, ideas change, sometimes rapidly. As in any science, ideas stack up and then get overturned. The ideas that seemed to be lost may return later, slightly changed or disguised. Psychological theories borrow from one another and at the same time psychologists disagree with one another; or they may work in 'silos'; that is they work so separately from one another that they never take account of what is happening outside of their own speciality.

In human sciences, for the reasons discussed in the previous two chapters, it is difficult – or impossible – to provide a coherent theory that deals with all the psychological aspects of human life. No theory has yet managed to get anywhere near the rich mixture of psychological attributes that make up human life – feelings and memories; physical energy and sensual responses to the natural world; learning and creativity; sociability, conviviality and talk. Child development research has provided great insights into the lives of young children, but its findings are not fixed, and it has many subdivisions. It does

not offer a magic potion which we have only to swallow in order to understand children. It is more like a large indigestible lump with lots of gristle.

There is also a time-lag factor. It often takes a long time for theories to
become popularized, and by the time they become well known, science has
moved on. Practitioners and policy makers used to find it hard to keep up with
academic knowledge; the books and journals they needed were not readily
available. It is much easier now for those with access to the web to become
familiar with the debates, disputes and changes that are taking place. But
access to the web is exaggerated, and in poorer countries it is fairly limited.
Consequently, many practitioners who have studied child development are
stuck in the time-warp of their initial training. It has been hard to do
otherwise.

The theories of child development offer signposts to different routes to
understanding young children. This chapter gives a brief account of some of
the signposts. One route goes in the direction of children as learners and
thinkers. Another route leads to feelings; how children try – with or without
adult help – to tame their powerful emotions. A third route is socio-cultural;
how children are shaped or socialized by the community or society in which
they grow up. A fourth concerns language, the most complex and important
skill that we acquire.

There are so many contradictions and paradoxes that, for all the signposts,
you end up in a maze. It prompted one famous psychologist, Jerome Kagan, to
say that children were like nothing so much as a rubber band, stretching into
any shape. For instance, children are 'meaning-makers' but they can only take
their meanings from or test them on other people. Children are highly individualistic (at least in some societies) but they must learn to live with and
through others. Children are highly creative and expressive, but they have to
learn to express their creativity – in music, dancing, storytelling, painting or
whatever – by consistent practice. The paradoxes are many.

The chapter is divided into four sections: learning and thinking; learning
in context; emotions and feelings; and language. Child development as a discipline is about much more than this, of course. The chapter is intended to
provide a short introduction to some of the main debates about understanding
young children.

Learning and thinking

Jean Piaget

A generation of practitioners was educated on the psychology of the Swiss
psychologist Jean Piaget. His ideas now permeate a lot of basic practitioner
training in early childhood. To learn about child development is to learn about
Piaget. Most students at university who have come through a vocational route

have been given a watered-down version of his theories. Piaget now belongs to history; his ideas have been superseded, and the classroom practices which arose out of his theories have largely vanished. But his theories represent the time-warp in which so many people are stuck.

Piaget focused on how children acquire knowledge. He considered that the most sophisticated form of thinking and understanding was scientific thinking; that is, testing out ideas, learning about quantification, reasoning logically, and arriving at new solutions. He tried to understand how children changed the way they think. Babies show intense reactions to the stimuli around them. How do they end up being able to reason deductively or logically? How do they learn to cope with mathematics, which is one of the most abstract ways of thinking? What happens in between?

Piaget suggested that there were various stages on the way to becoming a logical thinker. He based his ideas on close observation of his own children, from babyhood onwards. He suggested that children gradually learn to understand the properties of the objects they played with – whether they are hard or soft, or big or small; whether they have a wrong way and a right way up; whether their shape changes or stays the same; whether they taste or smell good, and so on. Babies have to learn to use and control their eyes and hands. Everything has to be learnt through seeing and touching. There are so many objects that learning how to manipulate them and what properties they have takes a lot of time and effort.

At the same time, children are learning words, and to give names to the objects they are manipulating. Gradually, they can use gestures, and then words to fix the objects in time and space; a teddy is furry and soft and has a snub nose and still is a teddy whether you hold him by an arm or a leg. Words are symbols, they are a short-cut to understanding.

Gradually children become more deliberate in their manipulations and deliberately and systematically experiment with objects; until finally they can do 'thought experiments', that is, work things out inside their heads without the need for any props. When children can solve problems in the abstract, and by reasoning establish cause and effect – *if* I drop the teddy in the bath it will become saturated with water and sink; I wonder how much water it will absorb before it sinks? – then they are thinking in a sophisticated way. (They are also no longer children but adolescents or adults playing with their younger sibling's teddy.) Mathematical reasoning is the pinnacle of thinking. Then the absorption capacity of the teddy can be expressed as a mathematical equation!

Piaget tried to categorize these stages of thinking, to *theorize* about them. He suggested that there were four main stages, each with a number of subsets. The first stage, *sensorimotor*, referred to babies coordinating what they see and hear and feel, and linking these sensory perceptions to their own actions, for example getting hold of an object and moving it about. In the next stage, *preoperational*, children can begin to use words and gestures to signify what they mean. But they are still fixed on surface appearances, what things look like rather than what they are. In the third stage, *concrete operational*, children can begin to systematically combine, separate, reorder and transform objects – to understand that water, for example, takes the shape of its container but remains the same. And finally at the stage of *formal operations* children (by now adolescents) can think logically and are interested in abstract ideas.

I have skimmed through these ideas (which fill many books), partly because they are already so well known. But I include them also because, looking back, it is possible to see how important they were, and yet how narrow a perspective they offer. When Piaget was developing his theory, in the 1930s, school was a place where children were taught the three 'R's: reading, writing and arithmetic. Teaching was didactic. The teachers made children read in groups from set readers (*Janet and John* was the most well known), memorize poems, practise their handwriting, learn to do times tables in their head, and copy sums from the blackboard. Teachers had to fill children up with knowledge. Piaget turned the tables. He argued that children had to find things out for themselves. They had to develop their own ways of thinking. They had to experiment, to take the lead themselves. It was the teacher's job to provide a well-resourced classroom, where children could have lots of opportunities to learn for themselves how things worked, with guidance and suggestions from the teacher.

These ideas chimed in with nursery school traditions of play. Children had always been allowed to play in nursery school. Piaget provided a theoretical legitimation of 'learning through play'. His ideas were especially popular with those working with young children.

Not only was Piaget a prolific writer, but his work inspired many other psychologists to test out his ideas. Academic journals and books reflected the interest in his theories. One of the most famous of these attempts was carried out by Margaret Donaldson, who tried to repeat some of Piaget's experiments in order to replicate aspects of his findings. However, she suggested that children could reason better if the task was familiar to them, and they understood the motives behind what they were being asked to do. In other words, context and relationships were also important in learning. Piaget underemphasized them; or rather he was interested primarily in *epistemology*, that is, how things come to be known, rather than in individual children's understanding of objects and events.

Piaget's ideas influenced education in a number of countries. In 1967 the UK government published its major review of primary and nursery education, known as the Plowden Report.[1] The members of the review board were impressed with Piaget's ideas and suggested that schooling should be radically changed to reflect his theories. Instead of children being taught from the front, by the teacher, there should be lots of workstations or corners, with many different kinds of resources, where children could experiment and try out different activities for themselves. Many nursery classes may have adopted these approaches, but it is unlikely that primary schools ever went overboard about them. But whether they did or not, there has been a backlash. Successive governments have condemned this 'child-centred' approach. They have demanded that education goes 'back to basics'. Teachers stand in front of the class again, children have to read and write in the literacy hour, times tables have to be memorized. The wheel has come full circle in England – while paradoxically, in many other countries, Piaget is still being introduced as offering a 'new' way of doing things.

Lev Vygotsky

'If Vygotsky didn't exist, someone would have to invent him.' This is the standard joke about Vygotsky. Piaget's theories relegated adults to unobtrusive helpers. Vygotsky put them centre-stage again. Teachers help learners learn. They are indispensable.

Lev Vygotsky was a brilliant Russian psychologist, working at a time when the Soviet Union was in revolutionary turmoil in the 1920s and 1930s. In Central Asia in particular, literacy levels were very low, and people were not used to education. Vygotsky tried to find ways of learning and teaching that drew on people's experiences, yet at the same time encouraged them to go further. Put in a nutshell, Vygotsky believed that learning should build on what the learner already knows, but that the teacher should demonstrate the next steps, and encourage the learner to move on. He coined the phrase 'zone of proximal development' to describe the intellectual space between the learner and the teacher. Children depend on adults to fill in the gaps for them, to tell them about the rules of any social encounter and to fill in missing information.

Piaget regarded play as a kind of scientific rehearsal, and thought that children would grow out of it once they had mastered abstract thinking. Vygotsky defined play differently, as a kind of mental support system which allows children to represent their everyday social reality. Play enables children to think and act in more complex ways, to invent their own rules and narratives. 'Let's pretend' gives children an opportunity to renegotiate reality. A small girl organizing a tea party in the home corner, for example, would not be able to organize a tea party at home, boil the kettle, make the tea and so on without help; a small boy mending a toy sink with a hammer is not likely to be able to repair the sink at home. Vygotsky wrote: 'In play a child is always above his average age, above his daily behaviour; in play it is as though he were a head taller than himself.'[2]

Vygotsky emphasized the social nature of development, the way in which most cues for learning are social. Piaget's child is a bit of a loner; by contrast, Vygotsky's child is context dependent. Children respond to the reality they see and experience around them, and what they learn reflects this reality. This is one reason why the Soviet state created a near-universal kindergarten system, in order to give children an orderly upbringing, in contrast to the sometimes chaotic life around them. Even now, even in remote parts of Central Asia, there are very good kindergartens where great attention is paid to the daily detail of children's lives.

Vygotsky's ideas took even longer than those of Piaget to become popularized. Although he was also working in the 1920s and 1930s it was not until the 1970s that his work became known in translation, when Piaget was already well known. Like Piaget, Vygotsky's ideas spawned many experiments and sub-theories. There is a vast literature about these ideas.

Jerome Bruner

Bruner describes himself as a polymath, a person whose interests range across many fields. He began by exploring some of Piaget's ideas about children's learning. Then, like so many others, he discovered Vygotsky. Inspired by the notion of the zone of proximal development, he popularized the idea of 'scaffolding' to describe how adults help children learn.

> If the teacher were to have a motto ... it would surely be 'where before there was a spectator, let there now be a participant.' One sets the game, provides a scaffold to assure the child's ineptitudes can be rescued by appropriate intervention, and removes the scaffold part by part as the reciprocal structure stands on its own.[3]

Bruner thought that schools could do a great deal to teach children, and that the teacher's role in fostering cognitive development is crucial. He suggested early on that 'any subject can be taught to any child of any age in an honest way'. Moreover, 'the task of teaching a subject to a child of any particular age is one of representing the structure of that subject in terms of the child's way of viewing things.'[4]

By the 1990s Bruner was describing himself as a cultural psychologist, although he had few connections with the group of cultural psychologists described in the next section (he was in another silo). He considered that psychology should be 'meaning free', by which he meant, in a somewhat postmodern way, that societies create their own meanings and systems of values. 'The very people and cultures that are its subject are governed by shared meanings and values.'[5]

Bruner did not put forward a substantial theory of his own. Instead he has been an intelligent mirror of the changes in theorizing about child development. He has moved from Piaget, through Vygotsky and Chomsky, to a view that to learn is to create meanings from the stream of events and activities within one's own society.

Learning in context

Learning and thinking has increasingly come to be seen as a social activity. The contexts of learning, and the part played by communities and societies in shaping the context in which learning takes place, have been the focus of much theoretical work in the past two decades.

Bronfenbrenner

Urie Bronfenbrenner was an American psychologist who visited Russia and China in the 1950s and 1960s. He was always concerned about the circumstances in which children grew up, but the visits crystallized his thinking. He was impressed with the kindergarten systems in those countries. They offered full integrated daycare and education and they were very well equipped. Children were well fed (even when food was scarce in the Soviet winters), and they had lots of opportunity for exercise and rest. It seemed to indicate that children and childhood was being taken very seriously by society. His book *Two Worlds of Childhood* contrasts Russian emphasis on childhood with the way children were treated in the USA. Whatever else communism did or did not do, Bronfenbrenner was impressed by the support given to young children. (Some people consider that Bronfenbrenner was fooled and only taken to the best places. But my own experience of kindergarten systems in Soviet Central Asia in the 1990s, after the fall of communism, confirms the picture that he gave.)

There is an African proverb, 'it takes a village to bring up a child'. Bronfenbrenner developed a theory, which he called the ecological theory of development, in which he tried to outline the different layers of influence on children growing up. Children were influenced first of all by the *microsystem* in which they grow up; that is, their home environment, their parents, siblings and friends. The next layer is the *mesosystem*, the neighbourhood, the school and other community influences. The third layer is the *exosystem*, the local government, local industry, the way in which life is formally organized at a local level. Finally there is the *macrosystem*, what the government does (or does not do), the beliefs and traditions of the wider society.

Two Worlds of Childhood is a very readable book, much more so than his later book *The Ecology of Human Development* in which he puts forward his ecological theory. Bronfenbrenner, despite his broad attitudes, was a positivist through and through, and this book is expressed as a series of theorems. He made many 'scientific' predictions and hoped they would inspire other scientists to test them out as rigorously as possible. But his theory was too wide and operated at too many levels to be testable. It was an important signpost; it reminded people that governments and local communities can have an influence on how children develop. We know the converse is true, that poverty harms children; it is harder to 'prove' the other way around. For although Bronfenbrenner wanted strict scientific enquiry, it is more or less impossible to set up large-scale experiments to see what happens when the government changes its policies, if indeed it does – in the USA childcare provision was a mess in the 1960s and is still a mess today.[6] There is no overall system of state-funded early education and care, as in most other developed countries. Instead there is heavy reliance on voluntary organizations and parental contributions; a private market with a bit extra for the very poor. Rosemberg has shown in Brazil how this patchwork model is implicitly adopted by the World Bank and other international donors and applied to poor countries. Bronfenbrenner tried to show how this wider political and policy environment affects what is provided on the ground for children.

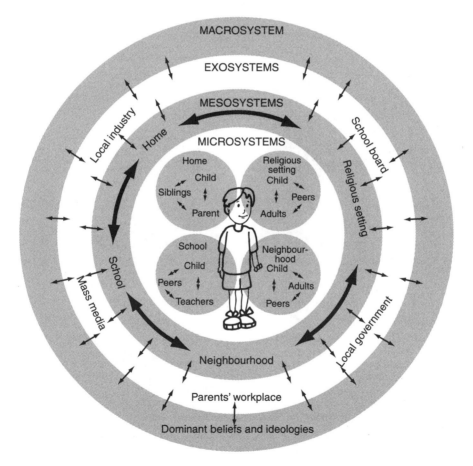

Figure 3.1 The ecological approach, which hypothesizes the layers of influence on a young child's development.

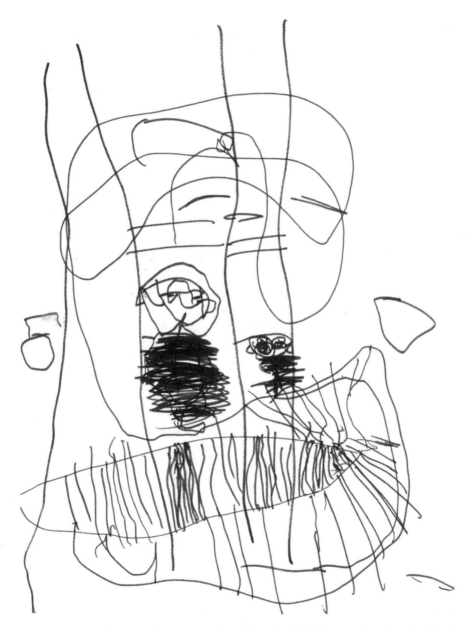

Figure 3.2 Bronfenbrenner's representation of ecological influences is schematized and orderly. In reality life is likely to be much more complex, and a more realistic diagram would be like this scrawl from Mothibi.

Bronfenbrenner has been very influential, as much in psychology as in social work and family studies. He is well known (and much quoted) for saying that every child needs an adult who is crazy about him (or her) in order to grow up.

Barbara Rogoff

Barbara Rogoff was inspired by Vygotsky. She was interested in exactly how adults shaped and guided children's learning and thinking, and she wanted to know if these processes were influenced by the community or society of which the adults were members. She carried out her most well-known studies in Mayan peasant communities in the mountains of Guatamala in South America. She systematically observed young children and noted how they took part in the same activities as everyone else, gardening, childcare, food preparation. They did not have childhoods apart from adults, as in North America.

In the Mayan communities there is a tradition amongst the women of weaving. Every household has a loom. Rogoff wanted to know how young girls learnt to weave. Weaving is a complicated process that requires a great deal of skill. Rogoff concluded that young children joined in the task gradually over days and months; they watched, then they were allowed to do a tiny bit, then a bit more, until they themselves became competent weavers. Rogoff called this process *guided participation* and explored it as a model of learning for children.

In her book *Apprenticeship in Thinking*, Rogoff argued that children do not think in isolation. Thinking is an everyday, social activity. The activities that take place, and the goals that underlie them, are culturally determined, and different in different communities or societies. She defines thinking as 'people's attempts to negotiate the stream of life'. Guided participation is the way in which adults help children to negotiate everyday life. Her position can be summarized as follows:

- Events and activities are inherently dynamic. Life is always changing.
- Events and activities are organized as goals – people only do things when they see the point of doing them (or are told to do them).
- Meaning and purpose cannot be separated out from their everyday context.
- Mental processes are part of this process of meaningful action and interaction.
- In order to understand actions and activities you have to look at the daily detail of what is happening.
- There is infinite variability in events, nothing ever repeats itself exactly. So there can be no single universal goal of development.

Barbara Rogoff's work has been very influential. Although she did important fieldwork in Guatamala and other countries, she is based in California and now concentrates on trying to improve local learning and schooling. She is part of a wider group of psychologists, loosely called cultural psychologists because of their belief that all learning is social and negotiated with others – a far cry from Piaget.

Michael Cole

Michael Cole is the most well known of the cultural psychology group. Like his colleagues in the group, he carried out his early work abroad, first in Liberia, amongst a group of people called the Kpelle. In Liberia he worked with Jean Lave (perhaps the most radical member of the group) exploring how children learnt to read and count using an unusual alphabetical and numerical system. In Russia, where he went next, he translated Vygotsky and first introduced his ideas in English.

He argues that ideas about development, about how the mind works and how children learn, are in a state of flux. 'We seem to be living in a period when orthodoxies no longer retain their holding power and new possibilities abound.'[7] Like Rogoff, he considers that 'the mind' emerges through the joint mediated activity and co-construction. He argues strongly against the more traditional view of thinking and learning whereby learning is an individual, isolated experience and there are universal laws that can explain it (the Piagetian point of view).

In his key book *Cultural Psychology, A Once and Future Discipline* he sets out his ideas. He considers that many aspects of developmental psychology are misguided, in particular the reliance on traditional experimental methods. His book is partly a discussion about the methodologies that cultural psychologists can adopt. He raises the question of whether the entire enterprise of scientific psychology is deeply flawed at its foundation. If culture takes so many different forms, if people are so different, and the places they live in so dissimilar, can developmental psychology deal with this variety of events and activities?

He thinks it can. But he is still wedded to the idea of a positivist science. (He named his research centre in California the Laboratory of Human Cognition.) He concludes that whilst methods must become more adaptable to the variety of human conditions, rigorous research is inescapable as a way of finding out about learning, thinking and behaviour. He concludes that it is necessary 'to create a methodology, a systematic way of relating theory to data that draws both upon the natural sciences and the cultural sciences, as befits its hybrid object, human beings'.[8] He suggests that psychologists should get more involved in everyday activities, as participant observers, and work out what processes are involved, and then try to investigate them through carefully controlled interventions. He and his colleagues, for instance, have recently been working on an out-of-school computer project for children with learning difficulties, to try to understand the learning tactics children and adults use in this situation. He does not underestimate the difficulties of trying to understand and record reality: as he concludes at the end of his book, inevitably 'the failures are sure to outnumber the successes'.

Jean Lave

Lave is a colleague of Rogoff and Cole. She took the same ideas about thinking and learning as a co-mediated activity in a slightly different direction. She was not a theorist of early childhood, as were most of the other people included in this chapter. But she was interested in describing the contexts in which learning takes place. Her catchphrases are 'situated learning' and 'communities of practice'. She thought learning in any situation was not only about the specific content of what was being learnt or taught, but also about the entire social situation in which that learning took place. So if there was a seminar for early childhood students about the work of Jean Lave, students would not only be learning about her work, but also what the lecturer thought about her, what fellow students thought about her, how those ideas fitted into other ideas being taught on the course, and how it fitted in with the experiences of practice the students already possessed. And so on. Nothing is learnt in isolation. She argued that 'learning is a process that takes place in a participatory framework, not in an individual mind. This means, amongst other things, it is mediated by differences of perspective amongst co-participants.'[9]

   She studied a number of 'communities of practice'. She investigated, for instance, how supermarket butchers learnt their trade; and how people learnt to keep off alcohol. She argued that learning was a 'trajectory of participation'. As people joined the group or community of practice, they are apprentice learners. They copy some of the practices they see, but it is not until they have a comprehensive understanding of the processes in which they are involved, and they can perform their tasks without thinking, that they become full members of the community of practice. The community or group itself changes as new members join and old-timers retire. In modern management-speak, this might be called an organizational culture. New members of the organization tend to be regarded with caution, but gradually come to be accepted, and might eventually be in a position to make changes. Lave argued that it is only possible to understand the culture of an organization or a group by exploring their everyday practices in detail, that is, by *deconstructing* what they do and why they do it.

   These views are so far away from those of Piaget that some developmental psychologists have found them hard to accept – or regard them as irrelevant. This perspective does not appear to allow for any differences in the way children learn from the way adults learn. Others have considered that Lave's ideas provide an interesting example into the way that, for example, schools work (or do not work) as places of learning.

These difficulties about incorporating ideas about culture into psychology, and overlaps with anthropology and psychology, are discussed further in Chapter 5.

Emotion and feelings

The great Viennese psychoanalyst Sigmund Freud, working in the first half of the twentieth century, claimed that emotional life and feeling were the core of human existence. Men and women might deny their emotions, or suppress them, but they inevitably shape our lives. The two most important emotions are love and hate; they are biological drives that we experience as feelings. Mostly these feelings are buried deep in our unconscious (the *id*). Most of us have developed an internal watchdog, our conscience, or in Freudian terms, the *superego*, to monitor our feelings and prevent them from breaking out and causing havoc. The rational, everyday self Freud calls the *ego*.

Freud was a psychiatrist. He developed his own case study method. This was a systematic way to explore people's feelings, even if they are long buried, by enabling them to explore their dreams and fantasies in a safe environment with a trained listener – a psychoanalyst.

Freud has inspired more followers and more interest in his theory of psychoanalysis than any other theorist, and in the middle of the last century most psychology drew heavily on his ideas. Susan Isaacs, for example, the British child development expert who founded one of the first departments of child development at a university (at the Institute of Education in London) eventually left her teaching and writing on child development to become a psychotherapist herself.

One of the most influential British psychotherapists was Melanie Klein (with whom Isaacs trained). Klein's view was that mother–infant relationships were very strong and powerful. Mothers had to tame the aggressive all-consuming passion of their infants. (Melanie Klein did not manage it herself, and her relationship with her daughter was always badly strained.) During the war, it became a commonplace view – a common-sense theory – that aggression was a natural instinct which had to be controlled. The *British Medical Journal* declared in an editorial in 1944 that 'Destructive impulses let loose in war may serve to fan the flame of aggression natural to the nursery age.'[10] Practitioners who learnt about child development, were, for a period, learning how children's emotions could best be channelled. For a long period in the 1970s and 1980s, psychology journals contained many studies of aggression, and whether daycare, in particular, made it worse. The history of childcare is discussed in Chapter 6, but in this section we consider the theme of emotionality and how it has been dealt with by child development theorists.

John Bowlby

John Bowlby was a psychiatrist based at the Tavistock Clinic in London. He was familiar with and influenced by Melanie Klein. Working for the World Health Organization after the war, he visited children in hospitals, nurseries and orphanages who had been separated from their parents, and was shocked by the fear, apathy and unhappiness of many of the refugee children he saw. As well as Melanie Klein he had also been influenced by evolutionary biology and ideas about young animals needing the protection of their parents until old enough to fend for themselves. He concluded that a child was necessarily attached to a caregiver. It was a biologically based behaviour for self-protection. He put forward his theory of attachment – that children needed a warm continuous relationship with a mother figure and without it they would be emotionally damaged. Lack of mother love was likely to lead to children, boys especially, turning to aggression and delinquency in adolescence.

Bowlby's theory of attachment struck a chord in the public mind. After the disruption of the war years, traditional family life appealed to many people. His theory was widely (mis)interpreted to mean that mothers should stay at home with their young children. If they worked they ran the risk of causing their children harm.

Bowlby's theory was more sophisticated than this. He argued that attachments went through several stages. First of all in pre-attachment phase, children just needed a caregiver to attend to their needs. They do not seem to notice or be concerned if the caregiver is unfamiliar. Gradually they begin to discriminate, and then, from about 6–8 months until about 18–24 months, they become firmly attached to one or two people and experience considerable anxiety when that person departs. Eventually mother and child establish a warm reciprocal relationship, where there is give and take.

Mary Ainsworth, a psychologist, systematically investigated the theory of attachment. She devised a test known as the strange situation test. A child plays with her mother in a strange room. Then the mother leaves and a stranger comes in. The child's reaction to the return of her mother is measured. There are three categories of reaction. An *anxious/avoidant* child does not take much notice of the stranger or of the mother when she returns. A *securely attached* child reacts positively to the stranger at first, but then cries and is upset when the mother leaves, and finally is comforted when she returns. An *anxious/resistant* child clings to her mother, is very upset when she leaves, and is not calmed when she returns. This test has been carried out with children in a number of countries. In some countries, for example Guatamala, far fewer babies show separation anxiety, although researchers claim that the overall pattern is the same. Separation anxiety is at its most acute when the child is 10–12 months old; it then drops off. Separation anxiety is most extreme in those westernized countries where nuclear families are the norm. In more communal or collective societies it is far less acute.

This test would now be regarded as unethical. Any procedure which deliberately causes children distress should be avoided. Bowlby's theory is still a prominent one in some psychoanalytic circles, for example at the Tavistock Clinic, but attention has switched to trying to understand the cognitive processes involved in babyhood, as the child learns to recognize her mother and gradually gains a sense of her own identity.

Judy Dunn

Judy Dunn is an English psychologist who carried out a landmark study of very young children growing up in their families. She was interested in what happened when siblings came along. Would children get jealous? How would they respond? She observed the children within families and followed them up over a period of years. She concluded that even very young children were capable of sophisticated emotional responses and emotional manipulation. Young children's relationships were rich, complex and varied, and even those of siblings might differ markedly. There were marked and poignant differences between children: 'one child is happily a member of a circle of close companions; another has just one intense and close friendship; another is without friends.'[11]

In her book *Young Children's Close Relationships*, in a series called 'Beyond Attachment', she suggests that theorizing about emotions and relationships has many gaps. Attachment theory was clearly inadequate. She suggested firstly that children are highly responsive to the quality of relationships and emotional exchanges within the family. They pick up tension, for example, or confidence or caution. They know when things are going wrong, even if they cannot voice their worries. Secondly, social competence is not general but person-specific. She argues that we should move away from a simple notion of a 'competent' or 'incompetent' child. Instead we should realize that competence depends on the company and the circumstances. Children behave differently towards different people, or even at different times towards the same people.

Methods for investigating children's emotionality and social relationships had to be devised in situ. These aspects of children's daily life could not be systematically investigated in a laboratory. But it is ethically problematical to be an observer in a family situation, and confidentiality is an issue. Dunn relied on controlled observations and interviews with parents for her data, explaining to them as she went along what she was doing and why.

She concluded that friendships are vital to children, not only for fun but also for fundamental social skills. Friendships can offer warmth and security, perspective taking, conflict resolution, moral understanding and a sense of self. Some young children have considerable powers of understanding, sensitivity and intimacy. Friends may quarrel more, but life with friends is more distinctive and more exciting.

> Friends can create a world of great involvement and high adventure, and they can do it at the tender age of 3 or 4. They must co-ordinate their efforts with all the virtuosity of an accomplished jazz quartet, and they must manage the amount of conflict between them. These things require enormous social skills.[12]

This does not sound at all like Piaget's egocentric child, who has to learn to share with others. Instead, Dunn concludes, children are emotionally aware, and understand the feelings of others.

> Most children recognize and respond to the feelings of others and behave practically to improve or worsen other people's emotional state. They understand the connections between other's beliefs and desires and their behaviour. They have some grasp of what is appropriate moral behaviour for different relationships. Such sophistication means that even young children can be supportive, concerned, intimate and humorous with others – or they can be manipulative, devious, and teasing and deliberately upset others.[13]

Other psychologists have studied children's friendships outside the family, in nurseries and schools. They have also concluded friendships are important. However, Dunn's point is that family is an incubator of emotions. Within the family, between parents and children, and between siblings, emotions are likely to be heightened. Social and emotional understanding (like the thinking and learning described by the cultural psychologists) is interactive. It does not lie within the individual; it is a product of the way in which people come together. Dunn and her colleagues, however, were investigating nuclear families, a Euro-American model of the family which is far from universal.

Her work is small scale. It does not claim to offer a grand theory or to make predictions – but it is widely cited. Both the methodology and the conclusions have stimulated discussion about young children's capacities.

Howard Gardner

Howard Gardner is an American academic who has been concerned primarily with theories of intelligence. I include him in this section because he has developed the idea that some people have an aptitude to be sensitive to the feelings of others. They are emotionally gifted.

He theorized that instead of there being one kind of intelligence, usually defined as being able to do well at school, there were multiple intelligences. These are:

- *Linguistic intelligence* – being clever with words, finding just the right phrase to express yourself, quick to understand new meanings.
- *Musical intelligence* – sensitivity to pitch, tone and rhythm, able to play instruments or sing easily.
- *Logico-mathematical intelligence* – ability to engage in abstract reasoning and to do maths (Piaget's intelligence).
- *Spatial intelligence* – to see, remember and create visual images; to have a sense of space, distance and proportions.
- *Bodily–kinesthetic intelligence* – to move gracefully, to use your body expressively in dance or mime.
- *Personal intelligence* – to have an accurate sense of yourself, to be able to understand your own feelings and motives (sometimes called wisdom).
- *Social intelligence* – to understand the feelings and motives of other people.

Gardner has criticized schooling heavily because it has taken so little notice of psychological findings – including his own.

> Put 20 or more children of roughly the same age in a little room, confine them to desks, make them wait in line, make them behave. It is as if a secret committee, now lost to history, had made a study of children and, having figured out what the greatest number were least disposed to do, declared that all of them should do it.[14]

His different kinds of intelligence are only schematized, although he does make various predictions and considers brain research will eventually substantiate the gist of his theory. In reality there is likely to be much more of a mixture of these aptitudes. They are a way of highlighting the great variety of human behaviour and the different values people hold. It is clear that in different societies or communities, different kinds of intelligence are valued. Euro-American societies (over)value linguistic and logico-mathematical intelligence. Other societies, for instance some communities in northern India or West Africa, may value musical and kinaesthetic intelligence very highly – for example the praise singers of Mali and Senegal. Robert Serpell has suggested that intelligence is defined in some African communities as learning how to be helpful to others; stupidity is being unhelpful. Pastoralist communities, who are constantly on the move, have a very finely tuned spatial intelligence. Young Inuit children in northern Canada, for example, can draw extremely accurate maps.[15]

There have been some efforts by neurologists and psychologists to find which part of the brain, if any, can be linked to these different kinds of intelligence. The psychologist Daniel Goleman has written a popular book entitled *Emotional Intelligence*. Getting on with other people, liking and being liked, are extremely important skills in almost every job. He considers that children can be taught to be more sensitive to others, but he also believes that the basis of emotionality is physiological. Joseph LeDoux, a neurologist, suggests that there is a part of our brain, deep inside the cortex, that regulates emotions. These claims for brain research are considered in Chapter 4.

Language

Language is what differentiates mankind from all other species. It is an extraordinary system of communication, making use of symbols – words – and a complex range of sounds. Societies have evolved many different languages. Each language uses a different set of symbols, stringing them together in different ways (grammar), and using different sound ranges (speech) and, for languages that are not oral, different signs on paper (writing).

If you compare the way people talk, even people who speak the same language and have the same accent, you can hear all kinds of variations. Speakers use different pitch, volume, tone quality, stress and patterns of breathing. Every language identifies a small number of distinctions in sound called *phonemes*. Some languages have as few as a dozen, none has more than 90. English has about 40 phonemes. The phonemes used for one language may be quite different in another, with little overlap. Some of the sounds we hear in English do not have a counterpart in, say, Chinese, which relies much more on tones and pitch. At birth, babies can respond to the entire range of phonemes, but fairly soon they learn to hear and reproduce only those of their own language. This is what makes second or third language learning so remarkable. Young children can learn two or more sets of phonemes, and never confuse them; and then match them to the vocabulary and grammar of the appropriate language.

Some languages have a high status. English is at the top of the pile. If you speak English, you can get by in most places in the world. It is an international language, the language of trade, diplomacy and academia. Other world languages are Arabic, Spanish, French, Portuguese, Chinese and Hindi. Other languages are at the bottom of the pile. For example, of the 50-plus languages spoken by the indigenous Indian peoples of Canada (now known as First Nations peoples), only two are expected to survive another generation – Ojibway and Cree.[16]

English speakers are under little pressure to learn other languages because they can get by in so many places. Other language speakers have as their starting point the need to recognize and speak several languages. In many ex-colonial countries, for example, children routinely speak three languages: their mother tongue (that is, that of their village or community), the regional language they need when they move out of their village or small community, and the colonial language, which is the language of schooling. In Tanzania, for example, a child who comes from the Kilimanjaro area will first of all speak Chewa, the village language; then Swahili, the language of East Africa; and finally English. In ex-colonial countries, and in many European countries, most children are bilingual or trilingual.

As one Latin American writer put it, 'el monolingualismo es curable' – monolingualism is curable.[17] It is worth bearing this in mind since much of the debate about language learning concerns English speakers, and assumes that they are monolingual. There are also relatively few studies of children who speak both high status and low status languages. It seems likely that the latter will almost always lose out.

Even though most studies of language learning have looked at an atypical group – monolingual English speakers – the phenomenon of language acquisition is startling. In a matter of a few years children acquire a remarkable number of words, and even more remarkably, know the rules for putting the words together – the grammar of the language. This is a skill of early childhood. Native speakers rarely get the pronunciation or the grammar of their language wrong. Yet adults learning a language, unless they are very talented or are used to learning languages, invariably make mistakes. How can children learn so much in such a short time, and why can adults not learn in the same way?

Children do not just learn a vocabulary. They learn that words are *symbols*. The word 'hot', for example, can refer to many different objects – a radiator, a saucepan, chips, water in the bath – and yet young children can grasp the concept of 'hotness'. Words refer to objects or to properties of objects, even when the object is not there. So the questions for language learning are how do children discover what words mean; how do they learn to arrange words and parts of words in a way that has meaning to others (grammar); and how do they do this twice or three times over, if they are bilingual or trilingual? These problems of language have not been solved. But as ever, there are many theories, and even more experiments and investigations into the minute details of language learning.

Behaviourism

Behaviourism, also known as *operant conditioning*, was a popular approach in the first half of the twentieth century. Its major theorists, John Watson and B.F. Skinner, believed that all behaviour is the result of instruction and imitation for which the learner gets systematically rewarded or punished.

In other words, parents and other teachers are very clear indeed about what they consider to be good or useful behaviour and what they consider to be poor or pointless behaviour; they reward the good behaviour and correct the bad.

Most developmental psychologists now favour more interactionist approaches to understanding young children – as discussed in the previous sections. But behaviourist approaches are still used in some circumstances, for instance in dealing with problematic behaviour in children. A major parenting programme in widespread use today, for example, is based on the idea that parents should consistently reward good behaviour with praise and consistently ignore bad behaviour, so that the child learns which behaviour is most appropriate.

Behaviourists considered that even the most complex activities, such as learning a language, could be explained by imitation and conditioning. So babies learn to talk by continually being talked to, and having their mistakes corrected. Like most theories, this one recognizes a partial truth: mothers usually do spend a lot of time with their children coaxing them to talk and structuring what they say. But children's language learning is so rapid that no one could ever talk to them enough to account for all the words and grammar they use. Experiments have shown that parents do not usually systematically correct their child's language; instead it is as if the language gradually slots into place. Children do not just learn to speak, they learn to generate language.

Noam Chomsky

Noam Chomsky is an American linguist. (He has a parallel life as a radical political theorist, for which he is still more widely known and respected.) He argued that language is so complex that it cannot be explained psychologically. Children do obviously acquire some of their verbal and non-verbal behaviour by casual observation and imitation of other adults and children, but their speech goes way beyond imitation. They produce sentences that nobody has heard before.

Chomsky argued that the capacity to understand and generate language is different from other behaviour. It cannot simply be learnt. The brain must be preprogrammed for language. Chomsky proposed that every child is born with a language decoder, what he called a *language acquisition device*, or LAD. This decoder enables children to recognize the underlying structure or grammar of any language they hear, no matter what the language. The experience of hearing a particular language triggers the decoder into action.

Chomsky's work has been to study *generative grammar*, that is, the rules that govern the way in which language is used.

There must be some set of principles that we are capable of applying in novel situations – without limit. . . . These principles have to be part of our nature, because there is no way to acquire them from experience. . . . It also follows that they must be uniform.[18]

Chomsky has tried to describe the rules, but he did not go further than that. 'It is pretty abstract, because when you deal with anything as complex as human beings, you're always on the surface.'[19] Nevertheless his theory, like that of Gardner, has given rise to neurological and genetic research. Can LAD be discovered? Neurological studies seem to indicate that language ability is located in the left hemisphere of the brain. This is discussed more in the next chapter.

Interactionist views of language development

Neither the behaviourist nor the LAD explanation for language acquisition is entirely satisfactory. One is impossible (children learn from the examples in their environment) and the other is miraculous (our brains are wired up for language). Interactionists try to find a third way.

Bruner, for example, proposed, in a much quoted article, that language was neither

the virtuoso cracking of a linguistic code, or the spinoff of ordinary cognitive development, [n]or the gradual take-over of adult's speech by the child through some impossible inductive tour de force. It is, rather, a subtle process by which adults artificially arrange the world so that the child can succeed culturally by doing what comes naturally, and with others similarly inclined.[20]

There are many interactionist perspectives. Most acknowledge that the brain has some sort of language decoder – although it is yet to be found – but are interested in the ways in which the environment influences language development. Interactionist research includes studies of deaf children; how teachers can shape language development; and, increasingly, bilingualism.

Summary

Child development is a sprawling discipline. It relies on a variety of methodologies and approaches. There are important theorists who have tried to redirect or rethink how we investigate young children and, as adults, relate to them. These theories have produced shifts in our understanding. But the bulk of the work in psychology is carried out by thousands of researchers beavering away at thousands of small (and not so small) experiments and observations to investigate young children's capacities, their behaviour and, increasingly, their views and opinions. Most of this work is written up in academic journals. It is an extremely complex field. This chapter has offered a few signposts.

Main messages from this chapter

1   Piaget was important but he has been superseded.
2   Learning is not a lonely activity but is inescapably social.
3   Feelings and attitudes are making a comeback; they may profoundly influence learning.
4   Language is at the heart of learning.

What to read next

The most comprehensive textbook on child development, giving the widest range of views, is

Cole, M. and Cole, S. (2002) *The Development of Children*, 4th edition. New York: W. H. Freeman.

Notes

1   HMSO 1967
2   Vygotsky 1978: 102
3   Bruner 1960: 60
4   Bruner 1960: 33
5   Bruner 1990: 20
6   For a recent description of early education and care in the USA, see the OECD's Country Note, USA, *Early Education and Care Thematic Review*
7   Cole 1996: 3
8   Ibid.: 330
9   Lave and Wenger 1992: 15
10   In Riley 1983: 1
11   Dunn 1993: 1
12   Ibid.: 3
13   Ibid.: 109
14   Gardner 1993: 138

15   Marshall 1940
16   Abley 2003
17   Quoted in Burman 1994
18   Chomsky 2003: 41
19   Ibid.
20   Bruner 1982: 15

4 Genes, Neurons and Ancestors

The brain with which you are understanding my words is an array of some ten million kiloneurons. Many of these nerve cells have each more than a thousand 'electric wires' connecting them to other neurons. Moreover at the molecular genetic level, every single one of more than a trillion cells in the body contains about a thousand times as much precisely coded information as an entire computer.[1]

The workings of human bodies – and almost all living creatures – are extraordinarily intricate and complex. We know a great deal about bodily processes and how the body develops, grows and ages. We know that it is possible to regulate and control those processes, with drugs and surgery and through the provision of more healthy and hygienic living and working arrangements. We have an entire public service – the National Health Service – dedicated to these ends. And yet we do not understand even very basic biological processes of the human body. Despite recent progress in genetics and the neurosciences, there are still immense gaps in our knowledge. In addition, we do not understand, and do not conceptualize very well, the relationship between mind and body. What is happening inside us and what is happening outside of us, and how are they connected?

Growth and maturation are influenced by diet, lifestyle and disease. The study of growth and maturation has been given new dimensions by recent medical research – for instance embryology or molecular biology.

Biological maturational processes are uneven. Different systems of the body run on different timescales. When we speak of biological maturation we refer to a composite account of intricately related molecular machinery. Norms of maturation have to be continually updated as circumstances change, and new facts are discovered. For instance, children in rich countries are bigger than children in poor countries. Obesity in children is a major health problem. Bodily changes reflect nutritional environments. The body gets accustomed to different kinds of food, and then cannot cope easily with changes in diet. For example, nomadic groups in very cold countries such as northern Canada and Mongolia have fat-saturated diets that would kill people elsewhere. In Mongolia, nomads claim that they can tell where an animal came from from the taste of its fat. An Inuit woman described to me how raw whale blubber is 'soul-food'. I tasted the rubbery fat but to me it was so nasty that it was impossible to imagine it as comfort food! Diet leads to distinctive and measurable changes in physique and wellbeing, but it is highly contextual.

The spread of new diseases such as HIV/AIDS affect morbidity rates (the death rates of the population). In some countries life expectancy has been reduced to 40 years or less. Similarly, changes in drug use seem to be leading to new reactive patterns to illness and disease. The emphasis on hygiene in the care of young children, and overuse of antibiotics and painkilling drugs, have probably resulted in children with less effective immune response systems and less resilience. For instance, a recent survey of mothers of 15-month-old children undertaken in London asked the question, 'Was your child on any kind of drugs last week?' It revealed that 50 per cent of the sample were given painkillers and 10 per cent were on antibiotics.[2] In some other European countries – for example, France – reliance on pills and prescriptions is even higher.

Certain kinds of cells – embryonic stem cells – seem to be what drive biological change. They have unique regenerative functions – they can repair and refresh. Stem cell biology is prophesied to hold the key to ageing. Stem cells are those which appear to operate the triggers or controls for the growth, development and possibly the regeneration of different bodily systems. This process is at its most dramatic when babies are growing inside the womb. Embryology – the study of the way a foetus develops in the womb – is an important area of research. Study of embryonic growth may tell us why certain bodily organs can repair themselves or regrow after damage.

Molecular biologists are attempting to chart the extraordinary inter-actions between nano-particles of bodily proteins. Too tiny to investigate without sophisticated equipment, body proteins – the chemicals of which the body is made up – seem to combine and recombine in unique ways in each of us. The uniqueness of the way each body is constructed – and wears out – suggests that medical interventions need to be highly targeted. Each ill person may need a different combination of drugs and diet to deal with malfunction-ing body parts. This is the next medical revolution.

Speaking of ages and stages in terms of biological maturation is to make crude assumptions about rates, sequences, sites and constancy of develop-ment. Charts of normal growth and development skip over or minimize enormous complexities and variations. Statistical norms constructed from large population samples may be useful for mapping gross abnormalities, but they do not tell us much more than this. Nevertheless, it may be helpful, in treatment terms, to know about certain abnormalities in given populations, for example defects of vision or hearing or thyroid deficiencies. Children's growth and bodily development are matched against population percentiles in order to decide whether those who lie outside the range of what is normal need medical treatment. About 6 per cent of children are likely to have some kind of problem. Clinical check-ups or follow-ups for young children are a good idea in case there are conditions that can be picked up and treated. But not all abnormalities can be treated or corrected, and, as the biologist Steven Jay Gould has pointed out, there are always inherent problems in trying to define what is normal. Definitions of normality easily slip over into racist eugenics.

In any case, an overview of these biological maturation processes would still beg the question of whether or not what happens in the body can ever explain or predict behaviour. On the one hand, certain psychological theories, such as those of Gardner and Chomsky, seem to beg the question about neurological underpinning. On the other hand, many psychologists are wary of using biological growth as a metaphor to explain the development of learning and behaviour in children. This is not only because of the inherent difficulties in understanding biology, but also because of the value judgements implicit in describing behaviour. As the psychologist Jerome Kagan put it: 'All societies invent categories that simultaneously describe and explain the 10–20% of children whose profile of behavioural accomplishments is least pleasing.'[3]

This chapter focuses on how information from the biological sciences is sifted and used to explain or justify ways of understanding and working with young children. The field of cognitive psychology, for example, is increasingly predicated on the neurosciences and understandings about brain functioning. Genetics is used to describe behaviour, for example as an explanation of why people are obese (a genetic predisposition to eat too much). Evolutionary psychology speculates about the operation of genetic inheritance and its modifications. These relatively new areas of work, genetics, neurosciences and evolutionary psychology, and what we claim they teach us, are discussed here.

Genes

DNA

Genes are made up of microscopic amounts of four chemicals, adenine, cytosine, guanine and thymine (coded A, C, G and T), which appear in long and varying sequences of several hundred repeated patterns in each gene. There are approximately 30,000 genes in the human body, arranged into 23 pairs of chromosomes held together on a chain of sugar and phosphate. The genes and the chain on which they are distributed are called collectively the

DNA. The DNA was referred to by its discoverers as the double helix, because it formed a chain which appeared to loop back on itself.

Most cells in the human body contain DNA in their nucleus. Each DNA forms a unique pattern. This uniqueness, coded in the cells of the body, has enabled forensic scientists, for example, to track down criminals on the basis of a scrap of skin tissue or a strand of hair.

The DNA is reformed with each new individual. The mother's and father's DNA combine at conception. Some of the genes which are inherited from parents are dominant, and manifest themselves in the new individual; others are recessive and are not apparent. Although recessive genes stay on in the DNA, they do not get activated unless two individuals with the same recessive genes conceive. In this case, because there is no dominant gene, their child may display the recessive gene. Some well-known conditions, such as haemophilia, are carried on recessive genes. These genetic inheritance patterns were discovered by the scientist Gregor Mendel in the nineteenth century, but it is only very recently that the importance of his findings about genetic inheritance has been understood.

Cells replace themselves continuously – no part of your body is older than ten years. The DNA contains genetic instructions for replication, so that each new cell that is created will contain the same genetic information – although as we age there is wear and tear on the DNA. The genetic information may

Figure 4.1   The double helix, a diagram of the structure of human genetic inheritance. From Dennis and Gallagher 2001.

become distorted and variations or mistakes occur. Some genes appear to act as housekeepers; as repair and maintenance genes switching on chemicals designed to correct, compensate for, or eliminate mistakes. With age, as the DNA becomes slightly more unstable, the 'housekeeper' genes are busier and may themselves fail to work. Cancer is an indication that the housekeeper genes are not working properly at their job of clearing the body of damage. Where there is a malformation in a particular gene, the instructions to replicate itself may be damaged, so it reproduces more damaged genes. (Genetic damage could, of course, be environmentally caused, for instance by a virus or radiation.)

Gene malformation may have all sorts of knock-on effects on other genes. It should trigger the housekeeper genes, provided they too have not retired. For example, some work on cancer is now focusing on one such housekeeper gene, called Tp53, on chromosome 17, which appears to deliver a chemical 'suicide pill' to cells which have mutated. If Tp53 is itself damaged, then the mutated cells continue to develop, that is, the cancer grows. The HIV/AIDs virus is an example of an environmental cause that appears to affect the housekeeper genes.

Genetic engineering or manipulation relies on the repair and maintenance functions of genes. In 1968, scientists investigating bacteria discovered 'restriction enzymes'. The job of these enzymes is to cut out strands of DNA when they encounter particular sequences of the chemical letters that signify that some damage has occurred. But there is also an enzyme, called ligase, which mends or stitches together loose or damaged bits of DNA. These mechanisms, restriction enzymes and ligase, are, very roughly, the basis of genetic engineering. Scientists use the restriction enzymes to cut out bits of the DNA, and then use ligase to splice them together again.

Genetic engineering raises all kinds of ethical problems (not least the huge profits which biotechnology companies might make if gene therapy proved effective). Most countries have strict ethical guidelines concerning genetic research with humans. The limited application to humans in the treatment of certain genetic diseases has not yet proved very successful, partly because of the enormous complexity of the human body. But there have been experiments with genetically modified animals, for example mice and monkeys, resulting in the creation of 'transgenic' animals. Techniques for genetically modifying plants are commonplace because plants are much easier to reproduce. According to the campaigning organization Genewatch UK, 60 per cent of all seeds sold commercially are now genetically modified.

The Genome Project

Most of the work on genes has been done on fruit flies and other creatures that reproduce very quickly. Some of it has been done on the great apes, with whom we share 98 per cent of our genes. For obvious ethical reasons, less has been done on humans. But the new techniques for extracting and analysing DNA, developed in the course of work on bacteria, fruit flies, and other plants and animals, has meant that it has become possible to isolate human genes and analyse them in greater detail. The Genome Project, described very well by the scientific journalist Matt Ridley, is an attempt to map all the genes on the human body, to identify them and show where they are located on the chromosomes. This project was completed in 2000, but it raises more mysteries than it solves. It has been described as being like a list of all the parts for a Boeing 747, down to the nuts, bolts and washers, with no idea about how the parts fit together and no understanding of the principles of flight.

The genome blueprint, then, does not tell us much. Some genes seem to have no obvious purpose. The precise function of most genes, and even more importantly how the genes interrelate with one another and with the

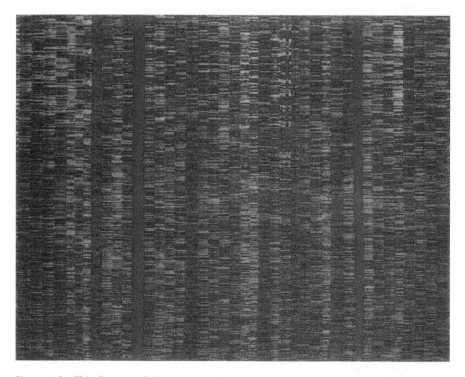

Figure 4.2   This diagram of the patterning of a human genome shows how complicated it is to decipher or decode genetic information. No one is really sure what these sequences signify. From Dennis and Gallagher 2001: 25 (Sanger Centre/Wellcome Photo Library).

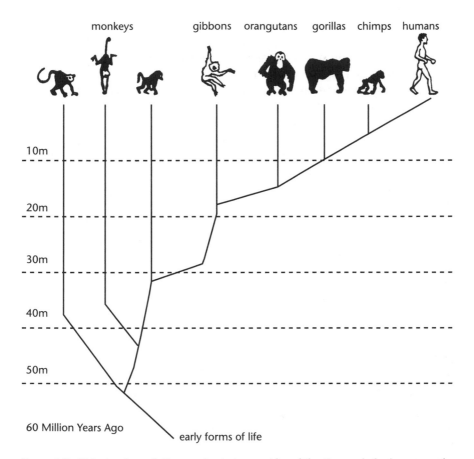

Figure 4.3 This simple evolutionary chart gives an idea of the time scale for human evolution. Evolutionary psychologists are concerned with the last 10 million years of human evolution.

environment, are not really understood. Genes operate digitally; they switch on and off, and trigger other genes to do the same, in immensely complex and little-understood patterns. There is a great deal of apparent overlap and redundancy and what appears to be junk information or spam.

Some people have argued that in order to understand the genome, it is necessary to take an evolutionary approach. Charles Darwin, the nineteenth-century scientist, in his book *The Origin of the Species*, suggests that evolution occurs through the slow adaptation of species to their environment over hundreds of thousands of years. Stephen Jay Gould coined the phrase 'deep time and endless motion' to describe the immense timespan and infinitesimal nature of these changes. All the time, species reproduce, and, in reproducing,

small variations occur. Change is ceaseless. The most successful new individuals survive, prosper and reproduce. The least successful die out. If there are
extraterrestrial events such as a meteoric impact, or even if there are local
microclimatic changes, the species which survive are those that best adapt to
the new environmental circumstances. Successful individuals then pass on
their genes to the next generation. This is popularly called 'natural selection'
and 'the survival of the fittest'.

Through this process of slow modification, human beings evolved. Descended from ape-like ancestors, we share a single common ancestor with all
other living things on Earth. This common ancestor, the first living thing,
lived about 4 billion years ago. It was very simple. About 600 million years ago
the first multicellular organisms began to appear in the sea. Then land-
dwelling creatures emerged about 500 million years ago. The first primates
appeared 55 million years ago.

Darwin did not know about genetics, but like Chomsky hypothesizing
about language decoders, Darwin speculated that genes must exist. The
geneticist Steve Jones, in his book *Almost Like a Whale*, has attempted to
use genetic information from the twentieth century to illustrate and elaborate
Darwin's theory, which was drawn up in the nineteenth century. Darwin's
theory does indeed fit very neatly with twentieth-century genetics. On the
one hand, genetics supports Darwin's speculation about the gradual
changes in species, and the way in which new variations and species
occur through spontaneous variations in the genes and through the
recombinations of reproduction. On the other hand, the theory of evolution
explains the curious composition of the genome, and the fact that there is
so much overlap between the human genome and that of other species. The
human genome contains in itself the history of the evolution of the human
species.

> DNA provides millions of links to the past some of which have
> revealed unexpected patterns. . . . Man and pig, or man and cow,
> share more than fifty long sequences [of DNA]. . . . The genes of
> many creatures have been read end to end. They reveal groups
> within groups beyond the imagination of earlier naturalists. Thirty
> thousand genes have been located in humans, almost as many in
> mice. PIGMAP, the cartography of swine is up to 600 or so. . . .
> A tiny nematode worm, the only animal to have had all its
> DNA letters read, has nineteen thousand and ninety-nine genes
> altogether. . . . Several bacteria and single cell parasites have also been
> deciphered.
>
> Their landscapes have much in common. Whole sections are the
> same in mice and men, and two thousand human genes have exact
> homologues in mice. A trudge along the DNA shows more than half

of a certain mouse chromosome to be more or less identical in the arrangement of one of our own; and cows are even more like us. Half of all plant genes have a mouse equivalent. The nematode worm shares a fifth of its own heritage with yeast (from which it split a billion years ago). . . . A gene that in humans causes an inherited disorder of the nervous system has an exact match in yeast (which has no nerves at all).[4]

Our genes therefore have accumulated, developed – and survived – over an unimaginable timespan. Some of the common ancestors from which we evolved have left their genetic mark on us, as on other branches of their descendants. And yet, despite knowing so much, we know very little. Whilst much of this genetic information is documented, much remains to be decoded. Are all the junk sequences in the genes, which appear meaningless and which have no obvious purpose, really junk? How do the genes programme the body into action?

The next stage of the Genome Project is called the *proteome* project. This is nano-technology at the frontiers of science. This stage of understanding genetics involves much greater molecular analysis of how genes produce the proteins that make our bodies, the science of 'proteomics'. The aim is to produce miniature machines, on a nano-scale, capable of swimming through our bodies to dispense drugs or perform micro-engineering works on targeted cells. Like atomic physics, this is the stuff of science fiction.

Genetic research consumes an enormous amount of time, energy and money. Some scientists argue that the results are not worth it. They distort our understanding and divert resources away from more practical research on killer illnesses such as malaria. David Horrobin, reviewing the evidence in the *Guardian* newspaper, claims that 'the idea that genomics is going to make a major contribution to human health in the near future is laughable'. So although the tabloids come up with sensational headlines about genetic research – 'gene for obesity discovered', 'aggression – it's all in the genes' – genetics, as yet, does not tell us very much about behaviour.

The big (and unanswered) questions in genetic research could be summarized as follows:

- Where do our genes come from?
- How do genetic blueprints affect everyday bodily processes?
- How do we interpret the effects of apparently redundant genetic material?
- How are genes related to behaviour?
- Should ethical considerations govern gene experimentation and manipulation?

Evolutionary psychology

Genetic research has spawned an industry of sub-disciplines. Sociobiologists explore how genes might predict behaviour. Evolutionary psychology argues the other way around: that certain behaviour patterns have only come about because of natural selection and genetic inheritance. Since these behaviour patterns emerged in response to certain environments, then understanding what environments may have been like in the past can tell us something about the origins and persistence of behaviour patterns now.

John Tooby and Leda Cosmides are two psychologists who are credited with 'inventing' evolutionary psychology.[5] As well as the genetic research and theories of evolution, they drew on some of the findings of the neurosciences and cognitive psychology (see below) to argue that the mind is made up of lots of different systems. Each subsystem evolved in response to certain evolutionary pressures. Cosmides argued, in a now famous analogy, that the mind is like a Swiss army knife. Like the knife, which has lots of gadgets to deal with lots of different tasks – corkscrew, tin-opener, file, scissors and so on – the brain has lots of intellectual gadgets which have been added through natural selection. Tooby and Cosmides believe these modular brain functions have evolved in order to deal with specific environmental problems.

The two authors hypothesize that the first humans were hunter–gatherers living in small groups in the African savannahs. They argue that these early groups of humans interacted closely with their physical and animal environment. They organized themselves into small and mobile groups of hunter-gatherers. Their dietary and work patterns created ecological and evolutionary characteristics that are still present today. For example, they ate as much as they could when the food was available, and ate very little when it was not. This pattern of eating does not work in today's (rich) world of plenty when food is always available, so that there is a temptation to gorge all the time. Understanding these early origins, Tooby and Cosmides suggest, will help us understand our behaviour in the present.

Leonides and Tooby claim that ultimately all behaviour will be traced to genetic programming of the brain, and theorizing about such behaviour patterns now will throw new light on genetic research. The evolutionary adaptations they identified in early human communities included dealing with such problems as:

- avoiding predators (learning how to avoid danger, fighting or flight);
- eating the right foods (finding high-fuel foods such as fat and sugar; disgust with rotten foods; eating as much as possible when food was available);
- forming alliances and friendships (living socially and in groups in order to maximize defence against predators);

- reading other people's minds (predicting and controlling behaviour);
- communicating with other people (signalling danger, improving cooperation, using language);
- selecting mates (finding people with good genes, avoiding those with bad genes);
- providing help to children and other relatives (enabling the gene pool to survive, rearing children, parenting).

It is these last two, the emphasis on distinctive, and essentially un-changeable, behaviour patterns for men and women, that have been most controversial. Men and women, the evolutionary psychologists claim, have distinctive adaptive behaviours. Men can spread their sperm (genes) without great effort and their best reproductive strategy is to have as many partners as possible. Female reproduction requires much more time and effort, and it is in women's interest to secure the attention and protective care of one male. Women therefore have had to develop strategies to ensnare men, and to ensure their investment in bringing up children. Women are more cautious than men in consenting to sex, and spend more time on their appearance. They are attracted to older men who have more resources. Men, on the other hand, prefer younger women, who have more reproductive capacity. Women are more likely to be jealous than men, in order to make sure they do not stray. Women's natural abilities will lead them to prefer childcare to work outside the home. And so on. What in other circumstances might be regarded as the most outrageous sexism has found an academic respectability in evolutionary psychology.

Bogin has attempted to summarize the evolution of childhood, that is, the gradual adaptations of genetic inheritance that makes childhood a good strat-egy for survival of the species. He hypothesizes that the smallness of infants and their relatively slow rate of bodily growth (relative to other mammalian offspring) confers advantages in feeding and babysitting. Children are easier to feed, consume less, and can be looked after by people other than their parents, yet have the long childhood they need to maximize the plasticity of their brains and learn about their environment.

> The five themes of childhood (feeding, nurturing, low cost, babysit-ting and plasticity) account for much of the evolution of and pattern of growth of our species. Understanding these themes helps resolve the paradox of human growth and evolution: lengthy development and low fertility.[6]

I have summarized these evolutionary ideas very briefly indeed. Since these ideas are in themselves offered at a broad level of generality, these summaries may appear rather crude. Critics such as Steven and Hilary Rose consider these evolutionary explanations to be absurd. However, such ideas have been considerably elaborated in many papers and books by evolutionary psychologists and their close ideological cousins, the sociobiologists. The sociobiologists are powerful popularizers. Perhaps the most well known is the American E. O. Wilson, who has written a series of books, including *Consilience: The Unity of Knowledge*. He argues too that human nature and human behaviour are governed by the evolutionary process of natural selection. In his view, all individual and cultural practices are governed by the impulse to get a Darwinian advantage for our genes. Natural selection shapes our behaviour, moral impulses and cultural norms. The way we feel about each other, the basic things we think about each other and say to one another are with us today by virtue of their past contribution to genetic fitness.

Richard Dawkins, the English sociobiologist, took the arguments still further in his book *The Selfish Gene*. His claim is that all life, and all explanations about life, are ultimately about the replication of genes. He and a number of other writers have speculated about cultural units, called 'memes', which mirror the action of the genes. Memes include catchphrases, tunes, clothes fashions, stiletto heels and so on. Precise predictions about human behaviour will be possible when we know still more about the composition of genes and can link them up with 'memes'. If we know that certain genetic malformations cause well-known diseases such as cystic fibrosis or sickle cell anaemia, then surely it cannot be long before we discover the gene for lying or the gene for flirting.

These reductionist arguments, that everything can in the end be explained by the genes, have also been adopted by some prominent writers in the field of child development. The American psychologist Sandra Scarr argued in her presidential address to the US Child Development Society in 1992 that children's development could only properly be understood in an evolutionary perspective. Genetic inheritance crucially shapes each child's life, and individuality can only be interpreted in terms of the reactions of genes to 'culture'. Like the evolutionary psychologists, Scarr regards genetics as unproblematical. In her view, the genes clearly determine more than 50 per cent of human behaviour, and it is only a matter of time before we understand the genetics involved. Her view is that we are pussyfooting if we pretend otherwise. (She also regards culture as easily described and assigned, an issue we return to in Chapter 6.)

The implication of saying that 'it's all in the genes' is that the environment in which children are raised is of relatively minor importance. At its most extreme, this argument has been used to justify neo-liberal economics. The poor are born to be poor and will stay poor whatever you do, and the rich are born to be rich and will become rich whatever you do. The economic marketplace is no more than a reflection of the biological survival of the fittest. Scarr's claims are along these lines. She regards most forms of childcare as 'good enough'. She claims that only in extreme cases is childcare likely to have very harmful or very positive effects on children. (In the absence of any systematic state funding for childcare in the USA the only regulated or funded childcare programmes tend to be early intervention programmes targeting very deprived communities – like Sure Start in the UK.) The debate Scarr provoked has focused a great deal on such early intervention programmes. Her critics argue that she is mistaken in relying so heavily on genetic evidence and evolutionary psychology, and even if she has not said so directly, her position supports the view that it is not worth intervening in poor communities with early childhood programmes. (This argument about intervention takes a different twist where neuroscientific evidence is concerned, as we shall see.)

The argument that 'it's all in the genes' does not mean, in the eyes of the sociobiologists and evolutionary psychologists, that we cannot or should not interfere with or manipulate the genes. The biological determinist argument that our genes control us is ironic, since we are also hoping to control our genes with scientific technology. If genes exist for criminality or other anti-social traits, gene therapy might be more effective than any other kind of intervention such as special schooling or prison. It has even been suggested that there is a gene for homosexuality, which has caused great concern amongst gay and lesbian communities because of the ethical implications of gene therapy.

> On the one hand ... our biology is our destiny, written in our genes by the shaping forces of human evolution through natural selection and random mutation. This biological fatalism is opposed by Promethean claims that biotechnology, in the form of genetic engineering, can manipulate our genes in such a way as to rescue us from the worst of our fates. It offers to eliminate illness, prolong life, grant our children enhanced intelligence and better looks – a cornucopia of technological goodies undreamed of even in the science fiction of prior generations.[7]

Aldous Huxley in his novel *Brave New World* described a society where some people – the alphas – are bred to be clever, and others – the betas and the gammas – are bred to be drones. It may be a long way off, but it is no longer an impossible scenario. Genetic manipulation and modification, and cloning are *already* taking place. The sociobiologists and evolutionary psychologists argue that genetic evolution could be used to understand, predict and control behaviour. In fact, Leonides has claimed that, in the future, evolutionary psychology will replace or overtake other forms of psychology.

The brazenness of some of these claims, especially those relating to the behaviour of men and women, and to 'memes' or 'cultural units of transmission' have sparked a considerable scientific debate. The arguments against using genetics and evolutionary psychology to explain behaviour can be summarized as follows:

- Genetic information is extremely complex. The biochemical processes involved cannot be translated into behaviour patterns except in the most extreme cases (such as Huntington's chorea, a degeneration of the nervous system that strikes in middle age or earlier).
- Darwin's theory of evolution put forward the survival of the fittest as an important, but not the only, mechanism to explain how humans evolved. Later writers have emphasized the random nature of many genetic changes, and the importance of major changes in the environment in skewing evolution.
- Human beings are so clever and competent that they can largely override their genetic inheritance. Children can, through learning, acquire all sorts of characteristics from their parents and other children and adults, without waiting for the generations' long process of translation into the genes.
- Evolutionary theories are too vague because they are based on speculation about human ancestry for which there is little or no direct evidence.

Ultimately, the argument revolves around scientific understanding and methodology. As we saw in Chapter 2, scientific theories deal with certainties, concrete phenomena that can be isolated and independently investigated, by a neutral scientist. Traditional scientific explanation is regarded as more robust and more predictive than any other type of explanation. Wilson even claims that we are programmed to adopt the scientific, atomistic model of thinking by our genes.

> The descent to minutissima, the search for ultimate smallness in entities such as electrons, is a driving impulse of Western natural science. It is a kind of instinct. Human beings are obsessed with building blocks, forever pulling them apart and putting them back together again.[8]

This traditional model of scientific investigation may need considerable modification when applied to the human sciences. Dawkins' idea of a 'meme' or 'cultural unit of transmission' or 'particles of culture' is an attempt to atomize culture and provide a 'scientific' explanation for it. Mary Midgley, a philosopher who has tried to address the issue of explanatory models in the sciences, argues that thought and behaviour cannot be meaningfully broken down into particles. They are more akin to ocean currents or wind force, where the overall pattern and context offer clues to understanding, rather than the miniscule constituent parts. The arguments about scientific modelling and Darwinism climax with brain research. Trying to understand how the brain works raises all the problems discussed above all over again with added emphasis.

The neurosciences

Neuroscience, that is the study of how the brain works, is an umbrella word which covers all kinds of disciplines and technologies. There is neuro-anatomy, neurobiology, neurochemistry, neuroendocrinology, neuro-physiology, neuropharmacology, neuropsychiatry, neurosurgery and so on. It is clear that there have been remarkable advances in neuroscience in the past two decades and in particular in the past five years. The afterlife of a scientific finding is cynically reckoned to be about seven years; after that, unless it is exceptional, it is out of date. In philosophy, ideas are still worth considering after two thousand years; but in experimental psychology anything over ten years is beginning to look dated, and in brain research, as in computing, if it was published last year it may well have been refuted or overtaken. The USA declared that the 1990s were the decade of the brain. Conventions on neuroscience attract not a mere 400, but 27,000 delegates.

What the brain is made of

The human brain is one of the most complicated structures in the universe. It appears to be organized in sections, and certain parts of the brain seem to be associated with language, seeing, hearing and so on.

The brain is made up of around 100 billion nerve cells, or neurons, and around the same number of glial cells, which are the supporting and nourishing elements of the brain. About half of the neurons are located in the cerebral cortex, an intricately woven tissue folded into six layers. Neurons vary in appearance. 'There are long thin neurons that send single snaking tendrils to the far reaches of the body; star shaped ones that reach out in all directions; and ones that bear a dense branching crown like absurdly overgrown antlers.'[9]

The functioning of the brain involves the flow of information through elaborate circuits consisting of networks of neurons. There is a microscopic gap in the junctions between the axon of one neuron and the dendrites of another. Information must cross these gaps via hook-ups called synapses. Each neuron may have between a few thousand and up to 100,000 synaptic connections.

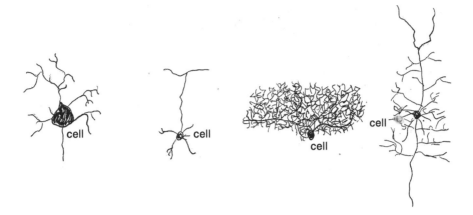

Figure 4.4 There are many different types of neural cells. This is an example of some characteristic shapes.

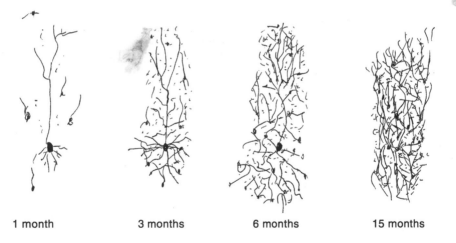

1 month   3 months   6 months   15 months

Figure 4.5 The connections between neurons develop rapidly after birth. This is a picture drawn from photomicrographs of infant brain tissue. Even so, it is only schematic, and not from one infant.

Communication between neurons involves both chemical and electrical signalling. There are other electrical junctions for communication between glia and between neurons and glia. No computer has ever come anywhere near the complexity, precision or speed that characterizes the human brain.

Some of the research about the development of the brain comes from embryology. We know that at the same time as the synapses are being

connected up, the axons or connections become protected or myelinated. Myelination is the laying down of a fatty sheath which insulates axons and reduces muddled connections, in order to speed information flows.

During foetal growth, neural cells divide at a phenomenal rate. Neural proliferation continues after birth, but at some point the instruction to proliferate is switched off – sometime in the late teens. At birth, a baby has billions of neurons. Many will be discarded and die off. Nature frequently overprovides and selects out. Redundancy appears to be a protective survival technique.

Each neuron is bathed in a continually changing chemical environment of neurotransmitters, neuromodulators and hormones, called neuroproteins. About 30,000 different proteins affect the neurons. Neurons react differently to these proteins. Some are profoundly changed; others may be washed with a potent sauce of aminoacids and yet be unaltered or unaffected. Some neurotransmitters act extremely fast, as superconductors; others have a modulatory or inhibitory effect. Understanding the effects of drugs on emotions and cognition may provide more information about the chemical architecture of the brain. But the starting point of investigation is that the biochemical processes involved in the brain are unimaginably complex.

Investigating the brain

A major difficulty in investigating the human brain is accessing it. The neuroscientist Steven Rose describes the struggle to *begin* to understand how the brain works. He discusses the methods and experiments needed to find out more about the brain, and the proteins that affect it, in his very readable book *The Making of Memory*. (In this book he also dwells on the difficulties of reconciling subjective individual experience and memory with objective chemical experiments on the brains of chickens.) Genetic inheritance can be investigated without too much damaging bodily intrusion. The brain cannot.

Until relatively recently, neuroscientists were highly dependent on three sources, all of which had grave limitations from the point of view of understanding the relationship between brain and behaviour. Firstly, they were dependent on animal studies – prodding or excising the brain tissues of partially electrocuted rats or kittens or squid or some other vivisected creature. Secondly, information comes from autopsies, from examination of the brain tissues of the dead. Embryos have been a very useful – but for many, ethically problematical – source for analysing the stages of development of the brain. Thirdly, neuroscientists have relied on studies of brain-damaged patients. But there are also great difficulties inferring brain function from brain-damaged patients – it is like trying to explain how tennis is played from watching the actions of a blind one-legged man.

New non-invasive techniques are being developed which rely on measurements somewhat similar to electroencephalograms (EEGs) that measure
electrical activity in the brain. There are surges of activity in the brain as we
think or act, which are expressed in metabolic changes. Unlike EEGs, new
techniques can measure not merely the level of activity, but also its location
within the brain. So, for example, if you recite a poem, you might get one
pattern showing up in your brain; if you gobble down a cake you may get
another.

There are basically three types of metabolic imaging:

- Regional cerebral blood flow (rCBF), in which an inert radioactive gas
  dissolved in blood indicates where blood flow has increased.
- Positron emission tomography (PET), where the radioactive analogue
  of glucose, or sugar, is injected into the blood to measure cumulative
  metabolism in different brain regions.
- Magnetic resonance imaging (MRI), which uses the response of
  water molecules within the brain to changes in the level of brain
  activity.

All these imaging techniques are extremely expensive to use. Such scanning
techniques can only be used in laboratory settings, and they usually require
subjects to keep very still. New techniques of brain imaging are constantly
being tried, but even so, the information gained is rudimentary. The coloured
blobs of the PET scan each represent assemblies of millions of cells or
neurons.

Cognitive psychologists are teaming up with neurologists to use and
develop these techniques. Systematic testing of children with brain disorders
suggests that children use a variety of learning strategies, some of which were
of use in circumventing their disability, some not. Studies suggest that infant
learning strategies, and the learning which ensues, develop very gradually and
in response to environmental stimuli. The brain appears to be very flexible,
rather than preprogrammed for modularity as the evolutionary psychologists
suggest.[10] However, tests on very young children also raise ethical issues.
Ethical guidelines exist but some query whether they are sufficient.

Theories about the brain

Despite all this intense research, the brain is so very complex that our
knowledge, despite constant new technologies, is rudimentary and highly
conjectural. No one has any kind of overall theory about how the brain
works. So it is hardly surprising that, as yet, neuroscience does not add up to a
coherent explanation of how we think and become the way we are.

Studying the brain and its activity is possible at many levels, from
that of the output of the entire system to that of isolated receptor
proteins . . . yet many of [these] subdisciplines continue to churn out
results relatively uninfluenced by . . . those working in adjacent parts
of the field. . . . We have masses of data and lots of limited theories . . .
but we still lack any grand unified conception of what it means to be a
brain and how it does what it does.[11]

Brains do many things at a time and with incredible rapidity. Despite Rose's
caution about there being no overall theory of brain functioning, some
popular writers on the neurosciences have made big theoretical leaps.

For the evolutionary psychologists, the most powerful evidence of the
genetic preprogramming of the brain into modules is demonstrated by 'the
language instinct'. Steven Pinker takes Chomsky further than he himself
wanted to go. In two influential and popular books, *The Language Instinct* and
How the Mind Works, Pinker claims that humans have a language instinct, and
are preprogrammed to learn language. Pinker argues that there is no way
babies can infer grammar, that is, the rules of language, from the number of
words that are spoken to them, yet all babies learn to speak their language
grammatically. Therefore, Pinker says, a baby's brain is preprogrammed to
learn a language, and once language is learnt, then in some way the preprogramming switches off; it becomes much more difficult to learn a second or
third language as we get older. The development of language in very young
children is taken as evidence that the first three years are so important.

Computer modelling has been another source of theories about brain
functioning. The metaphor of the computer as a brain is a powerful one.
Science fiction has always assumed that computers will eventually be
programmed to act like humans. Brain modelling has turned out to be more
difficult in real life. Deep Blue, the chess computer, can beat ordinary chess
players, but still gets beaten by the great chess grandmasters, whose human
tactics outwit it. But the most recent research on computer modelling suggests that if one abandons the supposition that human brains are merely
extremely powerful data storage and processing machines, but work, for
example, like neural nets, sifting and hierarchically ordering and recoding
information, then better approximations of human brain activity can be
developed.

This theory about neural nets has been developed by the evolutionary
neuroscientist Terrence Deacon. Deacon hypothesizes that, as a baby grows,
her brain develops a whole series of nets or sieves to sift through incoming
information. At first the net is so coarse, it catches only the most obvious
features of this information; then quite rapidly the nets get finer and finer. He
says that because babies know so little, and have no words, they have to scan
the incoming information for landmarks and signs, and grammar offers such

landmarks. So if you take the phrase, 'give the cup back to mummy', a baby might take some time to recognize words like 'give' and 'cup' and 'to' and 'mummy' and she will recognize first of all that there is an invariant pattern to the order of these words. It is rather like learning a tune; you can follow the tune before you pick out the individual notes – and the individual notes on their own mean very little without the tune.

Different languages have different grammatical patterns and these are what a baby picks up first of all in learning how to understand what people say to her. Deacon's ideas about language acquisition seem to be borne out by various computer modelling experiments. Computers cannot learn the rules of grammar from simply storing all the data that comes in and trying to analyse it. It is not logically possible. Human learning is simply not cumulative, least of all a baby's learning. But if the computer is programmed differently, as a kind of neural net, to pick up certain patterns, then, with great difficulty, it can learn grammar.

As the neural nets get finer, and the baby begins to sift out words, then this ability to pick up grammar is lost; the signposts are already in place, they form the layout of the next, finer neural net, and the baby's brain will now scan for more detailed information about words and meanings. This theory would explain why young children can learn languages easily and adults cannot. Language is the first and most special example of learning, and the symbols and meanings language gives us enables us, with enormous flexibility, to develop, continue and accelerate these processes – the coding, refining, sifting, comparing, storing, recalling and excluding. With language we can use and call upon a spectacular amount of information about the world.

A key question is the extent to which language is culturally determined. Language is essentially a question of prioritizing and relaying information from the environment: creating ways of interpreting information, deciding what is relevant, what can be coded, what should be stored, what it is necessary to recall, what can be emphasized and embroidered. These decisions are, in the last resort, cultural and value-based. These cultural issues are considered in Chapter 6.

Ideas about bodily, and in particular visceral, responses, and their influence on brain functioning, have been put forward by Joseph LeDoux in his book *The Emotional Brain*. He suggests that although we conventionally conceptualize thinking and feeling, the intellectual and emotional, as separate activities, in the brain they are not separate at all, they appear to be so interconnected as to make our conceptual distinction between them a dubious one. Other neuroscientists have commented on the effects of stress, and the way in which our perceptions of events influence bodily reactions. It is well established that certain kinds of drugs, such as cocaine or amphetamine, affect the way we feel, although exactly what is going on in the brain even the neuropharmacologists have difficulties in explaining.

Theories about brain functioning revolve around a number of key (and unresolved) issues:

- How does the brain develop? What kinds of cell division are taking place and with what rapidity?
- Are brain functions segmented or modularized, according to genetic preprogramming? Or is the brain preprogrammed only to be very flexible?
- How significant is the number of neural connections in brain functioning?
- Are there critical periods when neural connections and pathways are established? Or can neural connections and pathways continue to develop throughout life?
- Do certain kinds of environments enhance brain development?
- How does brain functioning respond to the many kinds of bio-chemical/hormonal influences to which it is subject, either naturally or artificially through drugs?

What kind of scientific explanation?

Even if we were clearer about the answer to these questions, would they lead to a greater understanding of behaviour in general, and of child development in particular? Both Pinker and Deacon, in different ways, argue that such understanding is within our grasp. Pinker concludes his book *How the Mind Works* with a chapter entitled 'The Meaning of Life'. He thinks we should reduce what we can to atomistic, scientific explanation and accept that we are not programmed to deal with the rest.

> Consciousness is activity in layer 4 of the cortex or the contents of short-term memory. Free will is in the anterior cingulate sulcus or the executive sub-routine. Morality is kin selection and reciprocal altruism.
>   . . . Maybe philosophical problems are hard not because they are divine or irreducible or meaningless or workaday science, but because the mind of Homo sapiens lacks the cognitive equipment to deal with them. We are organisms, not angels, and our minds are organs, not pipelines to the truth. Our minds evolved by natural selection to solve problems that were life and death matters to our ancestors, not to commune with correctness or to answer any question we are capable of asking.[12]

The attraction of scientific explanations, however incomplete, is that, as 'hard' evidence they promise greater predictive power than do psychology and human sciences. They also offer an enormous potential for social control. As Rose comments:

> Science is about both knowledge and power. The new neuroscience is not merely about understanding but also about changing the world. . . . Anxiety, depression, anger at social injustice are all now potentially to be explained in terms of disordered biochemistry, itself more often than not the result of disordered genes. . . . The technological thrust to generate a psycho-civilized society by brain manipulation, from psycho-surgery to tailored drugs is very strong.[13]

It is partly this enormous prestige, and potential for manipulation, that makes the neurosciences so seductive a resource for early childhood.

The next section explores how the early childhood literature has drawn on neuroscientific evidence to support its own, more tentative conclusions.

What lessons are there for early childhood from the neurosciences?

What do the neurosciences tell us about early childhood? According to the educationalist John Bruer, the answer to this question is 'absolutely nothing'. His exasperation is understandable. There are frequent claims that neurosciences 'prove' that intervention in early childhood is justified by scientific research on the brain. Some of these claims are explored in more detail below. It has become a commonplace (mis)understanding, put forward in many books and articles, and stated confidently from many conference platforms, that, although there is virtually no direct evidence, brain research offers us clues about how to promote the development of children.

In his book *The Myth of the First Three Years*, Bruer explores the limitations of the neuroscientific evidence and the way in which brain research has been sold despite these limitations. He argues that those who draw on brain research to explain and justify intervention in early childhood rely on three main assumptions.

- Brain connectivity – the development of synaptic connections – equals greater learning.
- Critical periods, after which it becomes harder to establish such synaptic connections.
- An enriched environment can promote faster and denser neural connections.

Explaining the sense of personhood, feelings and bodily sensations is hard to link coherently to discussions about neuronal growth and activity. Yet this is what authors have tried to do.

Synaptic connections

As discussed above, brain research is extraordinarily complex, multifaceted and fragmented. Almost all of it has been carried out on animals. Human tissue is available only from autopsies or from brain-damaged patients where intervention appears justifiable. Counting synaptic connections, given the density of the cortex, is scientific work at the borderline of the possible. Bruer recounts a series of studies by Pasko Rakic and colleagues on brain development in rhesus monkeys. This relied on electron microscopes to enlarge tissue samples by 14,000 times. They then counted the synapses in each of at least four specimens from dozens of animals. They counted over 500,000 synapses in 25,000 electron micrographs. Each micrograph required very careful analysis in order to distinguish synaptic densities from all the other brain information contained in the micrograph – the variety of neuronal cells, non-neuronal cells, sheathing, blood vessels. Bruer quotes one of the researchers as saying to him, 'This is a sparsely populated field. In fact one might say that the study of postnatal brain development is so sparsely populated that it does not really exist as a field of scientific enquiry at all.'[14] Tracing the development of synaptic connectivity in a given human individual has not so far been undertaken. Indeed, even in rhesus monkeys, the cortical interference involved in operating on the monkey and obtaining brain tissue is likely to skew any subsequent results obtained from the subject.

Critical periods

The evidence on critical periods is equally hard to prove using neuroscientific studies. The evidence that does exist comes partly from behavioural studies on learning and attachment in a variety of species, and partly from studies of language development. The neuroscientific evidence cited is usually that of a series of experiments carried out in the 1970s on the visual cortex of kittens. They systematically blinded kittens in one eye, and demonstrated that even if sight was restored, the kitten could no longer see out of that eye since the necessary neuronal connections had not been established.

My own introduction to this field of brain research began in 1999 in Canada when I read an influential policy report advocating intervention in early childhood, written by Fraser Mustard, a retired physician. He argued that the government should invest in the under 3s before it was too late. Instead of using social or political arguments, which are more controversial, he cited the kitten studies as a major – and incontrovertible – source of evidence on critical periods. When I checked the references in the report, I was shocked to find that there was so little recent or direct neuroscientific evidence. How could such claims be made about neuroscience on the basis of 30-year-old experiments on laboratory-reared kittens? I subsequently heard Fraser Mustard address a shareholder's meeting of the Inter-American Bank in Paris, chaired by Amartya Sen, the distinguished Nobel prize-winning economist, arguing that the neurological evidence on critical periods was too powerful to ignore and the bank should invest in early childhood programmes. This is an indication both of the breathtaking claims that are being made on the back of the neurosciences, and of the credibility that they are accorded even in very eminent circles.

Enriched environments

Our understanding of the effects of enriched environments on brain development is also drawn mainly from animal studies. However, even with animal studies there is a problem about defining a 'good' or 'enriched' environment. Generally, the word used is 'complex', but complexity only in relation to the normal environment of a laboratory animal, not in any absolute sense. Most of the work on the effects on the brain of living in a complex environment has been in relation to rats. There is fairly clear neurological evidence that rats' brains do develop, in fairly circumscribed areas, mainly visual, in relation to certain kinds of complex environments, but this development also appears to take place in rats of all ages.

As discussed above, other information about the plasticity of the brain comes from brain-damaged patients who are able, to an extent, to learn new skills and develop compensatory mechanisms in different parts of their brain. This hardly amounts to neurological evidence about the importance of enriched environments for young children. There are behavioural studies about enriched environments, which suggest that in behavioural terms they may be important; but the evidence about neurological mechanisms which mirror behavioural development is conjectural.

Information about neuronal patterning in children is very limited. PET scans, for example, involve the use of radioactive materials and cannot be given to young children unless there are substantial reasons for intervention. Yet one of the most frequently cited research findings, quoted, for instance, by NAEYC (National Association for the Education of Young Children) as evidence for their manual on developmentally appropriate practice (see Chapter 9) is that of Chugani *et al.* on brain development. The study reported the results of PET scans on 29 epileptic children, ranging in age from 5 days to 15 years, many of whom had been medicated since infancy and some of whom were medicated on the day they were scanned. Their results were compared with those of 7 normal adults ranging from age 19 to 30. This study indicates that, based on PET analyses of brain glucose metabolisms, the brain does show some maturational patterns. The interpretation of these glucose uptake patterns is very tentative indeed, and there is only indirect evidence that they are related to neuronal growth and the development of synaptic connections. Despite this very limited and atypical sample, this work is continually cited. As Bruer remarks:

> Chugani's 1987 PET study is . . . possibly one of the most over-interpreted scientific papers of the last twenty five years. . . . It is taken as the paradigmatic example of how neuroscience is providing 'hard data' about the first three years of life.[15]

Why rely on brain research to justify practice in early childhood?

Why, then, has there been such a furore over brain research underpinning child development? To use the word 'furore' is not to exaggerate. The following extracts are from the mass-market magazines *Time* and *Newsweek*.

> Experience in the first years of life lays the basis for networks of neurons that enable us to be smart, creative and adaptable in all the years that follow.[16]

> Every lullaby, every giggle and peek-a-boo, triggers a crackling along his neural pathways, laying the groundwork for what could someday be a love of art or a talent for soccer or a gift for making and keeping friends.[17]

> You hold your newborn so his sky-blue eyes are just inches away from brightly patterned wallpaper. ZZZt: a neuron from his retina makes an electrical connection with one in his brain's visual cortex. You gently touch his hand with a clothespin; he grasps it, drops it, and you return it to him with soft words and a smile. Crackle: neurons from his hand strengthen their connection to those in his sensory-motor cortex.[18]

Others using more sober language make very similar points. Anne Meade, in *Promoting Evidence Based Practice in Early Childhood Education*, summarizes neurological research, and whilst admitting there is little or no mention of play in the neuroscientific literature, goes on to claim: 'brain research contains considerable implications for the role of play in early childhood education. . . . Is this type of play where children use all modalities – the senses, physical activity, emotion and representations – particularly conducive to synaptic growth?'[19]

Mary Eming Young, senior adviser for the World Bank's $1,000 million loan programme to develop early childhood programmes in 29 countries, claims, at some length and citing Chugani, that brain research justifies the bank's investment in early childhood. I have traced elsewhere[20] how those responsible for early childhood programmes in the World Bank argue for early childhood intervention for targeted poor populations. These intervention programmes are based on the provision of 'enriched' environments (that is, American early childhood education programmes based on the NAEYC developmentally appropriate practice manuals). This is, for the World Bank, a more respectable and acceptable argument than the alternative, which is to admit the need for radical socio-economic intervention to change the lives of poor children.

Jerome Kagan also discusses this point about the nature of intervention – whether it should be on the level of the individual (an enriched environment) or at the level of society. He has been the most persistent psychological critic of the view that intervention in the first three years matters. He argues that the evidence about brain research is used in a very cavalier way:

> Psychological determinists have assumed that every kiss, every lullaby, or scolding alters a child's brain in ways that will influence his future. But if slight changes in synapses, like some amino acid substitions, are without functional consequences, then every smile at an infant is not to be viewed as a bank deposit accumulating psychological dividends.[21]

Kagan calls this popular emphasis on the developing brain capacity of infants the myth of infant determinism. The reason that such explanations are so popular, he claims, is that intervention protects the myth of equality in a society that, like that in the USA, is profoundly unequal. Instead, he argues that social class (and cultural context – see Chapter 6) are the most powerful predictors of future performance.

Arguing for the funding and provision of services for young children has been, at least in Anglo-American countries, an uphill struggle. Children have been a very low political priority in these countries. The so-called findings of brain research have given these struggles an extra edge. In particular, they appear to offer a solution to childhood poverty and inequality that can be addressed on an individual level – enriched environments for targeted populations – rather than on a societal level – redistribution of resources. (More than one in five children come from impoverished backgrounds in the UK and USA.[22]) They also appear to offer the possibility to individual parents to enhance their child's development, to hurry it along, hence the enormous popular interest in the *Time* and *Newsweek* articles quoted above, and the rush of popular books, like that of Kotulak. His

book *Inside the Brain: Revolutionary Discoveries of How the Mind Works* won a
Pulitzer prize.

> For millions of American children, the world they encounter is relent-
> lessly menacing and hostile. So with astounding speed and efficiency,
> their brains adapt and prepare for battle. Cells form trillions of new
> connections that create the chemical pathways of aggression; some
> chemicals are produced in over-abundance, some are repressed. . . .
> What research can now tell us with increasing certainty is just how
> the brain adapts physically to this threatening environment – how
> abuse, poverty, neglect or sensory deprivation can reset the brain's
> chemistry in ways that makes some genetically vulnerable children
> more prone to violence.[23]

Underlying these claims about the importance of brain research is our (by
now) familiar debate about scientific method. Although they also involve
speculation and conjecture, universally agreed scientific methods have been
extremely successful in revealing the physical world. The discoveries of science
have gone hand in hand with rapid technological developments, from computers and radar to bombs. Human sciences can boast no such successes. The
fields of genetics and neuroscience are extremely important and mesmerizing
areas of research in their own right, but their great attraction to the field of
human sciences is that they appear to offer an incontrovertible underpinning
to behavioural and social events. A new branch of psychology, evolutionary
psychology, rests on the exploration of such claims.

Meanwhile, philosophers doggedly persevere trying to explain the nature
of explanation:

> How can there be an objective world of money, property, marriage,
> governments, elections, football games, cocktail parties and law-courts
> in a world that consists entirely of physical particles in fields of force,
> and in which some of these particles are organized into systems that
> are conscious biological beasts such as ourselves?[24]

Mary Midgley, in a series of papers and articles, sensibly suggests that
there are many different ways of knowing and explaining the world and many
ways of being in it. Our contribution is to be alert, well informed and critical –
no mean task given the inevitable scientific dogfights about the status of new
knowledge in ground-breaking biosciences such as genetics and the neurosciences. Midgley argues that we should be concerned to justify our practices
not only in terms of what we know but also in terms of what we value.
Ethics, values and social commentary have their place in all methodological
enquiries.

Summary

This chapter considered the arguments that the understanding of behaviour can be enriched by brain research and genetics. It also briefly explored evolutionary psychology, which claims to be based on genetics. These are very popular topics for discussion and are frequently aired in the press. But the evidence that brain research and genetics can help us understand young children is at a very early stage, and might mislead us more than it helps us.

Main messages from this chapter

1   Genes are extremely complicated and, despite many recent findings, we know relatively little about how they work.
2   The brain is still more complicated, supremely so, and it is foolish to make predictions about young children's behaviour using current findings from the field of brain research.
3   You need to keep up with ideas about scientific research in the fields of genetics and the neurosciences, but do not be seduced by them.

What to read next

Dennis, C. and Gallagher, R. (eds) (2001) *The Human Genome*. Hampshire: Palgrave/ Nature Publishing Group.
Rose, S. (ed.) (1999) *From Brains to Conciousness? Essays on the New Sciences of the Mind*. London: Penguin.

Notes

1   Dawkins 1988: xiii
2   Wiggins 2001 (personal communication)
3   Kagan 1998: 13
4   Jones 1999: 304
5   See Evans and Zarate 1999
6   Bogin 1998: 37
7   Rose and Rose 2000: 4
8   Wilson 1998: 53
9   Carter, quoted in Meade 2001
10   See Rose 1999 for further discussion
11   Rose 1999: 5
12   Pinker 1998: 561

13 Rose 1999: 17
14 Bruer 1999: 72
15 Ibid.: 8
16 *Time* 1997
17 *Newsweek* 1996
18 Ibid.
19 Meade 2001: 22
20 Penn 2002a
21 Kagan 1998: 20
22 OECD 2001
23 Kotulak 1996: ix–x
24 Searle, quoted in Midgley 1998: 247

5 On the other side of the world

The previous chapter was about the extraordinary developments in genetics and neurosciences. It also suggested that those working in the field of early childhood have overreacted to and overinterpreted those findings. This chapter explores the other end of the continuum. In what ways do wider cultural and socio-economic circumstances shape how children grow and learn? What sort of notice do we take of those circumstances?

Anthropology

Anthropology is about the study of culture. Like all the other disciplines discussed in this book, there are no right approaches or right answers. There are certain major themes that crop up in the study of anthropology – self, identity, interpretation, meaning – but there are many perspectives in dealing with them. The doggerel verse sums it up: 'Two men look out from the selfsame bars; One sees mud, the other sees stars.'

Anthropology is above all about 'culture'. But culture is a very slippery concept. The classic definition is that

> culture . . . taken in its wide ethnographic sense is that complex whole which includes knowledge, belief, art, morals, law, custom and any other capabilities and habits acquired by man as a member of society.[1]

This is a long list and more or less impossible for anyone to investigate or describe. For instance, is culture what goes on in people's heads, their attitudes and understandings? Or is it what they actually do, the way they behave in certain circumstances?

A culture is taken for granted by those who belong to it. We think about what we ourselves do as (mostly) rational and self-chosen, but in fact we may be drawing on very traditional cultural ideas. Peacock, who wrote a useful textbook for beginners on anthropology,[2] uses the example of time. In Europe and America we tend to think of time as a line stretching between the past and the future, divided into centuries, years, months, weeks, days, hours, minutes and seconds. Every event we unhesitatingly classify along the time-line – births, marriages and deaths, jobs, any important event. The future is movement on the timeline. This notion of time is embedded in the English language (for example, English has several past tenses – some languages have no past tense). Our understanding of work, 'getting ahead', 'careers' and so on, is time bound. Time so ties us down that there are even those who protest against its demands. The 'slow food movement' is a (leisurely) campaign that makes the point that the quality of what we eat is more important than the time it takes to produce it – a movement that started in Italy, where good food traditions are very strong. There is now the 'hurried child' syndrome, a young child who is pushed to accomplish learning more quickly, by starting school early. But in other parts of the world, time is not such an obsession. In Buddhist tradition, time is circular, and comes around again. In parts of Africa it is rude not to come to a consensus in a discussion, however long it takes. Peacock, somewhat tongue-in-cheek, cites a Pacific Island society where 'time was not so much a line along which one moved as it was a puddle in which one sat, splashed or wallowed'.[3]

Another example is the concept of self. In Anglo-American societies, the individual is the elementary unit of human experience. The individual is the building block of society. 'Each child is an individual and must be treated as such', is a basic tenet for many early childhood practitioners. Yet in other societies a person is known not by their own individual name, but by a name that links them to other people. In some Moslem societies, a person is known by the name of his father or tribe. In some African societies people are called by the name of their children. When I visit some of my African friends I am called 'Mama Loveday' after the name of my eldest daughter. Many trad-itional societies are collectivist, and members of the society consider that 'fitting in' with others is far more important than doing anything by yourself. For all the emphasis on individualism in Euro-American societies, the indi-vidual is, paradoxically, a product of the group. What we term 'individual' is a cultural construct. Without belonging to a society or a culture, without speak-ing the language of the society or the culture, we would have no existence in it.

We take time and self for granted in Euro-American societies, yet to an outsider (and to some insiders), these aspects of 'culture' are rigid and ritual-istic, and probably irritating. For example, we asked my African son-in-law, visiting England for the first time, what he noticed most. 'People do not greet me in the street or on the buses', he said.

The anthropologist from outside tries to uncover habits and traditions that are so ingrained that people do not know they possess them. In one sense of the word, culture is a name that anthropologists give to the taken-for-granted but powerfully influential understandings and codes that are learnt and shared by members of a group, but seem mysterious to those outside of it. This is popularly known in anthropology as 'making the strange familiar and the familiar strange'.

'Culture' is also a shorthand word for describing a conglomeration of different, and sometimes incompatible, views and understandings in a given society or community. Within a 'culture', people hold different views about what that culture means, what it involves and how it should be upheld. There are arguments about 'British' culture, for example. Does it include Scotland, Wales and Northern Ireland? Has it been changed by immigration patterns over the twentieth century? Is the royal family still important or is it irrelevant? Are cricket and warm beer an essential part of British culture? There are many questions to ask about 'British culture' and the answers might differ radically according to who is giving their opinion. Anyone reading the *Guardian* newspaper, for example, might suppose the monarchy is obsolete and is now a joke; whereas tourists watching the changing of the guard at Buckingham Palace might consider that Britain is still a land of pageantry and ancient rituals.

Anthropologists have often chosen to carry out their work in parts of the world that are different from those where they usually reside. This encounter with other 'cultures' has the effect of sharpening up one's own cultural identity. By thinking about how other people do things, you become more aware of how you do them yourself – in something as minor as food preparation or as major as religion. As Peacock comments: 'A major mission and contribution of anthropology has long been, and continues to be, to enhance our awareness of the power and reality of culture in our existence.'[4]

The method anthropologists commonly use is called *ethnography*. This is a kind of participant observation, living the life of the people you are trying to understand, noting down as much as you can about it, as systematically as possible. Clifford Geertz, a well-known anthropologist, argues that anthropology is about interpretation of meaning. In his book *The Interpretation of Cultures* he defines culture as 'a web of significance'. The anthropologist can never fully understand a culture outside of his own, but he can learn how to describe it and analyse the meanings or significance of events very carefully indeed. This method of describing he calls ethnography, or 'thick description'.

'Thick description' is a useful way of documenting and understanding events from the perspectives of other people, but as other anthropologists have pointed out, it too is problematical. It is what we might call the glass bubble problem. Culture is essentially a self-contained world which an outsider is peeping into. The anthropologist is a peeper, trying to writing down or photograph what he sees. James Clifford and George Marcus, in a well-known book called *Writing Culture*, argued that anthropologists, in telling the story of their travels, exaggerate them and make them more romantic than they are. Bronislaw Malinowski, one of the earliest and most renowned of anthropologists, kept a diary during his trips to New Guinea and North Melanesia. It was a shock when it was posthumously published because it illustrated all too clearly how he stood apart from the societies he was investigating and was sometimes contemptuous of them.

Some writers have gone on to question vigorously the notion of culture. Renato Rosaldo, for instance, argues that people are misled if they think that culture is ever fixed or final. In all cultures there is a continual ebb and flow and reshaping of ideas, as the example of Britain shows us. Tolerance and understanding of culture is not merely about trying to understand and make allowances for someone different from ourselves. Culture, he says, is almost always fought over, it is 'a field of contention' in which the key words are 'change, experience, conflict and struggle'.[5] The cultural historian and anthropologist Eric Wolf also argues that 'culture' has for ever been 'assembled, dismantled, and reassembled'.[6] Sharon Stephens, an anthropologist particularly concerned with children's experiences and understandings, has pointed out the difficulties about investigating or upholding cultural traditions when they conflict with each other or with what we think is good for children.

> What sort of social visions and notions of culture underlie assertions within international rights discourses that every child has a right to cultural identity? To what extent is this identity conceived of as singular and exclusive, and what sorts of priorities are asserted in cases where various forms of cultural identity – regional, national, ethnic minority or indigenous – come up against one another?[7]

'Culture' is for ever being amalgamated and reshaped as people from different communities come into contact with one another. In certain places at certain times – as in most capital cities in the twentieth century – these cultural encounters are accelerated and intensified. The populations of major cities are swollen by refugees, immigrants and economic migrants. The issue then becomes one of *identity*. Should the newcomers try to keep to their familiar ways and traditions? Or should they drop them and try to become like everyone else – except, of course, everyone else is not the same. What kind of British person should a refugee to Britain become? A royalist? A cricket player?

And what about the people who were there before the latest wave of refugees arrived? How do they view the identity of the refugees and incomers? To settled populations in North America and Europe, it is *other* people, usually distinguished by the colour of their skin, who have these quaint blocks of irrational, or sometimes destructive, beliefs and practices; funny colourful clothes; strange, strong foods; and idiomatic or incomprehensible speech patterns. 'They' have 'a culture' which is sometimes tolerated and sometimes resented. Long-term residents of that country, especially if they are white, feel less need to question or comment on their own culture.

People newly arrived from poor or war-torn countries, especially children, often feel bad about their identity. The pressures are intense to conform, to adapt and to change. In his autobiography *Out of Place*, Edward Said, originally a Palestinian, describes his life-long struggle to fit in, to become American. As a child sent to a holiday camp he felt horribly peculiar. 'So beginning in America I resolved to live as if I were a simple, transparent soul and not to speak of my family or origins except as required, and then very sparingly. To become, in other words, like the others, as anonymous as possible.'[8]

George Lamming, the Caribbean writer, describing his childhood after coming to England, wrote: 'No black boy wanted to be white but no black boy liked the idea of being black. When you asked Boy Blue why he was so black he would answer, "Just as I wus going to be born the light went out."'[9]

Identity is even more of an issue in ex-colonial countries. Geographical borders of countries in Africa or Asia or South America reflect the past efforts of colonial administrators to rule, rather than sensible borders based on ethnic, linguistic, religious or class or even geographical boundaries. In Nigeria, for example, there are many different and competing traditions and histories, including long-standing religious, linguistic and ethnic divides. It does not make sense to talk about children coming from 'Nigerian' culture, especially when their families settle in the UK. Yet, as Brian Street points out, that is what all too often happens.

> Even though the concept of culture appears not to be rooted in biol-
> ogy (race) it is in fact very often premised on assumptions about fixity
> and permanence: the idea that somebody, for instance, might come
> from Nigeria and settle in England, somehow bringing along a bag
> with Nigerian culture in it, with which he or she is then stuck. . . . A
> person belongs to a given culture, that is how they are, they must
> think that way and behave that way.[10]

How galling, then, to be labelled as Nigerian, when Nigeria itself is made up of so many groups, many of whom are at odds with one another. The children of these 'Nigerians' may themselves have very ambivalent attitudes to assimilation, as Edward Said did in the USA.

Anthropologists then deal with a range of questions to do with culture. The word 'culture' is used by anthropologists as a useful abstraction to describe a holistic view of how a group of people, a community, or a society, live and communicate. But it is full of pitfalls as a workable concept. So much so that some anthropologists now focus more narrowly on concepts such as *identity*, or *beliefs* or *meanings*. They also no longer focus their research exclusively on far-away or exotic places, but find it equally challenging to use ethnographic methods to examine the everyday world where they live.

The contribution of anthropology to understanding childhood

Anthropologists have not spent much time investigating childhood – with a few notable exceptions. Margaret Mead and a group of like-minded colleagues, working in the 1920s and 1930s, wanted to investigate whether parenting was the same everywhere. She worked in a number of countries, including, most famously, Samoa in the Pacific Islands and in New Guinea. She demonstrated how different communities held very different views about childrearing and about sex roles in relation to parenting. In one of the tribes she studied, the Arapesh, men seemed to be very gentle and did most of the childrearing. In another, everyone was a bit rough with the children. Her accounts are very readable, even today, and like the best of anthropological accounts, make you reflect on the culture you are living in as well as the one she is describing. She has been criticized for exaggeration by male anthropologists who went back to the same place and, using the same ethnographic methods, came to different conclusions. Then she was exonerated again, by female anthropologists who argued that the sex of the anthropologist gave them different insights. Women anthropologists used women informants; whereas male anthropologists listened more to men. Mead and her colleagues were especially concerned with proving or disproving various aspects of psychoanalytic and personality theory. Psychoanalysis and personality theory no longer have the hold on psychology that they once had, so Mead's work may now appear dated.

Jahoda and Lewis have summarized work on the anthropology of childhood. They argued not only that psychologists had been unable to deal with cultural difference but also that these differences were so powerful and pervasive that it was nonsense to talk about universal norms of behaviour. They gave some remarkable examples of childrearing traditions. One contributor to their book describes musical games for children in a community in South Africa. The best musical results were obtained when all participants combined the maximum of individual skill and fellow-feeling in the realization and elaboration of a basic musical pattern. 'Pleasing others and pleasing oneself in musical performance were two interrelated aspects of the same activity.'[11] (This tradition was probably translated to the USA and re-emerged as jazz.) But it is at odds with the view in Anglo-American countries that children should be encouraged to be creative individuals, but they cannot be creative as part of a group; you can stress one or the other but not both together.

Montagu, who was concerned about arms build-ups and political aggression, questioned whether aggression was innate. He claimed that there were communities who were almost entirely non-aggressive. In his book *Learning Non-aggression* he collected anthropological accounts of communities where aggression in children was almost unknown. One such account describes learning amongst pygmy communities in Zaire. Children learn in turn security, dependence, independence, interdependence, coordination and cooperation. For instance, one game taught to younger children by older peers is swinging from ropes in trees. The game is to coordinate the swinging, so that everyone can take part and it becomes 'a perfect ballet' in which all children learn to demonstrate mutual coordination and agility. He describes games like this as 'the essence of co-operative communal life, to which competition is the antithesis'.[12] Montagu concludes that, 'whilst potentialities for aggression exist in all human beings at birth, such potentialities will remain nothing more unless they are organized by experience to function as aggressive behaviour'.[13]

Nancy Scheper Hughes, an American anthropologist, has focused on childrearing conditions that seem to damage children. She has written a brilliant and widely acclaimed 20-year account of the everyday life of women and children in a shanty town of Alto do Cruzeiro in the north-east of Brazil, *Death Without Weeping*. She tries to understand the neglect women appear to show their young children, and the apparent casualness and indifference with which they react to frequent infant death. This is behaviour which would appear to be abusive by conventional North American or European standards. She concludes that the way the women respond is not a matter of poor 'cultural' parenting practices that need correction, but a mirror image of the way in which the shanty women themselves are treated by their wider society as being worthless and of no account. Being able to accommodate and to accept and even joke about the unrelenting grimness and misery of their everyday life enables them to survive. They are often resilient in the face of tremendous odds. She writes that

> The problem is of course, how to articulate a standard or divergent standards, for the beginnings of a moral and an ethical reflection on cultural practices that takes into account but does not privilege our own cultural presuppositions.[14]

Robert Levine has described anthropology as a 'gadfly' to developmental psychology. He and his colleagues at Harvard University carried out a series of studies in Africa on childcare and schooling. He concluded that many of the assumptions that are commonly made about the need to stimulate young children and the need to talk to them in order to help them learn are more a reflection of concerns of Euro-Americans than hard fact.

The leap from factors to optimize school skills [in the USA] to universal prerequisites of cognitive, language and emotional development is misguided. . . . Children whose early environments lack these factors . . . acquired different skills, virtues and preferences in accordance with their own goals for human development. If these findings seem surprising in the context of existing theories of child development, then it indicates how far we have to go in integrating evidence from other cultures into our conceptions of what is possible during childhood.[15]

Increasingly in their studies of childhood, anthropologists are trying to use children as informants. Children often have wise views about their own position, and where they fit into their community. Sam Punch, for example, interviewed children in Bolivia about what they thought about being made to do household tasks. (They were ambivalent.)

Anthropologists have indicated some of the ways in which dearly held assumptions about childhood in the UK and USA do not seem to be borne out by anthropological studies. Their views link up with those of the cultural psychologists discussed in Chapter 3. But both anthropologists and cultural psychologists have to come to terms with the issues raised by Sharon Stephens and Nancy Scheper Hughes. Firstly, 'culture' is contested, it is not straightforward and whatever it is, it is constantly changing. Secondly, poverty and injustice cut across 'culture'.

The circumstances of 80 per cent of the world's children

The situation of most of the world's children is very different from those we conventionally study in North America and Europe. It is these Euro-American children who are taken as the norm in child development. In describing and analysing the situation of poor children from the other end of the world, we are faced not just with differing cultural descriptions but also with a global socio-economic system which, as some argue, always favours the rich over the poor, both across and within countries. The financial and ideological power of the developed world – from here on called the North – is undisputed. It is the North, and in particular the USA, that calls the shots. The recent war in Iraq is a clear example.

Children from the developing world – from here on called the South – are profoundly affected by this wider global economic context, over and above any cultural differences. The global statistics on children are appalling. An unacceptable number die at birth or soon after. The campaigning group Jubilee 2000 estimated that more than 7 million children die unnecessarily each year. Many of those children that survive have limited and falling access to education and healthcare, particularly girls in poor Asian countries. Many of the goods used and consumed on a daily basis in the North, such as food, flowers and clothing, are produced using cheap child labour in poor countries. Almost all cities have growing populations of street children. There has been a resurgence of endemic diseases once under control, such as tuberculosis, and a failure to deal with new ones such as AIDS – an estimated one in four children in Sub-Saharan Africa is affected by AIDS. Many millions of children are refugees fleeing from wars and natural disasters.

Every year UNICEF publishes a booklet entitled *The State of the World's Children*. This gives statistics concerning the position in countries in the South. In 2002 there were more than 100 million children without access to basic education, 60 million of them girls. Well over 4 million children have died of HIV/AIDS, and more than 13 million children under 13 have been orphaned. Two million children have been slaughtered (UNICEF's vocabulary), 6 million children injured and 12 million left homeless because of conflict.

Disease in poor countries has always been a problem, not least because of the unavailability of medicines. Drugs companies, for example, are reluctant to finance research into malaria, which is one of the biggest killers of children. This is because there is no money to be made in developing drugs for poor countries – people simply cannot afford them. The worst epidemic is now HIV/ AIDS. The *British Medical Journal* has run a special edition on HIV/AIDS. Amongst the many problems caused by the HIV/AIDS epidemic is the number of children who have been orphaned.

> AIDS has devasted the social and economic fabric of African societies and made orphans of a whole generation of children. Although donor agencies initially viewed the plight of orphans as a short term humanitarian disaster, they now acknowledge the long term social consequences of African children growing up without parental love and guidance. The potential of these children to form a large group of dysfunctional adults which could further destabilize societies already weakened by AIDS has increased the urgency of finding an effective solution to the orphan crisis. Africa is home to 95% of the world's 13 million children orphaned as a result of AIDS. The numbers will rise until at least 2010, by which time a third of African children will be orphaned.[16]

The most extreme condition that children experience, apart from HIV/ AIDS, is war. It turns daily life inside out, and leads to terrible suffering. War, unfortunately, is not a rare exception. There has been a long-running war in Afghanistan, another in Palestine. There are other, less well reported wars that have been going for many years in Sudan, Angola, the Congo, Liberia, Sierra Leone, Colombia, Sri Lanka and Indonesia, Chechnya and Kashmir. There are countries where wars have been fought and finished, leaving a dreadful unhealed legacy of bitterness – for instance, Iraq, Iran, Bosnia, Rwanda, Tajikistan. Women and children are the vulnerable victims of such wars. The world's population of refugees is at least 60 million, but the number of those affected by war and its aftermath is still greater. Mary Kaldor has argued that war itself has changed. 'Old wars' were fought between soldiers; 9 out of 10 people killed in wars used to be soldiers. Now the position is reversed: 9 out of 10 people killed are civilians, many of them children. 'New wars' involve organized crime (violence undertaken by privately organized groups, warlords, paramilitary units and so on for private purposes, usually financial gain) and involve large-scale violations of human rights. Such wars are often fought for precious minerals valued in the North such as diamonds or oil. These wars are aided by advances in technology – landmines, powerful small arms, cellular phones and computer links.

Graca Machel has edited for UNICEF a book about war entitled *The Impact of War on Children*. She details the terrible circumstances of many children affected by war. Amongst the children she describes are child soldiers. Rootless and orphan children, themselves victims of war and economic disaster, are drawn into war – or warlord armies – because it offers at least the short-term possibility of food and survival. The Polish journalist Ryszard Kapuscinski also describes child soldiers.

> I sometimes read stories about a child in America or Europe shooting another child. A child killing one of his contemporaries, or an adult. Such news is usually accompanied by expressions of horror and outrage. In Africa children kill children in enormous numbers, and have been doing so for years. In fact, modern wars on this continent have been, and still are, largely wars of children.[17]

One of the reasons that this picture is so shocking is that in the North we believe that young children will be nurtured and cared for. They should be free to be childish, and free to play. Child development assumes a benign environment. Child psychology is built on the assumption that adults should be protective towards children, or, as the journalist Madeleine Bunting expressed it, 'a parent's primary role is to convey . . . the reassurance that the world is a predictable, trustworthy, safe place'.[18] Much, indeed most, of the work undertaken in the field of child development tries to investigate the ways in which adults can create a benign environment in which children grow up and learn. However, *most* of the world's children grow up in environments that are far from benign. They grow up in circumstances of extreme poverty, pollution, danger and exploitation. Developmental psychology claims to be a universal science, but as yet has had very little to say about the extent or the effects of these circumstances.

Are situations like this inevitable? Could anything be done about AIDS, child soldiers and child poverty in the South? There are two opposing views about such child poverty. The first is that it is caused by the current economic system – sometimes called neo-liberal economics, or the global market – which inevitably leads to exploitation and inequalities, and makes the gap between rich and poor greater, breeding misery and discontent. The other view is that the global market is an economic fact of life. Poor countries are still developing, and they have to learn to cope with the global market. They need help to catch up to the education and health standards of the North, but in the future they will be economically better off. The best way to deal with illness, child poverty and warfare is to encourage more economic development and more democracy.

At the centre of these arguments are the World Bank and the World Trade Organization. The brief of the World Bank (and its sister organization, the International Monetary Fund or IMF) was originally to assist in the redevelopment and reconstruction of broken economies after the Second World War. It now acts as banker to all the world's poorest countries. It loans them money, at heavy repayment rates. Most poor countries are now heavily in debt to the World Bank. The money that was lent to poor countries to help them invest in production and develop their economies has been conditional on the adoption of neo-liberal market philosophies and 'structural adjustment' policies. The idea behind such policies is that competition is good, individualism and individual gain are the motors of development, and everyone should have an opportunity to become wealthy. State control, state interests and state regulation, where possible, should be minimized.

The World Trade Organization (WTO) is a body set up to regulate international trade. Although many people consider that it is important to have such a regulatory body (just as it is important to have international laws, and an international justice system which can bring dictators to trial), there has been a great deal of concern about how the WTO operates. Like the World Bank, it is accused of favouring big corporations over the needs of the poor. The example usually quoted concerns patents for drugs or genetic research. Should big drugs companies, for example, be able to fix the prices of life-saving drugs or take a patent out on a commonly used tropical plant? Or be able to charge prices for AIDS drugs that are out of reach of most people in the South?

> The UK charity ActionAid tried to launch an advertising campaign against patents. They tried to patent salted chips, as an example of the absurdity of claims for intellectual property that the WTO support. ActionAid has 'invented' a ready-salted chip, and have filed for a patent on it. If successful, we would have legal rights over the Action-

Aid Chip, and any chips that have salt added to them. So we could demand that chip shop owners throughout the UK pay for a licence to add salt to their chips. With 300 million servings of chips sold each year, we could stand to make millions.

Why can we do this? New patent rules allow companies to get exclusive rights over basic foods and even nature itself, simply by adding something to it or modifying it in a way that has not been done before.

Why has ActionAid done it? To draw attention to the threat that the patenting of staple crops by big companies is posing to poor farmers in the developing world.

Will ActionAid use the patent?

No, if the patent is granted, we have no intention of using it to make chippies pay royalties. We have done this to highlight the injustice of food patent rules.[19]

The World Bank acknowledges that in many poor countries health and education uptake has got worse. It has acknowledged some of its critics, like the Nobel economics prize-winner Joseph Stiglitz. It claims now to be investing in poverty reduction programmes. Much of its recent effort is directed at reducing poverty in targeted populations. Its attempts to measure the extent of poverty and, most recently, to solicit the views of the poor on the poverty they experience, are extremely sophisticated. It has one of the biggest early child-hood programmes in the world. The World Bank, like the WTO, argues that its interventions are more, not less, necessary as a vehicle for achieving economic stability and progress; and that more technological expertise can solve global problems. The problem, according to the World Bank and the WTO, has not been too much interference, but too little.

The critics of the World Bank and the WTO argue that they are not reducing levels of poverty, but making them worse. They argue that the effect of the global market, as defined and pursued by the World Bank and the WTO, is that the gap between rich and poor has increased. Many international non-governmental organizations (NGOs), as well as economists and other academics, argue that it is misleading to suggest that that neo-liberal economic development and global markets are neutral or culture-free or inevitable. They claim that there are other ways of regulating international finance and international trade.

In an editorial the South African journal *Children First* claimed that the international aid strategies promoted the interests of

a disgustingly rich elite. Development strategies in Africa with minor exceptions have tended to be the strategies by which the few use the many for their purposes. They are uncompromisingly top down.

> There is not, and never has been (since colonial times) popular participation in decision making.
>
> Aid is not directed at increasing and expanding the productive base and capacity to spur sustainable development and eradicate poverty. Instead aid is a tool to serve the commercial, political, economic and strategic interests of donor countries.[20]

Critics such as Susan George argue that the World Bank and the WTO primarily reflect the interests of big corporations in the USA and other rich countries. They create poverty because they rely on cheap labour and cheap imports. These critics claim that that indebtedness and rescheduling of international debts in poor countries 'violates all the most basic principles of the rule of law'. The organization Jubilee 2000 claims that debts totalling $450 billion arose from loans to corrupt and dictatorial regimes such as those of Mobutu, Suharto, various Brazilian generals and apartheid South Africa. These loans are still being repaid, yet they were loans that were prompted by the geopolitical interests of the USA, including the sale of armaments, rather than for reconstruction purposes. Debt repayment is now the biggest item on the budget of many poor countries. The Inter-Church Coalition on Africa has commented: 'Every child born in Africa is born with a financial burden which a lifetime's work cannot repay. The debt is a new form of slavery as vicious as the slave trade.'[21]

Majid Rahnema, an Iranian, has edited a collection of essays, mostly from authors in the South, called the *Post-development Reader*. This has now become a standard text critiquing ideas of development. He argues that ideas about development are the economic equivalent of the AIDS virus, in that they are so pernicious and have spread so rapidly. Traditional societies operate in a holistic and multidimensional way, minimizing risk to members. Ecologically, they are more likely to respect their environment, and regard it as a god-given source of life without which it would be unimaginable for anyone to live.

> Most activities have a multi-purpose aspect and are an opportunity for everyone to learn from others. Life organized around them often becomes the space for collective apprenticeship where the younger and the elder each in their own way, learn from each other. Children may not be sent to institutions specializing in education, but they are much less infantilized than their urban peers, whose world is reduced mostly to schools. Similarly 'technologies' are never just a collection of tools or imported 'gadgets'. They are organically incorporated into people's way of life. And they often require the co-operation of ever-widening human groups, beginning with members of the household. Far from leading to new forms of dependency they are tools that correspond to a profound need to be autonomous; not only an extension

of people's hand and brain, but also a constant reminder of their need for conviviality.[22]

This is the world of self-sufficient interdependent small communities that, in Rahnema's view, is being fatally infected by ideas of economic development and market capitalism. Whilst this may be a romantic view, nevertheless he amasses a good deal of evidence from the South that economic development has brought more harm than good.

These arguments about the role of the World Bank and debt relief may seem a long way from the concerns of early childhood practitioners. But as the Inter-Church Coalition on Africa suggests, the wellbeing of many millions of young children, that is about 80 per cent of the world's children, depends on who is right. It matters even more because the World Bank and a number of other international donors have decided to invest in child development. They argue that such an investment would bring economic returns. This is where we return to the ideas about child development discussed in Chapter 1.

Child development interventions in the South

There has been a dramatic expansion in early childhood provision in most of the world's cities. There are nurseries and childcare settings in every city throughout the world. A recent review of early childhood programmes in the South was carried out by Robert Myers for the 1999 World Education Forum Conference at Dakar, Senegal. Mostly, he suggested, these programmes are private businesses for the children of the better off, geared towards preparation for school. Ex-communist countries tended to have widespread and high-quality early childhood services, but UNICEF has shown that these are decreasing dramatically post transition to a market economy.

Myers commented on the understandings of children and models of services that have fuelled this expansion. He argued that ideas about childhood from the North have a near monopoly, and this makes for considerable tension.

> Frameworks and knowledge . . . continue to originate, for the most part in the Minority World. Accordingly a tension often arises between 'received truth' linked to Minority World knowledge base and values guiding an agency, and local knowledge linked to another set of values rooted in some part of the majority world. These may overlap, but are different.[23]

This chapter has discussed anthropological perspectives. These perspectives suggest that ideas about self-identity and culture are problematical. It is also hard to detach them from ideas about race and power. There are strong reasons to believe that there is tremendous variation in the way in which people construe their identity. But on top of issues of identity, there are pressing issues of poverty and the dreadful lives many children lead. Yet, on the whole, the view persists in child development that there is 'developmentally appropriate practice' that can be applied irrespective of time and place, and despite or in ignorance of these conditions. There are universal and essential truths about young children and how to care for and educate them. These are said to apply everywhere in the world, with minor cultural variations. The overriding assumption, which appears in the literature on early childhood practice, is that the ages and stages children go through, and the familial contexts in which learning takes place, are similar everywhere. Leading American educators have claimed that 'children are pretty much the same everywhere and the people teaching them have pretty much the same ideas'.[24] International agencies promoting child development have also made the same claims and appeals to universal standards.

> Given the right opportunities and the right learning environment children will develop in similar ways whatever their background. Culture may affect, and sometimes even determine, the topics, methodologies and techniques we use, but there is an underlying universality. As long as we keep in mind that everything we do is concerned with the development of the whole child, we are all doing the same sorts of things for the same sorts of reasons.[25]

This is also the World Bank's view. Mary Eming Young is a senior public health specialist at the World Bank. She argues for a targeted intervention approach for poor children. Using evidence exclusively from the USA, she argues that

> Evidence suggests that [ECD] programs are effective in addressing such vital human development issues as malnutrition among children under five, stunted cognitive development and unpreparedness for primary education. . . . Early childhood interventions can increase the efficiency of primary and secondary education, contribute to further productivity and income, and reduce the cost of health care and public services. . . . Deficits in individuals caused by early malnutrition and inadequate care can affect labour productivity and economic development throughout society. Properly designed and implemented interventions in the early childhood years can have multi-dimensional benefits.[26]

The World Bank in particular funds early childhood programmes in poor countries, based on assumptions about better parenting and improved life chances from early childhood education. This view that targeted early childhood interventions to poor children will improve their life chances, irrespective of inequalities or cultural traditions of the society in which they grow up, is a powerful one. It is a very common approach towards poor children, in rich countries as well as poor. For example, the Sure Start programme in the UK is based on this approach, as are Head Start programmes in the USA.

Why do programmes for poor children ignore social economic conditions? One of the reasons is that child psychology as a discipline works at a micro level. It focuses on individual circumstances and individual learning. Many studies detail the effect of certain kinds of education or care programmes on young children. They examine 'what works', what makes a change in the outcomes for children, what enables them to do better at school and so on. The most famous of these 'what works' studies are intervention studies carried out in the USA. On the basis of such studies, it is argued that for every dollar spent on a child under 5, seven dollars is saved later on, because children perform better if they have a good early childhood environment. One of many assumptions underlying these types of investigations/interventions is that it is not the job of researchers or teachers to change the socio-economic circumstances of children. That is more properly seen as the job of politicians. The only change that can be brought about at the micro level of child psychology is to influence the individual actions of children, their carers and teachers.

How does child development take account of socio-cultural and economic conditions?

Psychology has, for most of its history, been a positivist science that claims to seek universal truths and to uncover universal patterns. Developmental psychologists largely believed that psychological processes can be investigated through the study of the individual behaviour and learning of children; and by aggregating the findings from many children and from many studies universal norms or laws can be established. Children are assumed to pass through the same stages and to show the same age-related characteristics whether they live in remote parts of Nepal or in Chicago. This view is shifting rapidly. Here I consider some of the criticisms from within child development, besides those of the cultural psychologists.

Critics of child development argue that psychology cannot be the same as biology, and the society or community a child grows up in makes a critical difference to the way he learns and feels. Child development, in seeking universal norms, has been based on too narrow a sample to be able to establish any norms satisfactorily, even if it were possible to do so. Robert Levine, an anthropologist concerned primarily with childhood, has surveyed psychological handbooks over a period of 50 years in order to explore the extent to which environmental issues and cultural impact are taken into account. Although there have been substantial changes in developmental psychology in that time, for example in awareness of infant capacities, the narrow sample base of psychology has, in his view, always been a problem. He points to the language studies of Ochs and Schiefflin as an example of the misperceptions of developmental psychology.

> To most middle-class Western readers, the description of verbal and non-verbal behaviour of middle-class caregivers with their children seem very familiar, desirable and even natural. . . . The characteristics of care-giver speech [e.g. baby-talk] and comportment [the way babies are held] that have been specified [by psychologists] are highly valued by members of white middle-class society, including researchers, readers and subjects of the studies. [But] the general pattern of white middle-class caregiving that has been described in the literature are characteristic neither of all societies nor of all social groups.[27]

Cross-cultural psychology is a rapidly developing field. It recognizes the narrow sample base of psychology, but considers it can be addressed by investigating the behaviour or learning styles of children and their parents from different cultures or communities by systematically comparing them. But cross-cultural psychology itself begs the question of scientific methodology. Can behaviour and culture be broken down into little sections and compared? Paul Eldering and Lotte Leseman argue that research studies on 'culture' fall along an axis. One end is behavioural universalism. Behavioural universalism is the view that the same behaviour traits and patterns appear in children wherever they are, perhaps with minor variations according to culture. These minor variations can be charted accurately through cross-cultural surveys. This view accepts the positivist approach: cultural behaviour patterns can be broken down and compared.

The other end of the axis is cultural relativism. From this perspective 'cultures' cannot be usefully compared. Each community or society generates its own meanings and ways of behaving and in any case these are themselves continually changing. So no comparison could be straightforward. Many cross-cultural studies operate somewhere between these extremes. For instance, the well-known study by Tobin compared children in nurseries in China, Japan and the USA. He and his colleagues filmed the children in the nurseries in each country and talked to the staff. Then he showed the films to staff in the other countries, and asked them to discuss what they saw. This method revealed the assumptions held by the workers in each country, but also gave them a forum to comment on their own beliefs in the light of what they saw.

Many of the socio-cultural psychologists discussed in Chapter 3 have steered clear of any wider analysis of culture. They have avoided the anthropological and socio-economic debates raised in this chapter. They have focused more narrowly on specific groups. They have used the phrase a 'community of practice' to describe a particular set of circumstances entered into in a particular place at a particular time. Culture in this sense is not synonymous with nationality or ethnicity.

Jerome Bruner concedes that culture is nuanced and conflictual. He argues that culture 'rarely conforms to anything resembling a cookbook of recipes or formulas for it is a universal of all cultures that they contain factional or institutional interests'.[28] But not even he acknowledges the socio-economic circumstances that affect so many children. Developmental psychologists may see culture in very broad terms, and even try to reconcile cultural arguments with genetics. The influential North American psychologist Marc Bornstein argues that culture shapes how societies and individuals develop. 'In essence culture (plus genetics) determines the structure and nature of the social and physical environments the individual is reared in'.[29] But even psychologists sympathetic to ideas of culture cannot make the next jump and face the possibility that the culture to which they belong may be doing more harm than good to the prospects of the majority of children in the world.

The ethics of childhood

There is some common sense in the traditional micro approach of child development that emphasizes that children and their parents must learn to cope with bad circumstances and change them from within. But increasingly this approach is being challenged. One of the grounds for doing so is that it is *unethical* to stand by and see so many children suffer. We certainly consider that we have obligations to protect children within the UK and have many mechanisms in place to do just this. On an international basis, the UN Convention on the Rights of the Child lays an obligation on all signatories to the Convention to ensure 'protection, participation and provision' for all children. (The USA is one of the two countries that has not signed the Convention; the other is Somalia which has no government.) Whilst this obligation is open to many interpretations, it is clear from the above discussion that the rights of children to grow up in safe environments are not being met. The UN has a mandate to pursue the Convention.

The sociologist Zygmunt Bauman argues that through the media of television and telecommunication, those who live in rich countries see and read about those who live in poor countries. And with such knowledge comes guilt and obligation.

> We live in a globalizing world. That means all of us, consciously or not, depend on each other. Whatever we do or refrain from doing affects the lives of people who live in places we'll never visit. And whatever those distant people do or desist from doing has its impact on the conditions in which we, each one of us separately and together, conduct our lives. Living in a globalizing world means being aware of the pain, misery and suffering of countless people who we will never meet in person. . . . Our world, whatever else it might be, is also a producer of horror and atrocity. . . . [There is] an abysmal gap between the suffering we see and our ability to help the sufferers.[30]

John Rawls, the American philospher, argued in his weighty and landmark book *A Theory of Justice* that justice is most required when life is brief and there is a struggle for scarce resources. He argued, in effect, for the old maxim 'do as you would be done by'. To apply his argument, if you were reincarnated as a female child orphan in Tanzania, or a child soldier in Sierra Leone, would you receive just treatment?

There are not only empirical issues, but unavoidable ethical and moral issues as well in trying to confront and intervene in the practices of others. Neither developmental psychology nor neuroscientific and genetic research can, by themselves, produce answers to such very difficult questions. But nor can we afford to disengage from such moral difficulties, if only because so many children suffer.

Summary

This chapter considered how the differences in attitudes and behaviour between groups and communities of people have been investigated, and how significant those differences might be in terms of understanding children. Anthropology has been an important discipline in carrying out such studies. These differences are usually summed up as 'culture'. The chapter concludes that the word 'culture' is used in such a blanket way as to be misleading. The chapter also points to the inequalities in life chances between children who live in prosperous countries such as the UK and USA, and those who live in poor countries. Being poor in a poor country also shapes how young children grow and what they learn.

Main messages from this chapter

1 Beware of using the term 'culture'. It raises more problems than it solves.
2 Poverty and injustice cut across 'culture' and make life very difficult for young children wherever they are growing up.
3 When children die in their millions, this raises profound ethical and practical considerations for everyone.

What to read next

Penn, H. (2004) *Unequal Childhoods*. London: Routledge.

Notes

1 Taylor 1971, quoted in Peacock 1986
2 Peacock 1986
3 Ibid.: 5
4 Ibid.: 7
5 Rosaldo 1993: 105
6 Wolf 1990: 391
7 Stephens 1995: 3
8 Said 1999: 137
9 Lamming 1979, quoted on cover
10 Street 1999: 54
11 Jahoda and Lewis 1987: 110
12 Montagu 1978: 184
13 Ibid.: 7
14 Scheper Hughes 1993: 21
15 Levine *et al*. 1994: 274
16 *British Medical Journal*, 26 January 2002: 185
17 Kapuscinski 2001: 148
18 *The Guardian*, 31 December 2001: 14
19 Salil Shetty, Chief Executive, ActionAid. www.actionaid.com
20 *Children First*, Aug/Sept 2001: 38
21 *Fifty Years is Enough*. Factsheet produced by the Inter-Church Coalition on Africa, on the 50th anniversary of the founding of the World Bank, Toronto
22 Rahnema 1997: 115
23 Myers 2000: 25
24 At the NAEYC conference held in Toronto in 1999, two of the most well known US educators, David Weikart and Lilian Katz, made these claims

in a seminar on international perspectives, to the dismay of some of the audience.

25   Department for Education and Science 2003

26   Young 1998: 209–10

27   Ochs and Schieffelin 1984: 283

28   Bruner 1996: 14

29   Bornstein 1991: 6

30   Bauman, 'Quality and Inequality', *The Guardian*, 29 January 2001. www.guardian.co.uk/archive

6 Past, Present and Future

Everyone has a past, a history of life events that has made them into what they are now. In Chapter 1, I considered how we personally remember the past and how it affects us. But in a similar way, all ideas and practices have a past. The actions we take now, the policies that shape our actions, the places we work in, have a history. Is it worth knowing about the past? Many people would argue that it is not; the past is gone, done and dusted. Henry Ford, who founded the Ford Motor Company, is famous for saying 'History is bunk'. Some cynics say that the only thing you can learn from history is that you can learn nothing from history; its messages are always ignored. The argument put forward in this chapter is that history *is* important. The past helps us understand the present, and, contrary to the cynical view, even helps us shape the future. Studying history is a means of exploring the past, of understanding the continuities, the discontinuities, and the wider contexts of what we do and how we behave. History is also a useful discipline in studying early childhood.

Science is about establishing general rules, and making general predictions. History, like anthropology, is concerned with understanding the uniqueness of situations, the special features that make a person or a place, or a time, different from any other. History is also concerned with the play of power. Who pulls the ropes behind the scenes? Isaiah Berlin sums up the particularity of history very well.

> Historians, whose business it is to tell us what actually happened in the world [consequently] fight shy of rigid theoretical patterns into which the facts may sometimes have to be fitted with a good deal of awkwardness and artificiality. And this instinct is a sound one. The proper aim of the sciences is to note the number of similarities in the behaviour of objects and to construct propositions of the greatest degree of generality from which the largest number of such uniformities can logically be deduced. In history our purpose is the opposite. When we wish to describe a particular revolution – what actually took

place – the last thing we wish to do is to concentrate solely upon those characteristics of it which it has in common with as many other revolutions as we can discover, ignoring the differences as irrelevant to our study; and so what a historian wishes to bring out is what is specific, unique in a given character or series of events or historical situation. . . . The historian is concerned to paint a portrait which conveys the unique pattern of experience, and not an X-ray photograph which is capable of acting as a general symbol for all structures of a similar type.[1]

History in some ways is the most challenging of disciplines. Historical scholarship usually requires detective work, tracking down documents, pictures or other artefacts that are lost or forgotten, tucked away in dusty archives or sitting unlabelled on a computer disk. History involves interpreting, sifting through, juxtaposing and comparing many different sources of information, written, visual and oral, to build up a picture of a certain set of events. Perhaps more than any other discipline, it requires imagination, judgement and the ability to weave all the disparate elements into a coherent tale about why and how change and transformation has occurred. No communities or societies are static or without a history.

Nowadays, history books are best sellers. They set people and events in a wider context, sometimes offering a romantic view of the past, making it seem much more interesting than our own colourless, muddled times.

At worst, though, historians and history books glorify the past in order to justify certain actions in the present. Eric Hobsbawm, a distinguished economic historian, argues that history has been used ideologically to justify nationalistic or religious interpretations of events, so it is very important that historians 'tell the truth' and, to the best of their ability, establish the 'facts'. For example, both Jews and Muslims argue that 'history' supports their claim to ownership of the holy city of Jerusalem. The evidence suggests that the history of Jerusalem was more muddled and complex than either version will allow. A few historians have claimed that the holocaust of Jews and gipsies in Nazi concentration camps never took place. Disputes of this magnitude illustrate how important it is to establish the historical accuracy of events and the range of perspectives involved. Modern historical scholarship is generally very painstaking, although, of course, historians themselves may emphasize or favour one interpretation of the facts over another. The evidence may not be crystal clear, or may even have been falsified or destroyed. But positivism and relativism are not quite the battleground that they are in some other disciplines.

The history of childhood

The history of childhood, now a lively subsection of history, tells us how expectations of children's capabilities and behaviour have changed.

Philippe Aries, a French historian, is credited with making historians take childhood seriously. In his famous book *Centuries of Childhood* he claimed that childhood did not really exist until the sixteenth or seventeenth century. Before that, children had been treated as small and inadequate adults. He considered they were often maltreated, and that today we are much more careful about protecting children. He substantiated his claim partly by using pictorial evidence. Pictures and illustrations that remain from that time often depict children as little adults: small but with adult proportions and adult clothes.

Whilst historians recognize the importance of Aries' work, many now dispute his claim that children were not allowed to be children. Linda Pollock, for example, claims that parents have always shown a range of emotions towards their children, from great fondness and indulgence to punitive coldness. Nicholas Orme has written an illustrated history of children in medieval times. He also suggests that children were part of everyday life – they played, annoyed their elders and betters, and were loved by their parents.

There was a spectrum of opinion about childhood in all the historical periods that we know about. But at certain periods or amongst certain groups or classes, particular ideas were very powerful. In Chapter 1, I quoted the example of well-to-do children in Tudor times. The learning that was expected of them was phenomenal by today's standards – oral and written fluency in several languages; a sophisticated understanding of rhetoric, law and religion; exquisite handwriting; an appreciation of art; an ability to play an instrument; and the physical dexterity to step out in intricate sixteenth-century dances such as galliards. And if that was not enough, they might well ride, hunt and fence. All this by age 11 or 12.

There was a widespread view amongst the well-to-do in Victorian England when universal education was under discussion that the poor were not fit to learn. Offering them education would mislead and confuse them and give them ideas above their station. Hugh Cunningham has written a history of the way that poor children have been treated in England. As industrialization swept through England, families moved from the country into the towns and cities. Instead of helping out in the fields or with animals in the homestead, children were left to fend for themselves in the streets. Children just hung around with not much to do (and probably not much to eat). There were constant complaints by the middle classes about the children of the poor. They were always in the way. They formed unruly gangs. They were out of control. In the eighteenth and nineteenth centuries, the predominant public view was that these children should be put to work and not idle about in the streets. There were many attempts to set up industrial schools for them, where they were found small repetitive jobs, for example knitting and nail-making. The trouble was that these schools were expensive and did not make enough money to cover their costs. The children did not earn enough or work fast enough to make it worthwhile.

As more industry became established, poor children were put to work in factories and mines. A small proportion of children were employed as chimney sweeps. Because they were so small they could climb up chimneys more easily. But social reformers were concerned about what work did to children. Children spent very long hours in harsh conditions, with very few breaks. They became stunted, pale and tired. The child chimney sweeps attracted a lot of attention. They were more visible – and very dirty and sooty – and they were compared to slaves. Books and poems were written about their plight.

> When my mother died I was very young,
> And my father sold me while yet my tongue
> Could scarcely cry 'weep! weep! weep!'
> So your chimneys I sweep and in soot I sleep.[2]

Gradually legislation was introduced to restrict the number of hours children worked, first of all to 10 hours a day. But as children worked less, they hung around again. Middle- and upper-class children had been attending school for a long time, although in Victorian times, boys were much better educated than girls. Perhaps schools could also keep poor children off the street, and give them a smattering of education? Universal education was finally introduced in 1872, but it only ever had limited aims. Schools were like education factories for poor children. It kept them from being idle and a public nuisance. It gave them just about enough of an introduction to the three 'R's – reading, writing and arithmetic – to enable them to be more employable. Children were allowed to bring their younger brothers and sisters to school – otherwise they would have had to stay at home and look after them.

As Robin Alexander has pointed out, this mean-spirited conception of education has dogged education in England to the present day. We still use the Victorian education-factory buildings in the cities and we still have narrow aims for education. We still want to keep poor children off the streets. (The history of education is rather different in Scotland, where education was more highly valued and private schools were less common.)

The debate about the poor has never really gone away in the UK. Some countries have reorganized their economy and have more or less abolished poverty – in Scandinavia, for example, poverty rates are very low indeed. But in the UK, poverty levels are still high. In 2000, around one-quarter of all children in the UK were deemed to be living in poverty.[3] At the beginning of the twentieth century, many people, including some very eminent psychologists,[4] believed in eugenics or population control. There were arguments about whether the poor were a degenerate strain of the population whose rights needed curtailing (a eugenic argument that took a different, and terrifying, turn in Germany). In 1938 the National Council for Mental Hygiene organized a conference at Central Hall Westminster on the topic 'Is our national intelligence declining?' The organizers concluded that it was, since the more intelligent had fewer children, and the poor bred uncontrollably.[5] Nowdays in the UK there is an educational programme called Sure Start aimed at poor children. A key component of the programme is to educate parents so that they bring up their children not to be a nuisance. A historian might say *plus ça change* . . . 'nothing changes'.

One of the biggest changes in our attitude to childhood has been towards expectations of survival, at least in the North. Nowadays if a young child dies it is a catastrophe (but it is still an everyday event in the South). Children's survival rates used to very low everywhere – on average perhaps 50 per cent of children might survive into adulthood. In the UK, public health measures (sanitation, clean milk supplies, immunization and so on) were gradually introduced in the nineteenth and twentieth centuries, which brought down the death rate. Until then everyone had frequent experience of the death of friends and relatives. Stepmothers and stepfathers, stepbrothers and sisters were very common. Trying to make sense of death was a normal experience for children and their parents.

Religion was a primary source of explanation for, and an attempt to come to terms with, death (spiritual explanations, spells, witchdoctors and malign fates are still common explanations in countries with high infant mortality). Many books for children were about death and the meaning of death. Bedtime stories might include an account of the death of a good child, with angels hovering; or the death of a naughty child facing everlasting torment in hell. Heaven and hell were part of every child's vocabulary. Religious understanding was an important aspect of education – the UK magazine *Nursery World* used to carry regular religious features. These speculations about life and death and the meaning and conduct of daily life have largely dropped out of current thinking about childhood.

Stoicism and resilience were necessary survival skills for children. (They still are for many millions of children in the South.) These aspects of character were highly valued. The Victorian writer Charles Dickens always portrayed children in this way, bravely putting up with adult wickedness and cruelty. But as children's survival becomes more or less assured, society values other attributes of childhood besides stoicism and obedience. Concepts of risk have changed dramatically – children are protected against every eventuality. Contemporary parents in the North invest a great deal of time, money and effort in individual children. As they have become the focus of intense parental attention, children have become more cosseted and shielded against the tasks and duties of everyday life. They have become more 'childlike'. Zelitzer, in a famous book called *Pricing the Priceless Child*, gives an account of the changes in views about the economic value of children. She gives examples of various insurance scams involving the illness and death of children. Charles Dickens was familiar with such scams. In the following extract from *Nicholas Nickleby*, Squeers, the proprietor of Dotheboys Hall, a boys' school, explains how he paid for his own family's medical bills.

> The fact is we have only one extra with our boys, and that is for doctors when required – and not then unless we are sure of our customers. . . . After my medical bill was run up, we picked out 5 little boys (sons of tradesmen as was sure to pay) that had never had the scarlet fever, and we sent one to a cottage where they'd got it, and we put the four others to sleep with him, and they took it, and then the doctor came and attended 'em once all round, and we divided my total among 'em and added it on to their little bills, and the parents paid it. Ha . . . we always do it. Why when Mrs Squeers was brought to bed . . . we ran the whooping cough through half a dozen boys and charged her expenses among 'em, monthly nurse included. Ha.[6]

This may seem like horrific cruelty now, but there is a comparison to be made in current thinking about the status and worth of children. For example, some economists (and some leading psychologists such as Sandra Scarr – see Chapter 3) routinely calculate the financial trade-off between investment in childcare and outcomes for children. If investing in childcare makes little difference to how children perform later in life, it is not worth making the investment. Poor childcare is 'good enough'. It does not matter if many young children are cooped up together with bored caregivers. The quality of children's lives in the here and now, and the pleasures they might get from their daily life, are of no consequence in this economic reckoning. This economic argument is used as a justification for avoiding regulation in the USA. Children have been termed by the journal *The Economist* as 'negative equity', suggesting that the public should be compensated for the trouble they cause to others. One example *The Economist* gave was of air travel: children should be charged more because they are a nuisance to sit next to on a flight, they wriggle, cry and make a mess. Are these assumptions about the worth of young children so very different from Dickens' accounts of childhood?[7]

Children have always had their own subculture, their own rhymes, games and plays that get passed on from one generation to the next. This subculture has been described by Peter and Iona Opie. They collected rhymes and games from school playgrounds, and traced some of them back over several centuries. More recent studies, such as that of Bishop and Curtis on school playgrounds, suggest that these rhymes and games are still practised, even although the places that children can play have become much more restricted because of worries about safety.

Changes in our understanding about childhood happen before our eyes. Some people argue that children nowadays are profoundly affected by consumerism. (This subject is dealt with in more detail in Chapter 9.) The Canadian author Stephen Kline has demonstrated how children have been ruthlessly targeted by advertising. In his book *Out of the Garden* he illustrates how children's favourite domestic objects have changed. Children's toys used to be relatively simple and homemade – as they still are in most parts of the world. But in rich countries children have come to judge happiness by what they possess – the latest toys or trainers or computer games.

Studying the history of childhood illustrates just how much what we think of as normal is particular to a time and a place. The history of childhood gives us yet another angle to understand the present. Child development as a discipline tends to assume that understanding about childhood is cumulative and scientific; and that the knowledge that we have today is the best of all and supersedes that of the past. This is unlikely to be the case, for the reasons that have been explored here and in previous chapters.

The history of policy making for young children in the UK[8]

What follows is the history of policy making for early education and care in the UK. History is about particularities, not about generalities, so in this chapter I am focusing on one example, the UK. In other European countries this history would be different; even more so in the southern hemisphere. The common thread is perhaps the disregard which governments show towards young children, and the persistence of this failure of compassion in English-speaking countries.

Historical methods can also be usefully applied to childcare policy and practice. Those who make the rules and regulations for nurseries and other forms of provision and training for young children are influenced by a number of factors. They try to take what is best from the 'scientific' understanding of the child development of their day. William Kessen, one of the most famous of American developmental psychologists, described the history of child development as 'a history of rediscovery ... with some modest advances towards truth'.[9]

Christine Hardyment has shown just how much scientific advice to mothers has changed over the years. In the twentieth century, there has been a complete turnaround. She contrasts Truby King, writing in the 1930s, who said that science showed children should be brought up with the utmost regularity, with the liberal advice of Benjamin Spock. King said babies should be fed on time, put out in the fresh air for a regulation amount of time, and never indulged. Half a century later, Spock was recommending the opposite. Babies should be fed on demand and looked after in a thoroughly relaxed way.

Upper- and middle-class mothers of the eighteenth century were expected to be genteel ladies of leisure. They employed nannies and governesses for their young children. The nannies were mainly working-class girls, for whom looking after children was a form of domestic service. Yet, as Gathorne-Hardy points out, these nannies were entrusted with the upbringing and education of the young children in their care.

The role of women in the family is a recurring theme in the history of childcare and early education. The emancipation and economic independence of women and the gradual dismantling of sexual stereotypes are some of the greatest historical changes of the last century. The perception of women, their inclinations and capacities – their noble, but submissive character – as mothers, childcarers and teachers, shaped the availability and scope of provision for young children.

Well-to-do women expected someone else to care for their children. Friedrich Froebel, an Austrian teacher, argued that it was a noble role for women to teach children. Froebel is credited with developing the first nursery school, in 1836. He had a following in the UK, and some private nurseries were set up to demonstrate his ideas. He felt that children should have great freedom to play and to develop their innate spiritual responsiveness to nature. But he also thought it was a woman's job to bring up children. Trained and dedicated women would make excellent kindergarten teachers.

> She is in duty bound not only to watch the unfolding of the powers and capabilities of her pupils but also to teach them to love the good and hate the bad, to awaken in them new desires, to develop new interests, to arouse their higher instincts, and then to satisfy these cravings after higher ideals by opening up to them the wonderful world of nature, of art, of literature, and so give them a glimpse of the joys that await them and the rich heritage that may be theirs for the asking.[10]

The arguments about women's role in relation to children crop up again and again.

Nursery education has often attracted radical thinkers. Robert Owen provided the first workplace nursery at his factory at New Lanark in Scotland as early as 1818. He argued that children needed caring for in an enlightened way, and their mothers would work better knowing that their children were being well looked after. (His bottom line was the profit of his factory.) As well as Froebel's disciples, the Italian educator Maria Montessori also set up nurseries in the UK in the early twentieth century, some of which still continue. In

1927, ten years or so after Montessori visited the UK, the philosopher Bertrand Russell and his wife Dora set up an experimental school, Beacon Hill, that attracted a lot of attention. Russell was inspired by the new 'science' of psychoanalysis, somewhat contradictorily mixed with behaviouristic ideas about regular training to inculcate good moral habits. But the overriding idea was that repressing emotions and feelings in children would prove destructive in later life – especially sexual repression. 'Education consists in the cultivation of the instincts, not in their suppression.'

Russell spelt out his ideas in a book, *On Education, Especially in Early Childhood*, first published in 1926 and reprinted many times. He scandalized people with his psychoanalytical explanations about the dangers of repressing children's basic instincts. Outraged critics protested. 'If the old fashioned virtue of obedience is to be ruled out of a child's life . . . the children of the future will be exterminated by the process of eating what they like, going to bed when they like, playing with fire when they like . . .'[11] Russell argued that the rich were at liberty – in fact had a duty – to pave the way for others with their experiments. In his book, he argued that we should start with values, the attributes that civilized people should encourage and foster. His values included vitality, courage, sensitivity and intelligence.

Perhaps the most famous of the radical nursery experiments was Malting House School at Cambridge, run by Susan Isaacs. Like the others, this was a school for the young children of professionals, mainly academics. One-third of the children were residential. The regime was inspired by the theories of the psychoanalyst Melanie Klein about childhood aggression and repression, and the need to fully express emotion. The job of the wise adult was to chronicle every nuanced step each child took on his or her emotional and intellectual journey. The school became legendary for the freedom it allowed to children. Reporters clustered on the doorstep for salacious copy. Susan Isaac's own tone was more sober. She scrupulously observed the young children under her care, and subsequently wrote two highly regarded books about this experience. She became a columnist for a popular magazine, and gave authoritative and dignified advice on childrearing to a generation of its readers, before finally becoming a Kleinian analyst.

Whilst the well-to-do were experimenting, the poor were stuck. In 1900 more than half of all 3- and 4-year-olds were in school. Katherine Bathurst, an inspector for the Board of Education, castigated this system in a famous report published in 1905.

> Let us now follow the baby of three years through part of one day of school life. He is placed on a hard wooden seat with a desk in front of him . . . he is told to fold his arms and keep quiet. . . . He is surrounded by a large number of babies all under similar alarming and incomprehensible conditions. . . . A certified teacher has 60 babies to instruct,

> many of whom are hungry, cold and dirty . . . They are heavy eyed
> with unslept sleep . . . What possible good is there in forcing a little
> child to master the names of letters and numbers at this age? The
> strain on teachers is terrific.[12]

Her report shocked people. But the result of her campaigning was to exclude
young children from school. In 1907, funding was withdrawn for children
under 5 in schools. By 1910 the number of children under 5 in school was
halved, and by 1920 it was down to only 15 per cent.

But leaving young children outside of school was no good either. Poor
children had nowhere else to go if their mothers were working – as most then
were. Margaret McMillan, a leading nursery education campaigner, did her
best to argue for nursery schools.

> What young children require is fresh air, play and rest, and this is
> what the nursery school offers them. The development of nursery
> schools would tend greatly to raise the standard of physical health
> among the children.[13]

In 1923 the Nursery Schools Association (NSA) was formed to campaign
for more nursery schools. It produced a series of pamphlets on nursery education, some of which sold more than 200,000 copies. It also issued an authoritative policy statement in 1927, arguing that nursery schools were places where
children could be free and well looked after, unlike their cramped homes in
cramped streets.

> Underlying all mental and bodily development lies the need for free
> activity. Without it neither healthy growth of body and spirit, nor
> training in self-control is possible. . . . Free activity involves the provi-
> sion of spontaneous and purposeful activity in spacious open-air
> conditions . . . as well as an atmosphere of love, joy and freedom. . . .
> The daily routine must provide for the right alternation of rest and
> activity through the day. . . . It is undesirable to accept the hours of
> the ordinary school day as the limit for Nursery school.[14]

Despite this vigorous campaigning, by 1939 there were only 118 nursery
schools; together with under-5s in infant schools they catered for 180,000
children.

The NSA vigorously campaigned for state nursery schools but there was an
older, rival organization, with a different campaigning focus. The National
Society of Day Nurseries (NSDN) was founded in 1906 to set standards and
register day nurseries and crèches. It described itself as 'the only voluntary
body specifically devoted to the problem of the care of young children whose

mothers go out to work'.[15] By 1914, 80 day nurseries were recognized, many of them mill nurseries. The officers of the Society met in the drawing rooms of Piccadilly, and held fundraising balls at the Carlton Club, the bastion of the Establishment. Despite their fashionable charitable image, they made serious efforts to support the training of girls for nursery work or to raise standards of private day nurseries and crèches. Their work eventually led to the founding of the Nursery Nurses Examination Board (NNEB).

At the beginning of the Second World War, it was important to evacuate children from the towns and cities because of the danger of bombing. The government tried to provide nursery centres for billeted mothers and evacuee children – to be staffed, if possible, by voluntary workers. It was also obvious that more needed to be done to encourage women workers in industry. There was an argument about funds, but once they were sorted out, nurseries were set up very quickly. By the end of the war there were 1450 wartime nurseries, each catering for children from birth to 5 years, and open from 7am to 7pm. Their cost was estimated at £10 million over the course of the war.[16]

The disputes in the war about nurseries had been as much about mothering as about children. Mothers were working and childcare had to be provided. But after the war, mothers had to make way for returning soldiers. They were encouraged to give up their jobs and stay at home with their children. The theories of Bowlby about mother–child attachment provided a rationale for closing nurseries. By 1947, predictably, 700 nurseries – nearly half – had closed. Some of the remainder changed into nursery schools; others continued as social services day nurseries.

The NSA objected that nursery schools should not be closed. They still had a useful role to play providing outlets for emotion and instinctual expression in young children. During the war there was much concern about whether young children were learning to be aggressive; controlling aggression in children was regarded as being very important (see Chapter 3). Nurseries could support mothers in dealing with nervous, clinging children.

> The way of life [in nursery schools] organized for the children is simple and childlike and is planned in relation to the physical and psychological needs of children. . . . Aggressive dominating 'toughs' discover the happiness that comes from friendly co-operation with others . . .[17]

The themes of aggression and loss, and inner emotional balance were explored in detail by John Bowlby in his theory of attachment (see Chapter 3). An article by a child guidance psychologist put it more romantically.

> We must remember that the child's inner world is a romantic one, peopled like a Breughel canvas with a crowded population of shining

> angels in armour wielding swords of justice on a host of goblins, dragons and bat-like figures with yawning mouths and scaly tails.[18]

Dorothy Gardner, head of child development at the Institute of Education, argued that

> we cannot educate a very unhappy child, or one who is even temporarily in the throes of jealousy, anger or mourning. We are also coming to realise that emotional satisfactions lie at the root of all intellectual interests and that feelings are the driving force between all intellectual effort.[19]

But no sooner had Bowlby become the accepted wisdom of those working with young children than there was a new theoretical giant on the scene – Jean Piaget. As we saw in Chapter 3, Piaget revolutionized thinking about young children. The government in the UK commissioned the Central Advisory Council for Education to produce a report entitled *Children and Their Primary Schools*. The Plowden Report, as it became known, after its chairwoman Lady Plowden, included nursery education. It endorsed the theories of Jean Piaget about the child as an individual, self-propelled scientist experimenting with the world. It highlighted educational inequalities, except this time working-class children were not physically stunted or unable to control their fierce emotional lives. They were now intellectually stunted, and the job of the nursery and primary schools was to reawaken intellectual curiosity.[20]

Plowden was influenced by Bowlby as well as by Piaget. She was hostile to working mothers – although she herself used nannies. Her report maintained that it was no business of the state to provide services for working parents. Nursery education from then on (as it still is today) changed from offering all-round full-time care, education and healthy living. It became a part-time service, with the more limited objective of fostering children's intellectual development. The hours of nursery education became shorter than those of any other comparable European country, between 12 and 15 hours per week.

For half a century after the war, from the 1950s to 2000, working mothers and their children were an unpopular cause. Simon Yudkin, a paediatrician, wrote a widely supported report that detailed the large numbers of (mainly working-class) women who went out to work and the lack of childcare they faced (and still do in the UK). He said there was no evidence for the common view ascribed to Bowlby, that working mothers harmed their children. He recommended a proper government investigation into what he considered was an intolerable situation, which weighed heavily against poor families; and in particular against black children. The proportion of black working mothers, particularly from Afro-Caribbean backgrounds, was far higher than that of any other group.

Instead, Margaret Thatcher, then minister for education, firmly endorsed the educational approach and commitment to nursery education set out in the Plowden Report. The government committed itself to providing 250,000 new nursery places within 10 years, for 35 per cent of 3-year-olds and 75 per cent of 4-year-olds, plus an additional 15 per cent of full-time places. Urban aid would be used to fund the first tranche of nursery places, and some local authorities drew up plans for expansion.[21]

Meanwhile, the shortage of nursery education places had prompted a mother, herself a teacher, called Belle Tutaev, to set up a campaign for more nursery education. She encouraged mothers to start their own schools – or playgroups.[22] The Preschool Playgroup Association (PPA, now known as the Preschool Learning Alliance) was founded. Mothers acted as volunteers, helping out in the playgroup.

Jerome Bruner was persuaded by the government to leave the USA for a few years in the 1970s to take up a post at Oxford University as director of a project that explored British policy on early years. He and his team provided a useful picture of the state of early education and care in Britain, but his policy recommendations showed up his prejudices. He thought mothers should stay at home, and playgroups – volunteerism – was the best way forward for early years services. 'No long term benefit could accrue by making early pre-school care seem like the domain of professionals. It would surely have a corrosive effect on the self-confidence of parents and reduce volunteer efforts.'[23]

Bruner's assumption of maternal involvement through volunteering was implicitly based on a traditional view of domesticity. Women stayed at home to look after their children; and, indeed, looking after their children was their prime, if not always fulfilling, function. As one contributor to the PPA magazine *Contact* put it: 'I seem to be fighting a battle between the part of me that is determined not to be a domestic cabbage and the part that wants to do well the job of looking after husband, children and home.'[24] For such middle-class full-time housewives, playgroups fitted the bill exactly. For the poor working mothers, the lack of childcare was a major problem. Lady Plowden, who had become chairwoman of PPA, now argued that state provision was completely unnecessary.

> It's no large overall system which is needed . . . only in the last resort is there need to provide a substitute for those who are completely unable to manage themselves. . . . When we are planning for the care of our young children we must also enable care in its widest sense to be given to those who have the day to day responsibility, their parents and in particular, their mothers.[25]

As a result of these attitudes towards women and the obsession with the misdemeanours of the poor, early education and childcare in the UK has always been characterized by a large voluntary and private sector.

The Labour government that took power in 1997 was as rigid as its predecessors in terms of what and how young children should be taught. Part-time nursery education was seen not as a broad experience for young children in their own right, but as the first stage of the long haul of education. It was made available to all children aged 4 years, but without any reference to the childcare arguments. The overwhelming majority of 4-year-olds are now admitted directly to primary schools, a similar situation to the one that Katherine Bathurst had so objected to a hundred years earlier. Rising fives in schools take part in literacy and numeracy hours; free play and free movement, the *sine qua non* of the nursery movement, has been reduced mainly to scheduled playtime breaks. As a final insult, although nursery education (in its various versions) has been made available for all 4-year-olds, the number of nursery schools has fallen to under 500. They are too expensive for the limited task the government now calls 'nursery education'.[26]

The 1997 Labour government did, however, review sexual equality. Women could and should work. Working women became respectable again. It was something of a disgrace *not* to be working. In any case, the government did not want to pay out lots of state benefits to mothers staying at home.

All the ambivalences and contradictions of a century of weak policy making for young children have come to a head in the government's Sure Start programme. Billed as a great success, and an indication of the Labour government's commitment to young children, in fact it is a mess of contradictory policies and financing.[27] Despite being 'integrated', it deals only with children up to age 3, and has an uncertain relationship with the separately administered school nursery education programme. It is a segregated programme that focuses only on poor communities (again). It started off promoting the partnership of those government and voluntary agencies concerned with poverty and young children but has often descended into professional squabbling over which profession or agency should take precedence.[28] It began by promoting parental education (for example, cutting smoking) but mid-stream was told by the government to concentrate more on getting poor women back to work. The money spent on the programme is still less than other countries spend on their universal and comprehensive early childhood services.[29] But the government fanfares would have us believe that, somehow, a corner has been turned. A better knowledge of history would indicate how little has changed, and how much more change is necessary to break away from the policies of the past.

The history of policy making in other countries has taken other routes. Most other European countries have state-funded and state-provided nursery schools. The first full-time state nurseries were set up in France in 1848 because the government was so concerned about falling birth rates and wanted to encourage women to have more children. Vygotsky in the Soviet Union was part of an educational movement to establish a nationwide system of holistic kindergartens. What these various histories tell us is that the policy making in childcare and education, as in other areas, is deeply rooted in the past.

Summary

This chapter has considered how history provides new insights on childhood and policies towards young children. It argues that history provides an essential and revealing context for understanding early childhood education and care.

Main messages from this chapter

1 History helps us understand the uniqueness and particularity of events.
2 History provides important perspectives about the way we understand young children.
3 History shows us that policies are not conjured out of a hat but draw on deep-rooted traditions.

What to read next

Aldrich, R. (ed.) (2003) *Public or Private Education: Lessons from History.* London: Woburn Press.

Notes

1 Berlin 1997: 22
2 William Blake, *The Chimney Sweep; Songs of Innocence*, 1789
3 Bradbury and Jantti 1999
4 Francis Galton, said by many to be a founding father of psychology, strongly believed in eugenics
5 *Nursery World* report 1938: 237
6 Charles Dickens, *Nicholas Nickleby*, 1839
7 Mum's the Word, *The Economist*, 5 December 1998: 20
8 The rest of this chapter is an abbreviated version of a much longer study by the author. See Penn 2004b
9 Kessen 1965: 2

10 Quoted in Steedman 1988: 83
11 *On Education* was reviewed in the *Times Educational Supplement*, 27 February 1926
12 Bathurst, K. *The Need for National Nurseries*, in *The Nineteenth Century and After*, TES, May 1905: 812–24, cited in van Eyken (1973)
13 *Nursery Schools*. Extract from the memorandum prepared by the Advisory Committee on Education, Labour Party, 1919
14 NSA 1927
15 NSDN 1923
16 Ferguson and Fitzgerald 1954: 203
17 De Lissa 1945: 3
18 Bodman 1945: 17
19 Gardner 1956: 11
20 HMSO 1967
21 Department of Education 1973
22 Tutaev wrote a much quoted letter to the *Guardian Woman's Page*, 25 August 1961
23 Bruner 1980: 231
24 Letter to *Contact*, October 1965
25 Plowden 1977: 9
26 See Penn 2002b
27 Information about the Sure Start programme can be accessed on www.surestart.gov.uk
28 See Tunstill et al. 2002
29 See OECD 2001

7 Children's Rights

A new approach to studying childhood

Priscilla Alderson

Differences between older and newer approaches to studying childhood

The study of childhood in the twentieth century tends to have been dominated by child development theory and the thoughts of two or three great psychologists. From the mid-1980s, interest has rapidly grown in rather different ways of studying children. This chapter reviews some of these newer approaches. It considers how older and newer ways broadly differ in:

- the disciplines involved and their views about science;
- concepts of the child, of childhood and adulthood;
- basic aims and questions;
- views about values, rights and ethics;
- methods of collecting and analysing data;
- links with everyday policy making and practice.

There is much overlap between older and new approaches, especially in social psychology, so that it is hard to draw clear boundaries and comparisons. These ideas are therefore offered for readers to consider and to discuss critically.

The disciplines involved and their views about science

Child development theory has strong roots in traditional psychology, and links with medicine, biology and natural science (see Chapter 3). These disciplines concentrate on observing the child's body and behaviour using methods from animal research, as when Charles Darwin observed, described and drew his own children. Traditional approaches value empirical evidence – what is known through the five senses. Perhaps this explains many psychologists' excitement that they can now 'see' the brain working, through magnetic resonance imaging (see Chapter 4). The biological bases of both psychology and medicine are shown, for example, in the belief that children's minds, like their bodies, grow through universal, gradual, definite stages, set by genetic blueprints.

The traditional disciplines search for general causes and scientific 'laws', such as that which says that children have to be ready and at a certain stage before they can learn how to sympathize with another person's point of view. Doctors and psychologists give advice about childcare based on 'scientific evidence', through many popular books and magazines, and via radio, television, videos and websites for parents, teachers and other concerned adults. Their practical concern is to promote the best ways to ensure healthy, happy, well-educated children, and to prevent and manage antisocial behaviour. Clinical and educational psychologists help to ensure that child development theory is the main approach not only to understanding and managing children in personal individual cases but also to informing public opinion and policy generally. Many teachers, nurses, social workers and other people who work with and care for children also take this directly practical, factual approach to studying and understanding children.

In contrast, childhood studies involve a wide range of disciplines linked to the social rather than the natural sciences: sociology, social psychology, media and cultural studies, anthropology, history, literature, geography, social policy, critical theory, economics, international studies and philosophy. There are too many disciplines to allow firm generalizations but, broadly, many people working in these areas do not aim to be directly practical. Instead, they often concentrate on asking critical questions and examining taken-for-granted beliefs and underlying theories. There is interest in children's real everyday lives, and the very different ways in which children live in different continents. Researchers ask how cultural backgrounds and human motives might explain behaviour, rather than searching for biological causes. They therefore examine invisible issues, such as people's different perceptions of the same events, and their thoughts and feelings. The emphasis is on understanding diversity, instead of trying to find universal patterns on which to base policies.

This can be irritating to practical people who ask: 'What is the point of your research if you cannot give clear general answers about what children need that we can apply? If you are not going to benefit children directly, why should anyone help with your research projects, or bother to read the reports?' These important questions will be answered throughout this chapter, but to start with here are some replies.

To examine hidden beliefs can be the most worthwhile and useful kind of research. For example, women used to be seen as fairly helpless, inferior beings. Yet, instead of carrying on with 'practical' research about what inadequate women needed, feminists began to show how strong and competent and equal to men women could be, and how mistaken, and harmful to women, the old ideas were. Have children been similarly misunderstood? If so, it is necessary to look at *how* we see and understand children. Some researchers review past misunderstandings about childhood and critically question present ones. They ask how adults' memories and values might colour their views of childhood. Some studies look at *why* adults might want and need to describe all children as weak and dependent. In a case study, for example, of a young boy having a 'tantrum', there would be interest in the boy's own views and motives, rather than relying on adults' explanations. What is he reacting to and why? Is he being provoked? Does he find that this is the only way to get adults to listen? Why do adults dismiss his reaction as a 'tantrum', just as women were once called 'hysterical'?

This chapter aims to show how stepping back and thinking critically about some of the basic ideas that we take for granted, before making decisions about what to do, can be useful in helping people to understand childhood more clearly.

Concepts of the child, of childhood and adulthood

Over the twentieth century, children have benefited greatly from new ideas about their gradual development. Their needs for play, protection and carefully graded learning aids became much more fully understood. It is said that, in the past, children suffered from being treated too much 'like adults', but now we know, scientifically, what children are 'really' like. Yet at the same time, views about what women are 'really' like have become much less clear. Table 7.1 shows what 'real' women (column 1) and men (column 2) were once assumed to be like.

Table 7.1 Half-people

1	2
Ignorant	Knowing
Inexperienced	Experienced
Volatile	Stable
Foolish	Wise
Dependent	Protective
Unreliable	Reliable
Weak	Strong
Immature	Mature
Irrational	Rational
Incompetent	Competent

Through gender studies, gradually, the following arguments have become widely accepted.

- Women seemed weak and ignorant because they were kept in helpless dependence.
- Women were not allowed to gain knowledge and experience, or to show their strengths.
- Many women believed so deeply that they really were, and ought to be, ignorant and immature that they remained so.
- Women who tried to be strong were punished for being masculine. People thought they threatened public order and morality.
- Women were caught in a paradox, being seen as weak and foolish either because they were women, or because they foolishly tried to be like men.
- Yet women did not have to remain in column 1; they were encouraged or forced to do so.
- This happened because it suited men to keep column 2 for themselves, and so to justify keeping control over resources and decisions. (Many men were very generous but in the end it was because they *chose* to be, and because women could not own property and most of their work was unpaid.)
- It suited men to persuade everyone that women could only be safe and happy if they stayed in column 1.
- The inequalities and power relations between men and women became clearer. Overprotection too easily becomes oppressive control, which cannot be questioned if people deeply believe the column format and see men as always wise and women as always foolish.
- The problems of sexism, of teaching little girls to stay in column 1, and little boys 'who don't cry' in column 2 – in other words, of teaching children to become split, one-sided people – are now widely known, and routinely tackled by parents and early years practitioners.

We now know so much about (not) teaching little girls to be 'girls' in terms of column 1. The next vital task is to tackle the problems of teaching little girls and boys to be 'little'. 'But we don't teach them, they are naturally weak, ignorant and foolish, it would be cruel not to protect and control them.' This is the usual reply – as most people used to say about women. It is partly true. People of every age are sometimes weak and foolish, we are all a mixture of both columns.

Babies and young children can be wise, whether from instinct, intuition or acquired wisdom.[1] Feminists argue that knowledge and wisdom are not simply column-1-type reasoning in our minds, but that they also draw on emotions and bodily feelings such as love or fear. Babies are very much in touch with their bodies and feelings, and they can relate to other people sensitively and intensely. Babies are expert, for example, in feeding. Breastfeeding is most easily established when mothers let babies set the timing and pace of feeds. Children aged 0–5 years are brilliant teachers, being largely self-taught in the basic knowledge they will rely on for a lifetime.[2] The psychologist Judy Dunn found that very young children are highly concerned about their siblings' and parents' feelings.

Examples from history (see Chapter 6) and from the South (see Chapter 5) show how young children competently share in housework and other work on farms or street stalls. Many are far more active, experienced, and interdependent with adults than they are often allowed to be in Britain now. As women once did, children gain through being protected in column 1 terms in many ways. Yet they lose in many ways, when they are underestimated and overcontrolled. Just as gender studies of men–women relationships explain why women become stuck in column 1, the new childhood or generation studies, of adult–child relationships, help to explain why children are too.[3]

- Children often seem weak and ignorant because they are kept in helpless dependence.
- They are not allowed to gain knowledge and experience, or to show their strengths (such as to walk around towns as they used to do).
- Many children believe so deeply that they really are, and ought to be, ignorant and immature that they remain so.
- Children who try to move into column 2 may be punished for being rebellious, and adults who encourage them also risk being punished. Many people (public opinion, the media) think they threaten public order and morality.
- Children are caught in a paradox, when they are seen as weak and foolish because they are children, or else because they foolishly try to be like adults.
- Yet even babies do not have to stay wholly within column 1, unless they are encouraged or forced to do so.
- It suits adults to keep column 2 for themselves, and so to justify keeping control over resources and decisions. (Many adults are very generous but in the end it is because they *choose* to be, and because children cannot own property, and most of their work is unpaid.)
- It also suits adults to persuade everyone that children can only be safe and happy if they stay in column 1.
- The power relations between adults and children become clearer through research in generation studies. Overprotection too easily becomes cruel control which cannot be questioned when people deeply believe the column format and see adults as always wise and children as always foolish.

- There is a wide difference between supporting children because they have to be in column 1, and keeping them there after they are ready to be in column 2. Yet the problems of making children stay in column 1 – as split, one-sided people – when they are willing and able to be in column 2, are not yet widely admitted or routinely tackled. The generation conflicts are so invisible because they are taken for granted as right and natural, that there is not even a word, like sexism, to describe them.

Basic aims and questions

Although, as we grow older, we become more experienced and informed, and perhaps more wise, children too can be profoundly experienced, informed and wise. Most western children are too carefully protected to encounter serious dangers, but researchers who are fortunate enough to listen to children who know about danger, such as refugees or those who face life-threatening illness,[4] discover how intensely experienced young children can become and how maturely they can cope with complex and distressing information and decisions. The aim then becomes to explore how competent children can be. And taken-for-granted ideas about childhood can be turned into questions.

- How do people construct and reconstruct childhood as a life stage of being volatile or reliable, weak or strong?
- How can beliefs/theories about childhood be stretched to fit the exciting newer evidence about how thoughtful and social very young children can be?

For example, researchers have examined children's work,[5] the experiences of disabled children,[6] children's contributions in their early years setting,[7] and how children actively take part in research.[8] Once they see children as people, researchers and practitioners can work respectfully with them to explore their complex and wide-ranging views and experiences.

'Traditional' child psychology, as mentioned earlier, tends to test and assess children in order to detect and potentially prevent and treat conditions that seem unhealthy or abnormal. Yet this can inadvertently harm children by showing them in such a negative light if the best a child can score is zero. A typical questionnaire asks parents to rate how much their pre-school child 'tells lies . . . has wet or soiled self this year . . . has stutter or stammer . . . has other speech difficulty [and] bullies other children'. Further questions ask if the child 'is so active it exhausts me . . . appears disorganised and distracted . . . has more difficulty [than other children] concentrating and paying attention'.[9]

There is no chance for children to give their views and perhaps reasonable explanations about their behaviour or to talk about their achievements.

A popular textbook about how to fit observations of children to 23 pages about 'milestones' of development sums up ten whole months in these words: 'Key features of 9–18 months: Growing independence can lead to rage when thwarted. Shows anxiety when left alone. Emotionally more stable but can be jealous of adults' attention to other children. Can be defiant – learns NO.'[10] No positive examples are given. Yet children aged 9 to 18 months have many lovely characteristics. The examples are biased in concentrating on children's unreasonableness and seeming limitations, which would make it hard to trust or respect the children or work with them as partners in solving their problems. Adults' positive questions, solutions and attitudes then risk being discouraged and even excluded from research and childcare.

Many books by early years specialists are positive, and give fine examples of competent children, their helpfulness and imaginative awareness of others. Yet phrases such as 'terrible twos' abound. Like racism, these are negative stereotypes of a huge and very mixed group of people, falsely grouped together for one biological feature, in this case their age.

Different tendencies between older and newer approaches to childhood could be summed up as follows. Older approaches tend to emphasize adults protecting and providing for children; newer approaches are more likely to see children as active contributors who can be creative partners with adults. The next section looks further at these contrasting approaches.

Views about values and rights

Childhood researchers vary but they tend to endorse the following values. Children's lives are worthwhile and they matter now in the present, not simply for their future effects. Children are not merely developing and practising, they are also accomplishing and contributing competently. Their views and values can be valid in their own right, and adults are not always correct about what it means to be right or wrong, good or naughty. Adulthood is not the perfect endpoint and instead we all go on changing and learning, forgetting and making mistakes throughout our lives. These values link to views about children's rights.

Concerned about starving European children, Eglantine Jebb promoted the first international Charter of Children's Rights in 1914, on their rights to basic goods and to protection from harm and neglect. These so-called provision and protection rights can equally well be understood under old and non-controversial headings of children's welfare, needs or best interests. The United Nation's (UN) first Declaration of the Rights of Children, in 1959, included protection rights against exploitation and discrimination. The UN

Convention on the Rights of the Child 1989 (UNCRC) took ten years to be written and agreed, and it added the third 'P' of participation rights (see Tables 7.2–7.4). The three Ps usefully divide up children's rights, although many rights overlap across them. Important articles also urge governments:

- To encourage the mass media to disseminate 'material of social and cultural benefit to the child ... that promote social, spiritual and moral well-being and physical and mental health'.
- To ensure wide publicity about the UN Convention to adults and children alike.

A convention is the strongest kind of international treaty. The UNCRC is by far the most widely endorsed treaty ever, ratified by 192 governments who thereby promise to implement it in law, policy and practice, and to report regularly to the UN on progress in so doing. Only Somalia, which has no government, and the USA have not ratified the UNCRC.

Many people see modern rights in terms of 'Keep out! Don't interfere with me. I have the right to do whatever I like, as long as it doesn't harm anyone else.' In this view, no wonder children's rights are unpopular, a nightmare vision of the selfish unmanageable child, careless of parental love, and of responsibility, duty, loyalty or concern for others. However, the UN Convention rights are quite different. They are about necessities, such as clean water, not luxuries. They involve concern for children's best interests, for public order, health and morals, and for parents' rights and duties. The preamble to the Convention asserts the importance of every child living 'in an atmosphere of happiness, love and understanding' – although no one can have the right to love because love cannot be enforced by law. Rights are shared equally: 'our rights' not 'my rights'. Children's rights respect the inherent worth and dignity and the inalienable rights of all members of the human family. They promote social progress and better standards of life in larger freedoms that lay foundations for justice and peace in the world. They are tools for change, when governments regularly report to the UN on how they are implementing the rights in law, policy and practice.

Children's rights can benefit everyone, when communities have clean water and play areas. Parents can benefit too. Eight-year-old Finnish children have one day a week off school while their parents are at work. All the parents take it for granted that the children can stay at home on their own all day or go out to play with friends, even on dark winter evenings. So when Scandinavian children have more rights and freedoms, so too can their parents. In Britain, after-school childcare stops children's freedoms of peaceful 'association and assembly' to wander freely around their district and play with friends when and where they choose. Childcare is also very expensive and a great contributor to child poverty. Beliefs have grown up in Britain that all children need

Table 7.2 Provisions rights

- Care necessary for the child's wellbeing
- Competent standards of care
- The highest attainable standards of health and necessary health treatment
- Periodic review for looked-after children
- Adequate standard of living for physical, mental, spiritual and social development
- Compulsory and free primary education
- Education that is preparation for responsible life in a free society in the spirit of understanding, peace, tolerance, equality and friendship among all people
- Rest and leisure

Table 7.3 Protection rights

- Physical or mental violence
- Injury or abuse
- Neglect or negligent treatment
- Maltreatment or exploitation
- Cruel, inhuman or degrading treatment
- Unlawful deprivation of liberty
- Discrimination
- Rights to the promotion of physical or psychological recovery and social reintegration of child victims after neglect or abuse, cruel treatment or armed conflict

---

Table 7.4 Participation rights

- The right to life and survival
- To a name, an identity, a nationality
- To contact with parents and family
- To play, and to participate freely in cultural life and the arts
- To respect for the child's ethnic, religious, cultural and linguistic background, humanity and inherent human dignity
- The child's right to express views freely in all matters affecting the child
- The views of the child to be given due weight according to the age and ability of the child
- The opportunity to be heard directly or through a representative during proceedings that affect the child
- Freedom of expression and information
- Of thought, conscience and religion
- Of association and peaceful assembly
- Disabled children should enjoy a full and decent life in conditions which ensure dignity, promote self-reliance and facilitate the child's active participation in the community with the fullest possible social inclusion

---

constant adult supervision, and when children are no longer allowed to exercise certain rights and responsibilities they are seen as unable to do so (see Chapter 9).

Views about ethics

When children are seen as real people with rights, new questions arise about ethics in practice and research. These concern researchers, practitioners and students when they observe or test children, interview or assess them, or write case studies or records about them. Ethical research involves respecting people's privacy and confidentiality and their informed consent or refusal, besides many other standards that weave into all aspects of research.[11] Too often, adults are respected but not young children, although the latter are even less able to challenge researchers, or get research methods improved or inaccurate reports corrected. Children should have the same privacy rights as adults.

Informed consent to research involves telling people what the project is about, what you would like them to do to help you, why, how this could affect them, and what you will do with the data. It involves respecting children if they refuse or want to stop or withdraw from a project. Even young children can understand and talk about these matters. When are children old enough to be competent to consent? Much depends on each child's own experience and confidence, the type of research, and the skill with which researchers talk with children and help them to make unpressured, informed decisions. Children aged 3 years upwards have willingly taken part in research, not only as subjects but also as researchers.

Modern medical ethics has forced medical researchers to change their methods. They now do less risky research with children, and they inform, respect and protect children more. It is time for social and psychological researchers to take ethics more seriously. Unfortunately, distressing research, such as testing how upset babies become if their mother leaves them with a stranger, is still often carried out, although psychologists criticize this (see Chapter 3).

One-way mirrors, or secret records such as case studies made without asking for the person's permission, are unlikely to be tolerated today in research with adults. They are no more acceptable in research with children or when training students to study or work with children. Adults may argue that if they tell children what they are researching, such as bullying or racism, the children will hide their behaviours and the research will be impossible. Yet this negative deficit type of research can be counterproductive and is unlikely to produce helpful findings. Alternatively, involving the children as informed partners can produce much more useful results. For example, 7-year-old children decided to do a survey about bullying. Instead of asking the usual question 'Who bullies whom?', they asked 'When and where does bullying mainly happen?' Their survey helped the staff to know the danger areas where they needed to be in the playgrounds, and the rates of bullying fell.[12] Similarly, research which asks children what they think racism means and how it affects them is likely to reveal ways for children and adults to work together to tackle racism.[13]

Ethical research involves sensitive methods for discovering children's own views and meanings. In one study, children said the book area was the least popular place in their family centre. Were they immature or was the book corner inadequate? When they were asked why, the children explained that they disliked the way that the book corner was used – sometimes rather like a prison to keep them quiet and constrained, and also to read stories to large groups. So the use of the book corner changed, and there were smaller story groups.[14]

Ethical and rights-based research also takes account of children's own views about good and useful research and not only adults' views. It is concerned:

- to protect children from harm, abuse, anxiety, distress, and dishonest exploitation during the research;
- to be aware of risks of published research reports that could increase shame, stigma and disadvantage for whole groups of children (such as all refugee children or all children of single parents);
- to consider ways of preventing and reducing these risks.

There are three main ways of involving children in projects:

- Unknowing objects of research who are not asked for their consent and may be unaware that they are being researched.
- Aware subjects who are asked for their informed, willing consent to be observed or questioned, but within fairly rigid adult-designed projects such as questionnaire surveys.
- Active participants who willingly take part in doing the research (see methods section below).

Asking ethical questions can help you to be a critical reader of other researchers' reports.

- What are the report's hidden values and standards relating to harm or benefit, honesty, fairness and respect?
- Who will the research recommendations mainly benefit – children or certain adults such as educators or therapists who claim that research shows their services are needed?

- Are children seen as problems, victims or contributors?
- Do the researchers aim to rescue, or criticize, or respect children?
- Do the researchers thank the children who took part?

Children are not fully equal to adults, adults have far more power and resources and authority. But many children have strengths, capacities and good sense that are respected by ethical researchers and professionals.

Methods of collecting and analysing data

In the past, research about children tended to be done through:

- surveys of parents' or teachers', but not children's, views;
- standardized tests of 'representative' children;
- measuring children against assumed norms to show their abnormalities, failings and deficits;
- artificial laboratory tests with complicated methods that younger children often failed, and asking standards questions instead of questions about the child's own experiences.

Some of the newer methods are described below.

Asking for children's own views

This can be done through observing, talking and playing with them, and helping them to take photos and make diaries, maps and videos about their daily life. In semi-structured interviews, children tell stories about their lives, in which they are the experts. Or they take photos or make videos, maps and drawings. Children who cannot read or write can do all these activities, such as when young Nepalese children made maps of where they herded their animals and collected fodder and firewood.[15] Children have plenty of interesting and useful views about their education, their rights (or lack of rights) at school, and how they have improved their schools, such as through their skilled peer mediation and conflict resolution.[16]

Taking account of context

Understanding childhood goes beyond the usual approach of looking at each child individually, by taking account of the social and political context. For example, approximately one in three children in Britain grows up in poverty, so that understanding childhood includes understanding how poverty affects children's lives and learning, and how children are seen and see themselves either as inferior beings or as respected, competent people. Children and young people helped to design and conduct a survey of nearly 3000 young Londoners' views which led to the Mayor of London working with children and young people to create his city-wide Children's Strategy.[17]

Moving away from testing failure

Other new research methods are moving away from testing children's failings to examining their own reasons for their beliefs and behaviours which can then often be seen as sensible – understanding each child's viewpoint, meaning and values. Susan provides a good example of the benefits of this method. Susan determined to be the first person in her family to go to university. She insisted on moving from her local reception class, when 4 years old, where she felt 'smothered and mothered', to be a weekly boarder at a special school. She is blind, though, like many children at that school, she is exceptionally far-sighted about life, values and, for some, politics, which they debate with great enthusiasm. Susan recalled how 'Mum had to drag me screaming down the [school] drive because I didn't want to go home.' Unlike many of her peers, Susan managed to keep a close friend at home. When Susan was 10, she visited several secondary schools and then chose what she believed was the best one, though she found it a hard choice to make. A year later she was very pleased with her decision, academically and socially. In some ways, Susan was the only person who could make a fully informed decision that took account of her experiences, values and plans. Like many other children I have met, her understanding was not linked to her age or assessed intelligence, but to her experiences.[18]

Practical research with and by young children shows their competence. For instance, a run-down housing estate was being upgraded. Almost by chance, an adult asked children about the plans. Eventually, ten children aged 3–8 years did a survey of the other children's views. They wrote a report about their results, adding their photos, maps and drawings. They met senior council officers to discuss the report, and advised that the play area should not be put on the edge of the estate as planned, beyond a busy road. Instead, the play area was set in the centre of the estate, where children could safely play without needing adults to be with them.[19]

Summary

Childhood studies examine how children live in the present, how they achieve and accomplish activities besides learning and practising. Everyone is seen as having mixed abilities, instead of being an inferior child or a perfect adult. Being able to do things well can depend far more on a person's experience and knowledge (even as a baby) than their age. Neither is moral awareness necessarily linked to age. Young children can be kind and responsible, and adults are sometimes selfish. Early years staff have everyday experience of sensible, sensitive young children. We therefore need to rethink older ideas about incompetent children and see how we can listen to and involve children in many aspects of their lives and choices, also how we can adapt professional practices and policy making to take greater account of children's informed views.

Main messages of this chapter

1   Babies and young children are competent people but too few people recognize this or act on it.
2   The UN Convention on the Rights of the Child has been a landmark in rethinking children and childhood.
3   Research with young children has undergone a sea change; the ethics of such research have been scrutinized and children are much more centre-stage.

What to read next

Alderson, P. (2000) *Young Children's Rights*. London: Save the Children/Jessica Kingsley.

Notes

1   Murray and Andrews 2000
2   Gardner 1993
3   Mayall 2002
4   Alderson 1993
5   MacKinnon 2003
6   Davis *et al.* 2000
7   Miller 1996
8   Clark and Moss 2001
9   Adapted from Abdin by Grieg and Taylor 1999: 128–9
10   Sharman *et al.* 1995
11   Christensen and James 2000
12   Highfield Junior School Plymouth 1997
13   Alderson 1999
14   Miller 1999

15 Hart 1997
16 Alderson 1999
17 Hood 2001
18 Alderson and Goodey 1998: 119–20
19 Newson 1995

8 Hoping for Health

Helen Penn and Val Thurtle

What is health?

Ask an expectant parent if they want a boy or a girl. Most parents will reply they do not mind as long as the baby is healthy. 'Healthy children' is a concept with which we can all apparently agree. But reflection on what is meant by health, and indeed what we mean by a healthy child, raises further questions. What is health? Whose view prevails? Who is responsible for keeping children healthy?

One key question is how to balance individual choice with the wider good of society. For instance, should parents be able to refuse vaccinations for their own children if it means that there is a greater chance of all children getting ill? Or should parents drive their children to and from school or other places, when more traffic on the roads is bad for all children – more accidents and more pollution? Or is fluoridation of the water supply a good idea to prevent tooth decay – everyone has to have it or no one?

Another key question is about access to health care. In the UK, children do, in principle, have equal access to health care. But why then are there inequalities in outcome, and why are poor children ill more often? If we look at global access to health care then the disparities are shocking. Children die in their millions in poor countries for want of basic health care. In its 2002 special issue *Global Voices on the Aids Catastrophe*, the *British Medical Journal* has drawn attention to these disparities between rich and poor countries, which it considers are unacceptable to anyone with a conscience.

A third question is whether we rely too heavily on doctors and on medical interventions such as drugs to keep us healthy, and to keep away pain and illness, instead of putting emphasis on trying to maintain a healthy lifestyle. In the research study quoted in Chapter 4, more than 50 per cent of children under 2 years in a mixed district of London were receiving some kind of medication.

This chapter seeks to address some of these issues but, like all the other chapters, provides few clear-cut answers.

A discussion on health of children of any age raises questions about what is meant by the term 'healthy'. For some parents and carers the child is healthy if she shows no symptoms of illness or disease. This view of health as the absence of illness or disease is much influenced by the 'medical model'. Medical science is concerned about the fitness of individuals and promoting good health. But it places more emphasis on disease and abnormalities. It seeks to prevent problems, to identify risk factors and spot the early onset of disease or illness. It also supports those who already have illnesses or diseases, through drug control, surgery and palliative care. It focuses on specific symptoms, and treats these symptoms in isolation, without taking account of anything else happening in the person's life.

Many argue that the 'medical model' is a simplified way of seeing things. Health practitioners, as well as members of the general public, may see health more holistically. Health is influenced by people's experience and knowledge, as well as by their values and expectations. This 'social model' contrasts with the medical model.[1] In this way of looking at health, an individual's health is affected not only by biological factors but also by the whole situation in which they live, an accumulation of political, economic, social, psychological and cultural effects. Identifying the cause of good or ill health is inevitably complex. Bronfenbrenner's ecology of human development (see Chapter 3) highlighted the interplay of different levels of experience. His model puts the child at the centre, living her life in embedded complex, interactive and inter-dependent structures. Her health might be affected by the way her parents treat her, by illnesses she might catch at nursery school, or by where she lives and whether or not she is rich or poor. As Chapter 3 also pointed out, it is hard to test this model and to work out what kinds of changes at what kind of level make a difference.[2]

All of us, parents, health workers or practitioners, hold several implicit ideas about health. Peter Aggleton gives a number of definitions of health. Health can be seen as personal fitness – the child may be seen as healthy because he can keep up with his peers on the football pitch or shows other kinds of stamina or strength or agility. Health can be seen as a commodity. Parents can try to buy extra health, for example at the dentist. Orthodontic work may not be necessary, but having nice teeth may make you feel better about yourself. Or a carer might want to buy extra nutritional supplements, vitamin pills or herbal remedies to boost her or her children's health. Health can be viewed as a personal strength, or as basis for personal potential. Some nursery and school programmes – for instance Head Start in the USA – stress the importance of self-esteem. This means bolstering a child's confidence and positive sense of herself.

Seedhouse talks of health as the *foundation for achievement*. This means judging the future impact of healthy lifestyles or the impact of disease. For instance poor diets, such as the sugar and salt in processed food, or sugary drinks like coke, might lead to the early onset of diseases such as diabetes. Severely overweight children are likely to be mocked by their peers and to be bullied, and their schoolwork might suffer. A physically ill child may miss out on education and find it hard to keep up with his peers. An unhappy child, who has low self-esteem, perhaps with mental health problems, is less likely to make friends. He may go on to have long-term mental health problems and develop a poor employment record and experience poverty. Health has an impact in the future as well as in the present, although it is never certain how things will turn out.

With such varying views of health, constructing a working definition is complex. This chapter focuses on a *holistic* approach and tries to look at a wide range of factors that might influence and help maintain children's wellbeing. It considers how children might avoid illness and disease or be treated for them. Such a holistic view is at odds with the more traditional medical model.

Measuring health

In many countries the health sector is an important part of the economy, employing huge numbers of workers and absorbing relatively large amounts of national resources. As we saw in Chapter 4, it is the focus of much techno-logical innovation and biomedical research. Most citizens come into contact with health services at several points in their lives, usually when they are at their most vulnerable. Because the nature of some decision making in health involves matters of life and death, health is more in the public eye than many other social issues. Like the law, health is highly professionalized and medical professions have a high status, so they also exert a great deal of power over policy making and decisions about health. It is difficult for a mother to stand up to a doctor and say 'I think you are wrong' or 'You are not listening to me', although this is changing as the health service becomes more responsive to consumer demand, and as consumers themselves make more demands.

Most areas of medicine are dominated by specialists and child health is no exception. Epidemiology (the statistics of health) is used to give an overall picture or norms about the state of children's health. The classic measures that are used in a community or society are the rate of survival at birth, called the *infant mortality rate*, and the number of children who survive to the age of 5, called the *under-5 mortality rate*. Boys are slightly more vulnerable than girls. In the UK, the infant mortality rate for boys is 6 per 1000 whereas for girls it is 5 per 1000.

In most rich countries (the North) these rates are low and falling. For instance, the infant deaths of children in the first year of life per 1000 live births in England and Wales has declined from 29.2 in 1950 to 7.1 in 1997.[3] More children survive than they did a century, or even a generation, ago.[4]

Mortality rates are also used to compare the effectiveness of health policies in different countries.[5] There is a clear difference between the mortality rates in the North (rich) and South (poor). In Nigeria, for example, mortality rates are very high: 11 children out of every 100 die at birth, and 18 children out of a 100 die before they are 5. Other countries have even higher mortality rates, especially where HIV/AIDS has taken hold. In recent years some poor countries have shown an improvement in mortality rates, but in Africa in particular, the rates are increasing sharply. However, in the South, collecting any kind of accurate data is difficult, and these figures may be a considerable underestimate of the true picture.

Mortality rates give a very general idea of the state of child health within countries. UK figures for infant mortality in 2001 show a rate of 6.4 per 1000 live births in the West Midlands compared to the significantly lower 4.1 per 1000 in the south-east. In the UK mortality and morbidity rates (the rate of incidence of serious illnesses such as respiratory disease or gastroenteritis) can be seen to differ at town and even ward or neighbourhood level. Pockets of advantage and disadvantage show up on such figures.

Many people consider that children and young people in the UK are much healthier than those of previous generations. There is, however, little evidence that the health of children as perceived by their parents has improved. Certainly, rates of long-standing illness for children over 5 years of age increased in the 1980s[6] (the most recent figures available). Children in western societies are living longer with medical conditions that would previously have been life-limiting. For instance, in the 1960s a child with cystic fibrosis might have died in his first decade, but he is now likely to live into his 40s. Premature babies are also more likely to survive, although prematurity is linked to various kinds of disability.

Definitions of health and disease change over time. Didier Fassin described the medical and public health difficulties in Paris in recognizing lead poisoning. Clinical cases suggested that children who showed symptoms of lead poisoning were primarily from West Africa. As a result, in seeking to find treatments (and despite contradictory evidence from the USA), doctors blamed cultural practices.

> When questioned on their profession, many fathers had mentioned that they were 'marabouts', i.e. Muslim healers – an activity that often serves to mask the reality of joblessness. Some professionals soon suggested they were dealing with 'a disease of marabouts' children' and looked for a possible source of contamination in the ink of Muslim prayer tablets. More broadly, African practices and objects were closely examined in interviews with parents and compared with lists

of dangerous products, before being subjected to chemical analyses: eye-shadows, craft pottery for cooking food, and traditional potions administered by parents. Faced with the authorities' incredulity as to the reality of the epidemic and its source, it was necessary, they explained, to eliminate all possible causes. Nevertheless, this excess of cultural zeal is astonishing if we consider that in North America, for more than half a century, paint had been considered as the main source of poisoning of children, and that tests on paint during the first Parisian inquiry had shown very high lead concentrations. However, it was not long before the role of old paint became difficult to deny.[7]

Even when lead paint was finally pinpointed as the cause of lead poisoning, doctors still tried to blame West Africans for their bad habits of letting children scratch the paint. Mothers were told to cut their children's nails short and wash their floors more often. Eventually it emerged that the reason the incidence of lead poisoning was so high in West Africans was that they lived in the poorest, most dilapidated housing with the worst concentrations of lead paint. It took over half a century, until 1998, for the French government to act and outlaw lead paint. By then, definitions of lead poisoning had changed, and much lower levels of lead intake were regarded as dangerous. What had previously been regarded as a few cases of brain damage affecting West Africans was now seen as a major environmental hazard which required public action.

Illnesses that have attracted more recent attention are conditions such as child suicide and behaviour problems such as attention deficit hyperactivity disorder (ADD) and autism. ADD, especially, appears to have shown a rapid increase, although there is enormous variation in both diagnosis and treatment. ADD and autism used to be very uncommon, but now appear to be frequent. No one is sure why the increase has happened: whether the diagnosis has changed, or whether the conditions in which children are being brought up have changed, or whether it is due to changes in diet or some kind of chemical pollution. Like the example of lead poisoning, it requires unravelling. Other illnesses that are attracting attention, at least in the North, are obesity-related illnesses. Obesity in children is also increasing rapidly, partly because of lack of exercise, partly because of poor diets relying on heavily processed food, saturated with fats, sugar and salt. (On the other hand, malnutrition in some poor countries is so widespread that it is an accepted condition of life.)

So although mortality rates are declining in rich countries, there is a real question about whether children are any healthier. These new sicknesses are part of what is called the 'New Morbidity'.[8] Indeed, as Titmuss pointed out convincingly over half a century ago, in general the increases in reported illness are linked with the circumstances in which children live, particularly the families' socio-economic status. Health status correlates with the difficult circumstances in which some children are raised. In addition, the demands of having a sick child are likely to have a downward effect on the socio-economic status of the whole family. Even if, in some sense, more children are sick, people are also more tolerant of disability and better able to manage conditions that before would have been regarded as very serious. A child could have an ongoing but well-managed condition such as diabetes, and not regard herself as ill or unhealthy. Such arguments reinforce the view that we all have different views of health, and the prolonged life of very sick children, for example, is not necessarily a measure of health and wellbeing.

Because of wide variations between countries as well as within countries, epidemiological statistics need to be looked at critically, particularly if they are a basis for health planning. In the South they appear to be shocking: UNICEF estimates that 7 million children die unnecessarily each year.[9]

Public health

Parents are inevitably preoccupied with their own children. They take the long-term view, imagining how their children might grow up and what they as parents can do to nurture, protect, help and influence them – the 'foundation of achievement' viewpoint. Parents want the best for their own children in the short term and in the long term.

In public health it is the overall health and wellbeing of the community or population that are at stake. Public health has been defined as the 'science and art of preventing disease, prolonging life and promoting health through organised efforts of society'.[10] A policy towards public health is just as important as parents' own individual efforts to prolong life and ensure the wellbeing of their children.

Traditional public health policy focused on the need to improve the health of many by improving nutrition and, just as importantly, sanitation. One public health policy, vaccination, has eradicated smallpox, which used to be a terrible scourge. Vaccination can also give children immunity to other life-threatening diseases. Measures to improve the food supply – such as controlling tuberculosis in milk production and preventing the decay and adulteration of food, especially meat – have contributed significantly to public health. Building effective drains has contributed more to reducing death and illness rates than have medical advances. Cholera and typhoid used to be endemic in the UK, and claim many deaths, but these infections are now rare where the water supply and sewerage are closely controlled. The greatest public health battles are now in poor countries; not only food hygiene and waste disposal, but combating diseases such as malaria, pneumonia and, above all, trying to prevent the HIV/AIDS epidemic from spreading.

Public health approaches are widening. The main thrust used to be control of infection (as it still is in the South). Now, public health is more sophisticated and complex. It means thinking about *how* the health service is administered and whether it is accessible to all children, and *if* it is responsive to users. But there is also a recognition that the *social* environment promotes positive and emotional wellbeing in children; or conversely damages their chances of wellbeing. Doctors and health workers alone cannot do this. Changing a poor, run-down environment means cooperation at many levels and sectors of government – housing, transport, education and employment as well as health.

In the UK there are relatively high levels of child poverty by the standards of the North. Child poverty in Britain rose in the last decades of the twentieth century.[11] Bradshaw notes the number of children living in UK households with an income below 50 per cent of the contemporary average after housing costs had risen threefold between 1979 and 1999. Other countries had a high child poverty rate but the rate rose faster in the UK than elsewhere between the mid-1980s and 1990s.[12] Child poverty is clearly related to ill health. The evidence on low birth weight, most congenital disabilities, chronic sickness, some infectious diseases, obesity and childhood accidents supports the argument that children living in poor socio-economic circumstances are likely to have poorer health that those living in more affluent circumstances. Poor children are ill more often, have more accidents, and have a shorter life expectancy. So in order to tackle ill health, the government must also tackle poverty.

Improving children's health

Chapter 6 showed how, in comparison with other historical periods, in the twentieth century children and childhood are more precious. They are more highly valued by their parents, if not by society at large. Reformers at the beginning of the last century argued that children needed much better preventative health services and regular medical checks.

Medical evidence suggests that very early intervention in children's health can be critical. Deficiencies and difficulties at an early stage may have repercussions many years later.[13] All young children in the UK, in theory at least, are screened through child health services. There is an extensive screening and surveillance system offered by the statutory health care services, although this in itself will not improve health unless an appropriate intervention is available. In the UK, some of the frontline health workers concerned with screening are health visitors. In the ex-Soviet Union states and some other countries with good kindergarten systems, screening is regularly carried out by doctors and nurses attached to nurseries. In other countries, such as Finland and France, child and maternity benefits are linked to attendance at a health clinic.

Screening is the identification of unrecognized diseases or defects using tests that can be quickly applied. The tests are not definitive but suggest that further investigation and further referral are necessary.[14] Child surveillance in Europe, the USA and the UK differs in terms of the procedures, weighing, measurement, vision and hearing tests and the frequency of contact offered. There is an ongoing debate on the effectiveness of routine universal surveillance. Some of the procedures, such as vaccinations, have been questioned. Testing may unnecessarily raise parental anxiety, especially if the next stage of investigation is delayed.

Providing a professionally led screening service for all children is expensive but may prevent the need for more expensive treatment later on. Inevitably, some children and families need more input than others. Poor families generally have more health problems. The 'inverse care law', however, suggests that those that have the greater need receive the lesser service.[15] This raises the question of whether certain children should be targeted for more intervention. Targeting, however, increases stigma. Universal child health surveillance means that the fact that it is taken up by everyone lessens any stigma.

The term 'screening' sounds formal and the term 'surveillance' has overtones of being watched. The historian Carol Steedman recollected how the visit of the health visitor was dreaded in her poor community when she was growing up. Health visitors do more than monitor for defects; they traditionally see themselves as having a positive health promotion role for parents and carers. They contact families, encourage and support breastfeeding, work with parents to address home safety issues and encourage the use of local service supports, although their heavy caseloads mean that such advice may be cursory.

Health surveillance is designed to diagnose and treat the very early onset of disease. For some years there has been a debate about the extent to which growth and health *in utero* and early life impacts on adult health in terms of blood pressure, strokes, respiratory function, coronary heart disease and diabetes. The methods used to investigate these possible connections are problematical. Many studies are retrospective, and all studies require very large samples to provide significant results. But all the evidence suggests that foetal health is likely to be important.[16] Consequently, health in pregnancy is important, and diagnostic services are widely available for pregnant women.

Childhood obesity certainly is linked to adult obesity.[17] One-third of obese pre-school children become obese adults and show signs of ill health – diabetes and fatty heart muscles – and as a result have a shorter life expectancy. The current generation of children is predicted to have a shorter lifespan than their parents. The problem of obesity is so widespread in the North that it has been described as an epidemic. There are two significant ways governments can intervene. Firstly, as in Sweden, it could control the advertising of processed foods. They could also introduce more stringent regulations concerning additives in food – reducing salt, sugar and fat. They could also introduce warning notices on fizzy drinks. Although governments have taken such preventative action in relation to smoking, they appear reluctant to do so for food, especially since the food industry lobby is so powerful. Secondly, governments could intervene by making exercise and sports more prominent in the school curriculum. In Finland, for example, children are usually expected to get 13 hours upwards of physical exercise per week, in nurseries and in schools. However, mostly governments do none of these things, mainly because ensuring adequate diet and exercise are seen as the *personal responsibility* of parents.

Mental health in childhood also has an effect. Unhappy and disturbed children are likely to grow up into unhappy and disturbed adults. The prison population, for example, contains a disproportionate number of adults who as children were in care. On the positive side, children who have good mental health are more likely to go on to make good and lasting relationships and to achieve academically and in other areas of life.[18] Again, a child's mental health is regarded to be more the personal responsibility of parents than the responsibility of government. In the UK, for instance, children who behave badly in nurseries and schools and are clearly showing signs of unhappiness and distress are generally treated punitively by the system, that is, excluded, in contrast to Scandinavian countries where they are likely to receive more support.

Two of the difficulties in investing in child health, or any particular health policy, are the increasing costs of medical intervention and the competing demands on the health budget from all areas of medicine. Surgical operations are very expensive. So are many drugs. How, then, should resources be shared out? Very ill children require a lot of resources. Should they automatically receive them or should there be some kind of health rationing, if there is not enough money to go round? And how should health services for children be weighted against, say, the needs of the elderly, who also require significant medical interventions? These ethical problems of making choices in difficult circumstances, and prioritizing certain forms of medical interventions above others, increasingly dominate the health field. Medical ethics is one of the fastest-growing areas of medicine.

School health

All children go to school, so schools could monitor and contribute to the health of children. As Chapter 6 showed, when universal education was first introduced in the UK there was a great emphasis on health, especially school meals and health checks. But much of this concern with schools as health-producing places has disappeared. Mayall argues schools in the UK are potentially unhealthy places.[19] The building may be a physically poor environment. The nutritional standard of school meals is poor. Some of those who need the hot dinner and are entitled to free school meals are reluctant to take up the meal because of stigma. As indicated above, the emphasis on the national curriculum has led to a reduction in physical exercise in school at a time when young people are undertaking less activity generally. Staff are reluctant to devote time to have extra health input at the expense of subjects that are assessed. The school nurse, speech therapist and other visiting health workers may share poor facilities. Meanwhile, as more mothers work, children are taking on the monitoring of their own health status, at least on a short-term basis, eating, drinking, resting and playing at their own pace according to their own promptings, even although once at school they are completely subject to adult control.

The low health status of schools is not always the case or inevitable. The World Health Organization's report called (rather optimistically) *Promoting Health through Schools* has been circulated worldwide and argues that schools need to see themselves as a healthy organism.[20] The physical environment needs to be safe and hygienic. Nutrition and exercise need to be part of the school regime. There should be a route into health services for children who need them – for example to psychologists, dentists and nurses. The curriculum itself should take on life-skills issues and what it means to be healthy. This is discussed further in Chapter 9.

In the UK this healthy school approach is being worked out in the Health School Standard.[21] This programme seeks to bring health and education together, investing in health to raise the level of pupil achievement. Schools are encouraged to work to standards, which they develop with health and school staff, including the children themselves, to meet their needs and promote the wellbeing of the school community. Healthy schools will be accredited. Some have already achieved this status.

However, children are in school for only a limited proportion of each day. A public health approach requires 'joined-up thinking' from a variety of workers and agencies, including those traditionally seen as health workers and many others as well.

Choice, participation and risk

One concept that is increasingly used in health, and in other social sciences, is *risk*. The concept of risk was coined by two sociologists, the German Ulrich Beck and the British sociologist Anthony Giddens.[22] Society, they argue, is increasingly characterized by a growing sense of uncertainty and ambivalence, and distrust of rapidly changing and contradictory expert knowledge. There are fewer certainties about jobs and employment, and also more generally about what should be done or what is right. Individuals have to imagine the future and calculate the risk of taking one option over another in terms of their life chances – decisions they might previously have left to someone else. Individuals have to plan for themselves and take more risks alongside a growing sense of uncertainty and threat. They are more likely to question the authority and relevance of oppressive institutions, to make their own choices and calculations of risk. The calculation of risk is now a way of looking at the behaviour of individuals and of organizations. In epidemiology, risk is defined more narrowly as the increased susceptibility to particular diseases; there are 'risk groups' and 'risk environments'.

The following two examples may be useful to illustrate the concept of risk. A nursery which, as well as offering childcare, ran a large training programme for childcare workers, had a very small, walled backyard for outside play. The ground of the yard was entirely rubber-coated and it was completely empty. The director of the programme explained that 11 years earlier, her child had fallen over in a playground and had had to have orthodontic treatment. She explained that she never wanted to see another child have a similar accident. So because of a freak accident, the director felt she had to provide a completely safe environment for the children in her care, even if it meant that the environment was sterile. She calculated that the benefits of letting children play outside were not worth the risk of another accident. She also took into account the possibility of litigation from parents if an accident happened. This threat of litigation for accidents or incorrect treatment hangs over the health service, and health authorities in the UK pay out large sums in compensation every year. Consequently, people who have responsibility for the care of others may tend to be cautious and conservative in their treatment, even if it means that the children they are looking after have much duller and more restricted lives.

Another, very different example concerns HIV/AIDS. This is a sexually transmitted disease, so the simplest way to prevent catching it is to abstain from sexual intercourse, or to have only one partner. In some African countries, HIV/AIDS affects more than one in three people, and health workers and teachers stress the importance of prevention. Yet in these countries, even though young people *know* that unprotected sex leads to HIV/AIDS, they continue to indulge in risky behaviour. Barnett and Whiteside point out that their calculation of risk is logical in a poor environment, where life is short and unpredictable and people have little control over what happens to them.[23] This is called a *risk environment*. For example, inner-city environments of many big American cities constitute risk environments, where people make choices that in other circumstances would not be wise – for example drug taking.

So, from the point of individual choice, people make decisions based on their calculation of risk. Women who smoke, for example, ignore the risk of tobacco-related illness because the gratification from smoking is worth more to them than a distant risk of their own or their children's ill health. This may be a logical choice in the circumstances in which they find themselves, if they live in a risk environment.

Some work is being done on how children perceive health risks. Backett and Alexander, working with 4–12 year olds from largely middle-class homes in the UK, found that they had a clear idea of the negative effects of unhealthy foods rather than stressing the positive aspects of healthy foods.[24] But, like many adults, their knowledge and beliefs did not necessarily relate to their behaviour. Knowing what is bad for you does not necessarily prevent you from doing it.

Pat Pridmore and Gill Bendelow compared children from differing schools and social backgrounds in both England and Botswana.[25] The researchers asked children to draw pictures and write about 'what keeps you healthy and what makes you unhealthy'. They found, as one might expect, considerable differences in the children's perceptions of health. English children cited responses such as healthy food, exercise, sport, hygiene, not smoking and sleep. Smoking, bad diets, violence, alcohol and a poor environment were seen to cause ill health. In Botswana, the Bushman children's responses reflected their very different social circumstances, their poverty and their acceptance of ill health as inevitable. Food, exercise, medicine and hygiene made you better; some children only mentioned the food. Some children suggested that ill health might be caused by drinking, smoking, fighting and accidents, but other children in the survey barely comprehended the concept of being unhealthy.

The children came up with a range of suggestions, those that impact on individual health as well as those that affect a whole group or community. The children's perceptions provided a clear illustration of their circumstances. They are affected by their poverty, by the health behaviours they observe around them, and the beliefs that are passed on to them by their parents, carers and wider community through schools, and, in the case of the English children, by the media.

Summary

This chapter discusses some ideas about health and health care for children. People have differing views about what health is, how to maintain it and how to measure it. The medical model of health of repairing the body as if it were a machine with parts is increasingly being challenged. The contribution of public health to reducing ill health is widely recognized. The disparities in health between rich and poor children within and across countries is a matter of great concern.

Main messages from this chapter

1   Good public health reduces illness and disease. Health is not just a private matter between you and your doctor.
2   Access to health care is inequitable, especially for children in poor countries. This is a major ethical issue.
3   The health and wellbeing of children in the North are at risk from overeating (and eating the wrong foods) and underexercising. The health and wellbeing of children in the South are at risk from HIV/AIDS.

What to read next

Barnett, T. and Whiteside, A. (2002) *AIDS in the 21st Century: Disease and Globalization*. Hampshire: Palgrave/Macmillan.

Notes

1   Jones 2000
2   See Antonovsky 1987
3   These statistics are taken from the website of the National Centre for Health Statistics at http://www.cdc.gov
4   Schuman 1998
5   Most basic international statistics on health are summarized in UNICEF's annual publication *The State of the World's Children*, available at www.unicef.org/statis/country
6   Botting 1995
7   Fassin 2004
8   Heussler *et al.* 2000
9   Always with the proviso that statistics are difficult to collect and bear a variety of interpretations
10   Acheson 1988
11   Bradbury and Jantti 1999
12   Bradshaw 2002
13   Barker 1992
14   Hall and Elliman 2003. Summarized at www.healthforallchildren.co.uk

15 Tudor-Hart 1971
16 See Wadsworth and Kuh 1997
17 Serdula *et al.* 1993
18 Mental Health Foundation 1999
19 Mayall 2001
20 World Health Organization 1995
21 User-friendly and up-to-date information on the *Healthy School Standard* can be found on www.wiredforhealth.gov.uk
22 See Beck 1992 and Giddens 1991
23 Barnett and Whiteside 2002
24 Backett and Alexander 1991
25 Pridmore and Bendelow 1995

9 Practice makes no difference

I have a postcard from an exhibition which says 'Practice makes no difference'. Yet it is a common-sense axiom that 'practice makes perfect'. Does doing things over and over again make you more skilled or more bored? Practice has a triple meaning. It means constant repetition – the sense in which it is meant in the postcard. It also means a repertoire of ideas and skills on a particular topic which are brought together by a group of people to create what is called a practice, or sometimes a community of practice. And thirdly it means doing things, as opposed to hearing or reading about them, as when you 'put your ideas into practice'. Sometimes all three meanings are conflated. The idea of 'practice' sounds straightforward but it is not. Most of the chapters in this book have been devoted to exploring ideas and approaches that have underpinned or informed practice (in the sense of a body of ideas and skills), even though they may fall outside of conventional thinking about child development. Now it is time to look at what people do in practice (in the sense of doing rather than reading or thinking) and whether practice (in the sense of repetition) leads to improvement or change.

Practitioners working in early childhood have accumulated a lot of experience, individually and collectively. For those who go to university to improve their learning and skills, this experience of practice should provide a rich seam to draw on. For many students, however, their experience seems to be irrelevant. Doing things, and doing things often, does not necessarily enable people to talk about them in any kind of abstract way. Linking practice and theory does not work easily. There are several reasons why this might be the case.

Book learning, especially for those who have been out of education for some time, is like learning another language. The language, expectations and conduct of university life are so different from everyday working life in a nursery that students sometimes have great difficulty in translating from one to another.

After working in the childcare field for many years, as an employee, then latterly as an employer, I felt I could draw on my skills and knowledge. I thought the degree would allow me to offer my services to others in the profession, and open doors to further opportunities. I soon discovered the lecturers spoke a different form of the English language when it came to allowing students to share their specialized field.

(Joan)

I have been working with children for six years and in a wide range of settings (I work for an agency) and I reflect on what has been said here, and try and put it into practice and match it up with what I do. I'm accumulating knowledge, it's there in the back of my head. I should have approached the lecturers more. I looked on them as aliens, they are above me, and I forget they are as human as me.

(Cynthia)

Like Joan and Cynthia, students may be very competent in their everyday dealings with parents and children, but analysing those actions and then writing about them are very different processes. Moreover, as this book has been at pains to show, many of the ideas about child development are highly specific or very subtle, or just plain contentious. They cannot be turned easily into prescriptions for practice in a classroom or nursery. On the other hand, if I thought that students did not benefit from learning, thinking, discussing and writing, there would be no point in writing this book.

Learning about child development, from an academic point of view, may give some insights into how children behave, but it does not tell you about the rules and regulations, explicit and implicit, which govern everyday practices with children. A nursery or childcare setting could be described, in the phrase of the cultural psychologists (discussed in Chapter 3) as a 'community of practice'. There are traditional ways of doing things that can only be understood as an outsider by analysing the significance of particular actions and events, and working out their meaning to those involved. The people involved often cannot explain what they are doing because they take it completely for granted, beyond explanation. Yet to the outsider, those actions may be strange and unfamiliar.

A well-known example is the study by Joseph Tobin and his collegues described in Chapter 2. He videoed daily life in nurseries in China, Japan and the USA and asked the staff to comment on each other's practices. In each country the nursery staff thought that what they did was drawn from the best available knowledge. They were well trained, and were putting their training in child development into practice. Yet each group of staff was shocked at what they saw elsewhere. In the Japanese nursery there was enormous reliance on peer pressure. In the Japanese class there was one child whose behaviour was very disruptive. Instead of correcting him, the teachers said again and again to the children, you must sort it out, you must deal with it. Japan is a conformist society, and the teacher's intention was that the children should learn how to make errant members of the group conform. In the Chinese nursery, on the contrary, the teacher was firmly in charge, and all the children obeyed her without any quibbles. The emphasis was on doing things together, as efficiently as possible. In the US nursery the children were aggressive and individualistic, and the teacher emphasized all the time the right, or necessity, of each child to make his or her own choices. When the staff saw each other's videos, and then met to discuss them, there was lively discussion.

As a researcher I have been fortunate to visit nurseries and other early years provision in rich and poor countries. I have mostly conducted reviews for governments or international agencies such as the EU, OECD, the Asian Development Bank and Save the Children. The methods I used were those of official investigators: interviews with key people; analysis of documentation (including financial statistics); and ethnographic observations in nurseries and other settings. As an official visitor I also saw a lot of performances by children, sometimes put on for my benefit, sometimes coinciding with an event such as a special holiday or end of term. I have spent months working in Italian and Spanish nurseries; I carried out official reviews of Belgian nursery classes and of the Canadian system of early education and care. I have a particular interest in South Africa. My work for Save the Children in particular has enabled me to become familiar with nursery education and childcare provision in many places in southern Africa. I have also spent time in Central Asia and Eastern Europe, initially for Save the Children, and subsequently for the Asian Development Bank. I have come to know the ex-Soviet system of kindergartens, which was, as Bronfenbrenner once commented, the most comprehensive system of early education and care ever devised.

I have, then, had a bird's eye view of many practices. What I propose to do in this chapter is to try to make the strange familiar, and the familiar strange, to use the anthropologist's phrase. What we take for granted as standard – for example the *developmentally appropriate practice* approach described in Chapter 1 – turns out not to be normal or standard at all, but a reflection of a particular, North American philosophy about childhood. Similarly, my friends in Central Asia are learning, painfully, that what they took to be hard scientific knowledge, proven and tested, is seen as old-fashioned and downright wrong elsewhere. As one indignant parent said to me 'They tell us that everything Russian was wrong. Well, I think it was a good education and what we have now is far worse.'[1] Meanwhile, the sunny philosophy of the best European nurseries[2] – the best, that is, in Denmark, Italy, Spain and the UK – holds yet another set of underlying principles about child autonomy and collective action.

What I propose to do is to explore some key topics of practice and discuss how they are viewed in different countries or in different systems of early education and care. It is a very incomplete list verging on anecdote and I will only skim through it. But it may give readers some rather different ideas about practice from outside their own particular community of practice. These topics are interrelated. I have introduced them to give some idea of the range of practices – and the range of assumptions that underlies them. To give them snappy titles, they are:

- *Holistic and whole* – some examples of practice which claim to offer children an all-round experience.
- *Suppleness, strength and stamina* – physical education and how it is undertaken in different countries.
- *Aunts, angels and teachers* – views about the role of staff in nurseries.
- *Catalogues of toys* – objects used in nurseries and their perceived use in 'stimulating' children.
- *Listening, speaking and singing* – who listens, who speaks, who sings, and when.
- *Learning your colours* – ideas about art and aesthetics.
- *Skeletons of frogs* – ideas about maths, science and the environment.
- *Grannies on the doorstep* – parents, grandparents and the wider community and their influence.

Finally, I discuss what facilitates 'good' and 'bad' practice.

Holistic and whole

'Holistic' is a word much used in practice. Holistic is taken to mean providing for a range of children's needs: for cognitive development, emotional development, social development and physical development. As I suggested in Chapter 3, these categories are themselves problematical.

Addressing 'the whole child' is a goal that many countries have adopted, perhaps nowhere more than in the ex-Soviet states. The interpretation given to holistic in the Soviet system indicates, by comparison, the limited way in which it is used in many English-speaking systems.

I have described, also in Chapter 3, how Vygotsky was involved in educational developments in Central Asia, where the Soviets' task was to transform illiterate nomadic people into conscientious Soviet citizens.

The Soviet state believed that if society was to fundamentally change, it would have to begin with the collective upbringing of young children. The Soviets also believed everybody could, should and wanted to work, men and women alike. Work and family life were reconciled by the provision of widespread childcare. Psychologists, doctors and many other experts worked on the development of the kindergarten programme, which was extended to some of the poorest and remotest regions in the world, for example on the steppes, or in the Gobi desert.[3]

Children needed to be developed intellectually, to be prepared for reading, writing and other intellectual pursuits. I have used the passive tense: 'to be developed'. Children were developed by good teaching – Vygotsky's zone of proximal development. They were set tasks appropriate to their age, and they were encouraged and monitored by their teachers in undertaking those tasks. Sometimes the tasks were arduous by western standards. For instance, children regularly gave end-of-year performances, or performances for special occasions, in which the level of performance – playing a simple musical instrument like a drum, or singing, or reciting poetry, or dancing – was of an exceptionally high standard and required collective discipline. Children had to perform together as well as separately. I have been privileged to see and hear some of these performances. It is a humbling experience to visit a kindergarten in a rough and remote desert area, and see immaculately costumed children singing, reciting and dancing; and also to watch their very proud parents.

Because the intention of the kindergarten was also to offer 'a good upbringing', there was a considerable emphasis on the class doing things together, in a disciplined way. No one could excel, or be individualistic, or different, but neither could anyone fail. No child fell behind her companions; all were expected to do and complete the same tasks, with extra help if necessary from the teacher or from other children. Bronfenbrenner wrote:

> From the very beginning stress is placed on teaching children to share and to engage in joint activity. Frequent reference is made to common ownership: 'Moe eto nashe; nashe moe' (mine is ours, ours is mine). Collective play is emphasized. Not only group games, but special complex toys are designed which require the co-operation of two or three children to make them work. Music becomes an exercise in social as well as sensory-motor articulation. As soon as children are able to express themselves, they are given training in evaluating and criticizing each other's behaviour from the point of view of the group. . . . Beginning in the second year of nursery (age 2) and continuing through kindergarten, children are expected to take on ever increasing communal responsibilities, such as helping others, serving at table, cleaning up, gardening, caring for animals, and shovelling snow. The effects of these socializing experiences are reflected in youngsters' behaviour, with many children giving an impression of self-confidence, competence and camaraderie.[4]

Bronfenbrenner also pointed out that there was congruence between the way parents treated their children and the way the kindergartens treated children; deliberately so. Both at home and in kindergarten, children were disciplined by withdrawal of affection. If a child was naughty, the mother, or the teacher, appeared hurt, as if saying, 'how could you behave like this to me?' This emotional disapproval, consistently applied, was extremely effective. The fact that the kindergarten discipline was based on traditional Russian upbringing meant that although parents did not spend much time at the kindergarten, they and their children did not experience discontinuities between home and kindergarten.

As the kindergartens were also providing care for working parents, they were open for long hours, from 7 or 8 in the morning to 5 or 6 at night. In some kindergartens, catering for shift workers, or for very poor parents, children would board during the week and go home at weekends. These long hours meant that great attention was also given to children's physical development. They received carefully monitored diets, with agreed portions of meat and vitamins. They slept every afternoon – most kindergartens were built with separate restrooms. Each kindergarten had exercise routines. These physical routines are discussed further below. Many kindergartens had their own swimming pools, gyms and dance halls.

The kindergartens held clinics, and children had health checks from doctors and nurses at least weekly. Medicines were issued at the kindergartens, and most kindergartens had a full-time nurse in attendance.

Bronfenbrenner, Kessen, and other eminent American psychologists visited kindergartens in Russia and China in the 1960s and 1970s. They were impressed, not only by the extraordinary level of investment, unmatched in any non-communist country at the time, but also because, to their psychologists' eyes, the children seemed relaxed. They appeared to show none of the signs of stress and disruptive behaviour so common in nurseries in the USA. Kessen concluded that although this level of conformity was not the American way, nevertheless it offered children a security and a predictability that benefited them at least in the short term. Table 9.1 summarizes the differences between the Soviet and Anglo-American regimes.

After transition in 1990, communist regimes fell apart. Kindergartens, like many other social services, closed down. Many kindergartens had been attached to state factories and farms, which were sold off or simply shut. In Kazakhstan, for example, more than 50 per cent of kindergartens were closed,[5] and the rest had to introduce fees which in effect put them beyond the reach of poor families.[6] Other ex-communist countries also struggled to maintain what they once had. Teachers' salaries fell or failed to rise with the exponential rise in the cost of living post-1990. Initial and in-service training more or less ceased. Buildings were not maintained. Worn-out equipment was not replaced. Visiting these countries now, in Eastern Europe and in the ex Soviet

Table 9.1 Comparison of the Soviet and Anglo-American regimes

Soviet	Anglo-American
Historical role for a society trying to achieve radical change. Kindergartens have a key role to play in bringing about societal change	Kindergartens/nursery a peripheral service with no particular role to play in understanding society
Dual care and education. Starting point is care for working mothers which is also at the same time profoundly educational	Education and care as separate systems. Cognitive development a separate and distinct issue from the provision of daycare
Knowledge consciously defined and prescribed by the educational system, to be learnt by child	Emphasizes the individual construction of knowledge: constructed by the individual in her own particular way
Importance of educators in delivering knowledge. Importance of educational institutions over the family. Child as product of kindergarten	Care of young children a marginal occupation. Emphasizes the roles and responsibilities of the family. Child as product of parenting
Collective character of education: the group is more important than the individuals within it	Education is the education of individuals not a welding of the group. Young children are seen as individuals for whom group life is an imposition

Source: Adapted from Penn 1999: 34

Union and its satellite states such as Bulgaria and Mongolia, what remains is the wreckage of an extraordinarily ambitious – and holistic – system.

The system in transitional countries could legitimately have been called holistic. It provided for mind and body in an encompassing way. It once seemed to be an outstanding system to visitors like the psychologists from the USA. Now it is widely perceived as repressive and institutionalized, and certainly not a model to be encouraged in the new global capitalist environment. For sure, not everyone remembers kindergartens kindly. One of my Kazakh colleagues described them as being like army camps. Physical punishment was not unknown, especially when children expressed reluctance at having to sleep for two to three hours every afternoon. (This was said to be neurologically necessary for brain growth.[7]) The Soros Foundation – and many other consultants – recommended that staff be retrained in western, Piagetian models, where children had freedom to choose what they wanted to do, and individuality was encouraged. The irony of this suggestion, that Piaget replace Vygotsky as a theoretical model, escaped them. Or perhaps, as suggested in Chapter 3, many of those consultants recommending change were experiencing a time-lag, and harking back to their own remembered training.

However, the question these experiences raise is, what is meant by holistic, or catering for the 'whole child'? Can provision that is available only for two or three hours a day, and that offers neither food nor exercise – as in much of the UK and other English-speaking countries – be described as holistic? In these countries, 'holistic' usually means trying to think broadly about what a child needs. But at what point does catering for the whole child slip over into being unacceptable and encroaching on the rights and duties of parents? Where I have spoken to parents, for example in focus groups in countries as diverse as Bulgaria, Kazakhstan, Mongolia and China, it is evident that they still have a high regard for the Soviet model. Those who can no longer afford to pay for kindergarten care feel bitterly excluded; conversely, the most wealthy gladly pay the cost.[8]

Suppleness, strength and stamina

I was recently the rapporteur (writer) of an OECD[9] team carrying out a review of Canadian early education and care. What struck the team very forcibly was the immobility of the children in most education and daycare environments. They seemed to be encouraged for the most part not to take any risks, not to move about too much, for fear of endangering themselves or other children. Canada is the land of the great outdoors, a challenging environment for hiking, climbing, skiing, canoeing and biking. Yet such is the lack of exercise in children that child obesity is a major health problem. Similarly in Australia, another country with vast amounts of space. Perhaps it is not so surprising after all. A leading Australian manual for young children gives safety checklists that insist on a pristine, hygienic environment.[10] It reads like that of a sterilized hospital ward for intensive care. The emphasis is on removing all conceivable hazards, rather than enabling children to deal with them. (I first came across these guidelines in a training manual in southern Africa. It was especially poignant to see them there, since there was no possibility such standards could be reached in a resource-poor country.)

It also seems likely that, from a medical point of view, the manual may be plain wrong. Children may need small exposures to risky environments to develop their immune systems, to control their body temperature, to improve their circulation. All these physiological systems may depend on exposure to challenges so that young bodies can adapt to changing environments, just as children learn how to adapt their thinking and learning by encountering novel situations.

Young children spending their days in nurseries are often very restricted in their movement, and protected against every possible – and impossible – contingency. In one daycare nursery I visited in the UK, the only exercise children had was to go to a carpeted exercise room, where they were allowed to walk on a beam 6 inches off the floor, provided they held the hand of a childcare worker whilst doing so.[11] In Chapter 8, there is a description of a nursery where staff were so concerned about risk that children were forbidden *any* physical activity or challenges – and a generation of students was being taught that this was the right approach.

An exaggerated notion of risk is only part of the problem. Physical activity is not conceived of as exercise but as a means to an end – learning. So children learn 'hand–eye coordination', 'manipulative skills' and the like. Rarely does one read in the Anglo-American literature of exercise for the joy and pleasure of movement itself. John Muir, the Scottish explorer who founded the National Parks movement in the USA, describes in his autobiography how, as a young boy of 8 or 9, he and his friends would run 12 miles or more for the sheer joy of it.

> In the winter, when there was little doing in the fields, we organized running matches. A dozen or so of us would start out on races that were simply tests of endurance, running on and on along a public road over the breezy hills like hounds without stopping or getting tired . . . we thought nothing of running right ahead ten or a dozen miles before turning back; for we knew nothing about taking time by the sun and none of us had a watch in those days.[12]

John Muir's energy seems inconceivable to us now. We would simply not expect children to run long distances for the sheer fun of it. Yet most small children are naturally exuberant. A 3- or 4-year-old will often run or gambol rather than walk. Our understanding of children's physical energy and capacity is very much bound by time and place.

Do other countries see physical activity differently? In Nordic countries, where winter weather is sometimes harsh, the view is that children must learn to adapt to their environment. In Norway, kindergartens organize outside camps in winter.[13] In Finland, children typically spend more than 13 hours a week outside, and they are encouraged to play vigorous games. In winter, they may do cross-country skiing or tobogganing.[14] In Denmark, children may build huts, light camp fires, or swim in the sea in their forest kindergartens.[15] In these countries the outdoor life is valued for itself, for the pleasures it offers and not merely as a means to improved intellectual performance.

In the Soviet and Chinese systems a great deal of attention is paid to physical fitness. Soviet kindergartens – which were usually very big so there were economies of scale – were routinely supplied with dance/gym space, and many had swimming pools. In Sofia, in Bulgaria, in 1998, 90 per cent of children in the relevant age group still attended kindergarten, and most of these kindergartens had their own swimming pool.

The kindergartens offer programmes for various kinds of highly specific physical exercises, including foot strengthening exercises (for children with flat feet), breathing exercises and so on. In the freezing Soviet winters, some kindergartens even offered cold outdoor bucket showers – an old Russian tradition for improving the circulation.[16] To those of us who live cosseted existences in rich countries, this seems positively barbaric, but one of the kindergartens I visited which had a cold showers regime was a special kindergarten for children with weak health. The doctors at the kindergarten claimed high success rates.[17]

In Chinese kindergartens, the emphasis was on callisthenics, exercises to develop strength, suppleness and stamina. These kindergartens, especially in cities, tended to be very big, about 200–300 children. After each lesson period, all children would come into the playground. Each stood on the spot which had been allocated. Loudspeakers would then relay the music and instructions for the movements. The children would bend, stretch, turn, balance and so on, all on their marked spot. Again this is derived from an old Chinese tradition, Tai Chi or shadow boxing. Groups of elderly people in the parks would be doing similar exercises. The result of callisthenics was that small children were fit, moving in supple, graceful and controlled ways. I have a video I made at a kindergarten in Beijing, which I sometimes show to English audiences. The children look extremely graceful, with the exception of a small American girl who was also attending the kindergarten; she seemed bemused and clumsy by comparison. For a long time after I came back, English children seemed to me to be very clumsy. They seemed to have relatively little awareness of or control over their bodies in comparison with the Chinese children.

In Africa, by comparison, nurseries and crèches are often makeshift affairs, with untrained care staff and little in the way of equipment. Yet dancing and singing in many nurseries is second nature. Children learn to dance rhythmically very early on. Dance has a particular status in society, as a collective expression of emotion. I recently watched a trade union demonstration for increased public sector pay in Swaziland, where the demonstrators danced their disapproval of the government. The government official who was watching the demonstration with me, said, 'They have been dancing for three hours now, soon they will be tired and go home.' All ritual occasions in the calendar require collective dancing in this small southern African kingdom, as in many other African societies. Children are not taught how to dance, but, as with the Guatamalan weavers' children described in Chapter 3, they join in adult dances, for a little bit, then for longer and longer until they are full participants.

In both the Soviet and Chinese kindergarten systems, activity is complemented by rest. In poor homes, children are unlikely to have their own rooms, and will go to bed when the family goes to bed. So rest regimes are deemed especially important. In the southernmost European countries there is also a siesta tradition – early afternoon is the hottest period of the day.

The body needs exercise and rest, but it also needs fuel. In the Soviet and Chinese systems, food is plain, local fare (partly prepared by the children in China, for example shelling peas), but it is nutritionally sound and always freshly cooked. Cook–chill and other forms of food processing, the norm in rich countries, are unknown and in any case would be too expensive in poor countries. But food – and its digestion – are also important in many European countries. One nursery I visited in Valencia in Spain had its own properly laid out restaurant, and the cook went round the classes each day to discuss the menu with the children. This may be an extreme case, but food in these nurseries is much more important, and part of a traditional way of life, than is the case in the UK or other English-speaking countries.

In all the communities and societies I have described, the physical regimes and expectations of physical prowess and body maintenance have a wider resonance beyond the nursery or kindergarten. It is undeniable, however, that the Anglo-American childcare tradition underplays physical activity and the need for rhythms of rest, activity and replenishment. Children are regarded as vulnerable and fragile and in need of constant protection and surveillance. Children are cocooned into inactivity.

Aunties, angels and teachers

In many societies, perhaps in a majority of societies, children are expected to be deferential – to older children, to those within their families, and to older people in their community. It is simply not tolerated to answer back or to disobey. Robert Serpell describes the way children are brought up in rural Zambia. He asked parents to define intelligence. For them an intelligent child was a helpful child, one who understands and anticipates the needs of others around him or her, a child who obeys instructions with alacrity. I have described elsewhere how nomadic families in Mongolia handle their children in order to make them constantly aware of the needs of others, to be alert to the effect their behaviour has on non-family members as well as on their mothers, fathers and siblings. Young children are shy, but extremely considerate.[18]

Children, then, are taught to relate to adults in different ways depending on where and when they grow up. Here is a very different example, from observations in a Spanish nursery where daily life was like an ongoing party:

> In this nursery the pleasure the staff take in one another's company, and in the children, is palpable. There seems to be an implicit view amongst most staff that of all the places in which one could choose to spend one's time, this is it. There is a kind of *joie de vivre* which expresses itself not only in the staff spending much more time in the

nursery than they are contracted to do, staying on to help on each other's shifts, but also with much physical affection and laughter. I watch a young member of staff and an older cleaner stroll up and down the courtyard, their arms around one another, deep in conversation. One member of the staff in particular gives enthusiastic kisses to every child, and to some of the parents, and their accompanying children, as well as to other staff. 'Handsome' she says to a small boy, and gives him a wet kiss, then kisses his older sister who is on her way to school; 'you are a delight' she says to another child as she bestows a kiss.

... Although this particular member of staff is extravagant with her kisses, almost everyone shows physical affection uninhibitedly. A toddler strays into the kitchen, the cook picks him up, kisses him and passes him outside, where he is passed around amongst several staff and children, all of whom also kiss him. The children often solve arguments and seal their peace with hugs and kisses, boys as well as girls.[19]

This was an unusual nursery in many respects and I do not wish to claim that its practices should be copied. But I am using it to show the range of ways of relating to children, from expecting instant and unquestioning obedience to this kind of partying.

The views of what adults should be doing – practising – in early education and care derive from what people consider to be education's goals, and what kind of view of young children they hold. These practices are transmitted through training (for those who actually undertake training) and through work experience. Most people believe that adults working with young children should be warm and patient; but not all believe that children should be treated as equals. Goldschmied and Jackson, in their book *People Under Three*, argue that a good way for practitioners to understand young children is to draw on their own experiences as adults:

Whenever possible we draw analogies between things that happen to children and those that we commonly experience as adults. As memories before the age of three are mostly lost, this is one of the few ways available to us of attempting to understand the sensations and feelings of a small child.[20]

Much of the practice in Anglo-American countries, especially with very young children, harks back to attachment theory. Attachment theory postulated that there is a tight bond between an adult carer and a young child. Without this bonding a child may grow up badly, either indiscriminately affectionate or affectionless. Nursery nurses and care workers often see themselves as substitute carers in this bonding process. In this scenario, just as children are viewed as physically vulnerable, so they are seen as psychologically vulnerable. Nursery nurses and care workers are often themselves vulnerable young women, taking up care work as a relatively safe and academically undemanding occupation. Being with young children weaker and more dependent than themselves gives them some kind of status.[21]

I have sometimes heard the expression 'he needs a bit of one-to-one' to describe the attention a nursery nurse gives an individual child, usually a naughty or disobedient one, who is made to sit down with her to undertake some small task. Nurseries are often organized to have 'key workers' who are, in principle, linked to a small group of children in order to be able to offer them the continuity of care and surveillance of a bonded relationship. In practice, staff turnover and staff absences, and irregular attendance by children, means that key workers are frequently unavailable at the moment when one-to-one care might possibly make a difference. A senior government official in the UK, who had a 1-year-old child in an expensive nursery in London, confessed to me that she felt relieved if she saw the same member of staff more than once when she took her child to and collected him from nursery. The fiction of continuity enables very poor practices to continue.

The argument has been made that in ordinary life, at least in rich countries, children get too much adult attention rather than too little. Non-intervention techniques, and a gentle distancing by mothers and carers, may be better for young children than a direct interaction initiated by an adult.

> The child expects to be the centre of attention all the time. He likes it. He of course doesn't do anything else any more; someone else is always busy doing something with him. . . . Such an infant will, in time, become increasingly whiney and cling to adults in an unhealthy way. He is only interested in adults, in having them around him, talking to him, doing things with him. None of this however gives him a feeling of joy and satisfaction, of quiet and well-being – at least not one of lasting duration. It leaves him restless and in need of excitement. It is precisely this kind of excitement a child gets accustomed to. He likes it. He cannot and will not do without it. We adults cannot do without lethal narcotics, once we have become addicted to them. In the same way, the infant who has gotten used to this kind of excitement does everything to be the centre of attention for adults.[22]

Who else does a child relate to if not an adult? As Judy Dunn suggested (see Chapter 3), very young children relate intimately to each other. A key question when children are together in groups is how children might be expected to relate to other children. Are they fierce individuals who must be taught to 'share'? Or are they natural allies in a mysterious and hostile world of adults? The sociology of childhood, expounded by authors such as Berry Mayall, suggests that children see and do things differently from adults not so much for reasons of immaturity and lack of experience, but because adults wield power and children do not. Generational differences are important in understanding childhood. The solidarity and subversiveness of children is posed against the authority of adults. Certainly for slightly older children in a school classroom where one teacher faces 20 or 30 children, this is likely to be the case. Maintaining control in a classroom is no easy task for a teacher, even in those countries where children are expected to be obedient. Devolving power to children and enabling them to support and regulate one another, so that the teacher is a kind of classroom resource, is a means of handling the imbalance between adults and children. This happens in a variety of ways, for example in the Japanese classrooms described by Tobin and his colleagues,[23] or the systems of group controls in the Soviet system, or in a few innovative schools in the UK where children are in charge of classroom discipline.[24]

Carers are commonly women, although there is a growing literature on men as carers. There are various arguments put forward for men to work with young children. These include providing equal opportunities for both men and women to be represented in the profession; and offering boys male role models. Yet sex is a highly problematical area. How (and if) men differ from women in the way they treat children is an open question.

Listening, speaking and singing

There are many communities in the world that are still mainly oral. Talking, listening, remembering and recounting, declaiming, reciting and singing, people have learnt to rely on memory and performance. Some of the greatest ancient Greek literature, for example Homer's *Iliad* and *Odyssey*, tales of Greek heroes, were composed in this way. But oral communication is essentially collective and public rather than individual and private; it requires speakers and an audience.

In her book *Ways with Words*, Shirley Brice Heath describes young black children growing up in an essentially oral community in the south of the USA. People used to gather around the doorstep in the evenings to chat and entertain themselves. In order to be heard and noticed in a group, young children, especially boys, had learnt to perform, to express themselves vividly and amusingly. When they got to school, their verbal wit was regarded as showing off, and their way of speaking was regarded as impertinent.

The skills of listening and speaking have to be taught and practised, just like the skills of reading and writing. In some communities this is a respected tradition. Certain people, for instance the elders in First Nation communities in Canada, are given the task of making representations on behalf of the group they belong to. The praise singers of Mali and Senegal are a semi-hereditary group whose job it is to be the official memory of a community – a tradition translated to the North in the popular singing of Baaba Maal and Youssou N'Dour.

In some systems, most notably the Soviet system, there was considerable emphasis on memory and performance. When I first saw some of these extra-ordinary performances in remote places, where young children recited poems, sang and danced, I thought they were embarrassing demonstrations designed to showcase the kindergartens. I think now in retrospect that they were much more important, an attempt to recognize and preserve heritage and tradition, as well as a useful training in listening, memorizing and speaking.

In some countries the routine of the nursery or crèche or childcare setting regularly includes 'circle time', an opportunity for children to come together and to listen to one another. But this opportunity for self-expression within a group, important as it is, is only a start. Oral fluency, listening and memory are skills that are essentially collective rather than individual and private. My grandson took part in a rather chaotic end-of-term performance at his nursery. His group were dressed up as animals and the children had had to learn songs as part of the performance. Several weeks later, when his parents and I were on a long journey in the car, he began to sing one of these animal songs. 'Who are you singing the song for?' I asked. 'I'm singing it for us,' he replied.

In some European countries, particularly those where school does not begin until 6 or 7 years of age, the pre-school curriculum emphasizes the skills of listening and speaking as a necessary precursor to reading and writing. The evaluation of the primary school outreach project by the National Theatre in London in the UK suggests that children who have taken part in dramatic performances also do better in their school work.[25]

Catalogues of toys

In one nursery school I visited in the UK, a spacious building with a big garden, I counted over 100 different activities that were available to the children. Some of them were innovative, for example making a sand tray into a desert, with desert animals and shrubs; or the boot box where children could try on differ-ent sizes and colours of Wellington boots; or sorting and grading apples fallen from an apple tree in the garden for sale or for jam. This was besides the more usual nursery activities: many different kinds of bricks for building; painting with different types and thicknesses of paint; outside workstations with clip-boards for writing and drawing. The nursery school in the UK has a long tradition of providing a stimulating environment for children. Margaret McMillan, one of the pioneers of nursery schools, saw children romantically as creatures of nature, and insisted on removing the barriers between inside space and outside space in her famous nursery school in Deptford. She believed children benefited from having great scope for autonomy and freedom of movement.[26]

This practice has endured within nursery schools, although nursery schools themselves are being dismantled by a short-sighted UK government. (It is quite unlike the separate UK care tradition which, as pointed out above, regards children as vulnerable and in need of surveillance. Chapter 6 explores the contradictions of UK history.)

This wealth of activities pre-dated Piaget, but Piaget's theories lent them additional legitimacy. But alongside the theory, parents and childcare workers alike have absorbed the consumerist messages of the societies to which they belong. They have come to believe that nurseries should resemble shopping malls, in their reproduction of continuous multiple choice. Writing about American pre-schools, Tobin comments that

> Consumer desire is reproduced by the material reality of our pre-schools. The variety of things and choices offered by middle-class preschools is overwhelming to many children. We create over-stimulating environments modelled on the excess of the shopping mall and amusement park. . . . We have become so used to the hyper-materiality of our early childhood care settings that we are oblivious to the clutter; settings that provide more structure and are less distracting seem stark or bleak.[27]

Brian Sutton Smith, in his important book *Toys as Culture*, suggests that young children have proved a lucrative market for the exploitation of care-giver and parental inadequacy. Parents, especially busy or absent parents, fear that they are not doing enough to promote their children's development. All manner of toys are marketed as 'educational' to tap into those fears. The statement below is a typical marketing ploy.

> Our mission is to provide families with a HUGE selection of creative and stimulating products in a customer-friendly entertaining and interactive shopping environment because we believe kids learn best when they're having fun.[28]

Stephen Kline documents how marketing to children of toys, foods and other products increased in the second half of the twentieth century in rich countries.[29] He illustrates the enormous sophistication, complexity and reach of market campaigns aimed at children and their parents. Advertisers of commercial products encourage children to demand and challenge in order to obtain what they want (or what is being promoted) and at the same time play on the guilt feelings of their parents. Kline claims that TV is used relentlessly to make sales pitches towards children. Although commercial toys have been advertised and sold in increasing numbers for the last century or so, it is in the last 25 years that the process has accelerated. For example, in 1987 (the last year Kline quotes), American toy manufacturers spent $350 billion on toy advertising. The commercialization of childhood extends to nurseries. Beatrix Tudor Hart, writing in 1938, gave a simple and ingenious list of toys that she used in her (very good) nursery. Today's nurseries are grossly overprovided by such standards. Magazines which aim at early childhood practitioners are replete with advertisements for new toys and equipment that are apparently indispensable for learning. Advertising pressurizes parents into buying all kinds of non-essential items for their children.

Seiter comments that children's vulnerability is exploited by the makers of cartoons and commercials.

> Children's cartoons and commercials] portray an abundance of the things most prized by children – food and toys; their musical themes and fast action are breathtakingly energetic, they enact a rebellion against adult restriction; they present a version of the world in which good and evil, male and female, are unmistakably coded in ways easily comprehended by a young child; they celebrate a community of peers.[30]

A recent Australian study suggested that although children, even as young as 3, were knowledgeable and capable of exercising some scepticism about the claims to reality of what they saw on TV, videos, and computer games, they did not question at all the market culture that gives rise to such advertising and promotion. They took it as normal that such goods would be provided for them, and that they would have endless opportunity to choose amongst them.[31]

If this seems a bleak picture, there are also contraindications that children continue to create and pursue their own interests and identities independently from those of adults when time and space permit. In 1969, Peter and Iona Opie recorded children's games in close-to-home spaces – driveways, pavements, streets, car parks. They identified more than three thousand games played by children. They argued that this rich children's culture was carried on in the interstices of everyday spaces, the 'child-to-child complex of people going about their own business within their own society . . . fully capable of occupying themselves under the jurisdiction of their own code.'[32] Indeed, they were dismissive of the idea that this children's culture could be shaped or controlled by adults in any way.

Although it is now much less likely that children would be allowed to play out and find spaces for their own use, recent evidence suggests that 'schoolyard lore' or 'childlore' is still vibrant in school playgrounds. Despite the overwhelming contemporary pressures to which they are subject, children, as they have done since time immemorial, have their own games, rhymes, chants and crazes, their own ways of amusing themselves. This childlore is still the daily currency of the playground for most children.[33] It has been charted in Australia, Britain, continental Europe and North America, and in ethnographic studies in the South. Childlore and childplay reveal dimensions of creativity, artistry, musicality and complexity. Some of it, such as ball and skipping games, is highly active and requires dexterity and physical coordination. It is 'performative, carnivalesque, subversive and parodic'[34] – including elements of parody of the very features of advertising that seem so threatening. It includes narratives, epithets, jeers, taunts, riddles and dirty jokes. It is fun, but not necessarily all the time for all of the children taking part, and it sometimes verges on bullying (although bullying, too, is subject to interpretation). The persistence of such childlore, despite all the concerns to the contrary, suggests that there are overwhelming reasons for its continuance. Brian Sutton Smith, the guru of children's play, argues that

> childlore deals with behaviour that has traditionally been regarded as non-serious, but as this behaviour appears to be a systematic part of the human repertoire, to think, therefore, it is unimportant might be a mistake.[35]

Marc Armitage claims that the layout of playground space inadvertently affects the nature of the games that are played in it. He carried out 90 play-audits of school playgrounds over a five-year period. He pointed out that designating an area as a particular kind of playspace is no guarantee that it will be used in that fashion; on the contrary, the most unlikely – or, to adults, unsuitable – places will be commandeered for games. Playgrounds have shrunk, as land has proved more profitable for other uses; and playtime has shrunk as teachers have become more obsessed with curricular and supervised activities. Playgrounds with nooks and crannies – round the back of steps, in corners – are commandeered for games, for example marbles on drain covers, cops and robbers games by metal grilles or fences. Games of imprisonment were a feature which occurred in all the play audits, and witches frequently prepared potions in gaol-like places.

Armitage comments that:

> The primary school children of today can quite easily be left alone on the playground and their spontaneity will do the rest. This is in fact what already happens. But for them to be able to make use of this spontaneity to the best of their ability, and to do so without the need

for direct adult intervention in their play, the environment provided for them as a place to play must respect the finding that children themselves are informally organizing their available spaces and features to meet their own needs. As adults, our role should be to support this and provide an environment that caters for what children actually play as opposed to what they should or could play, or even what we think they play.[36]

The debate about consumerism and toys is a debate from the rich world. Toys are simply not manufactured or available in the South, and the avenues for advertising do not exist. Rossie has made several studies of children's use of toys in the South. For more well-to-do children, imported toys have status, but for the majority of children age-old homemade toys are in frequent use. Goldschmied, in *People Under Three*, describes her 'treasure basket', a collection of household and natural articles, such as corks, chains, a sponge and fircones, that she offers children and which she claims interests babies far more than any manufactured toys.

Learning your colours

Art is as old as mankind. Decoration and images are present in the oldest archaeological sites. Even today, the art of Aborigine groups in Australia, or the San people in southern Africa serve to remind us of the veneration and ritual involved in creating representational art such as pictures of animals. Art is also functional and takes many forms besides the trendy conceptual art of rich countries: the weaving of South America; the carpet making and embroidery of the Middle East; the pottery and tiles of North Africa; the calligraphy of Arabic countries, to name but a few.

An Italian artist, doubling up as an infant teacher in an English nursery, said to me indignantly that she was expected to teach children their colours. 'There are more than 150 shades of blue. Which one is the blue that I should show to the children? Sapphire? Indigo? Aquamarine? I am teaching them to blur their colours, not to tell their colours apart.'

Neuroscientists such as Steven Rose have argued that children see the world very vividly, but that they learn to screen out the intensity of their perceptions in order to take in essential information more efficiently. My Italian colleague felt strongly that aesthetic information – in this case colour – was important and that its importance should be recognized. In her view, adults should be required to know, and children should be required to learn, about gradations of colour, texture and pattern. I have described elsewhere[37] working with another reception teacher (another artist supporting herself by teaching) who insisted on obtaining raw pigments and on grinding the colours herself with her groups of South London children – who under her tutelage found the task fascinating.

There is no doubt that young children are capable of very fine visual discrimination. Children who are required to look after herds of cows (or in the steppes, of herds of horses) can easily discriminate amongst several dozen – or even more – animals which to an outsider appear as a blur of brown, grey and white. The distinguished writer on Central Asia, Owen Lattimore, described the visual acuity of some of the nomad tribes with whom he worked. For them, being able to see, and judge what they saw, was a survival mechanism.[38]

Languages with ideographic (picture) scripts have a different pattern for every word. In order to become literate in Chinese, a child would have to learn to recognize about 2000 different patterns – as opposed to the 26 letters of the English alphabet. Accuracy in pattern making is therefore very important. Chinese children are taught to copy very carefully, and a less than good copy is discarded because it might mean something else. The drawings of Chinese children tend to be very detailed and realistic and to display a sophistication that is regarded with some disbelief by Anglo-American colleagues. Similarly, in the Soviet kindergarten accurate representation is valued above self-expression.

By contrast, in Anglo-American nurseries children are encouraged to be expressive, and all expressions are valued and, if possible, displayed, careless blobs and blurs as they may be. At the same time the commercial pressures described above have led to a proliferation of kitsch cartoon images. Many nurseries in the UK and the USA are immediately recognizable because of their friezes of cartoon figures such as Donald Duck and Mickey Mouse; a recreation of a make-believe world that is supposed to have a special attraction for children. It is a very curious practice to use cartoon figures so ubiquitously, and it persists despite rarely appearing in any training guides.

There is a debate amongst architects about whether the creativity and design of the buildings in which children are taught and cared for contribute in any way to the children's own creativity. Mark Dudek's book *Kindergarten Architecture* provides an overview of the range of buildings that are used for children, from the grimly functional to the fantastic – fairytale castles and grotesque attics.

Paints, felt-tip pens, plasticine, colouring books and the other staples of 'creativity' are simply not available in poor countries. On the other hand, everyday life may offer unparalleled artisan opportunities, of weaving, thatching, carving, pottery and so on.

Skeletons of frogs

I recently visited a nursery in the island of Mauritius. The nursery was not very interesting in the sense of its having only a limited range of activities and training materials. But someone had gone to town on mock-up biology. On one table was a set of dissected plastic frogs; the pieces of the frogs' skeletons and organs could be dismantled and reassembled. On another table was a similar set of plastic digestive organs. The digestive tract could also be taken apart and reassembled. I do not know, and did not have the chance to ask, where these biology models came from, whether they were an unsolicited gift or whether a misinformed teacher had ordered them from a catalogue. Then I thought that perhaps I was being unfair, and the 5- and 6-year-old children at least could grasp the concepts involved.

Those growing up in rural environments (or whose fathers are butchers) are likely to be more familiar with slaughter and dissection. Mothibi, my grandson, was playing in his African grandmother's yard with the chickens, throwing them pieces of corn, and then chasing them. Two of the chickens were for the pot. His African grandmother wrung their necks, then chopped off the heads and took the chickens away to be plucked. Mothibi picked up the chicken heads and went on playing with them. This familiarity and unconcern with the processes of animal husbandry are widespread in some societies. Animals are herded and milked, they are fed, they reproduce, and they are slaughtered.

Similarly, as Barbara Rogoff described in relation to South American Indian communities, rural peasant children are involved in everyday horticulture. They help sow, weed, water and pick and prepare the plants that will be their food. They learn about cycles of growth, water conservation, and insect depredations not as special subjects but as part of their lives.

Science is the systematic investigation of natural phenomena. It must be more difficult for those children who only experience nature second-hand, and whose understanding of it is a sentimental one in which, for example, ducks dress up in sailor hats and mice wear shorts. But in all countries there is some kind of natural life to observe. Below is Mothibi's drawing of a dead grasshopper. Its serrated and immensely strong legs are accurately drawn. Mothibi noticed that ants swarmed over the corpse of any dead creature, so after he finished drawing the grasshopper, he insisted that we put it back outside for the ants to eat. (We did find another dead grasshopper, and dug a hole to bury it in the vegetable bed. Mothibi muttered a prayer over it, but then dug it up the next day to see how far it had decomposed.) These kinds of minute natural phenomena are everywhere to be explored.

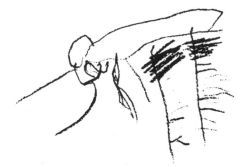

Figure 9.1   This drawing of a grasshopper by my 5-year-old grandson illustrates the fascination children can have with the natural world. The life, death and decomposition of the grasshopper preoccupied him for days.

Grannies on the doorstep

'Parents' is a sex-blind word, used in the name of equal opportunities. It is almost always mothers who make and take part in childcare arrangements; men are regarded as a special catch if they take part in such arrangements. There is invariably ambivalence about how men should be treated, so I will use the word 'mother' rather than parent as a more accurate reflection of the situation.

In the Soviet system, as I have noted, mothers and grandparents value kindergartens very highly. But they do not have very much to do with them. The teachers are the experts to whom they willingly defer. In the Anglo-American tradition the relationship between care workers, nursery nurses, teachers and parents is more ambivalent.

The mantra 'the parent is the child's first educator' is often used as a covert attempt to educate the mother into replicating the activities of the crèche or nursery or school at home.

Typically, in the UK, a child will have three or four different experiences of childcare before starting school: a childminder, a playgroup, a private nursery, a part-time nursery class. Because provision is ad hoc and often expensive, and turnover of staff is high, the goal of parental involvement is a paradoxical one. The mother may have to go to great lengths to find and/or pay for suitable daily arrangements. Often these arrangements are less than satisfactory. Yet she is required to acquiesce in these arrangements, and to appear to endorse them, by becoming 'involved'.

One rationale for parental education is that, because of the shrinking of family size and the increased mobility of families, mothers have little prior experience of children and few people to turn to. Often they do not know what to do with their children, and are puzzled by their behaviour. There are no grannies on the doorstep to fulfil their time-honoured role of giving advice and helping out. Some kind of non-judgemental advice from an experienced person might be useful to combat the isolation many mothers experience.

But in the case of low-income mothers or 'multi-problem' families, the mothers are considered as more than a little bemused by the responsibilities of motherhood. They are regarded as perpetuating 'a cycle of poverty'. This view that poor mothers are basically ignorant, and this ignorance can be addressed by education about parenting, stems from a concept of poverty as a personal failing. It permeates much of the literature on early childhood in the USA, and in turn reappears in a good deal of the World Bank and UNICEF literature.[39] Mothers who do not understand and apply basic hygiene, or do not talk to or 'stimulate' their children, run the risk of endangering their children's lives and atrophying their brains.

Another rationale for parental education is that it offers an opportunity for mothers to catch up on lost educational opportunities. Early childhood offers a 'window of opportunity' when mothers are newly conscious of the effects that they might have on another human being and are therefore especially willing to learn about new things. The emphasis in the UK is now to get mothers off benefits and back into the labour force as a saving to the economy. The government subsidizes many education programmes alongside crèche facilities for mothers seeking to return to work. Childcare is regarded as an appropriate work avenue for relatively unskilled women, and a good deal of the training available is to encourage women to become childminders or nursery nurses by undertaking some kind of basic vocational training. (The training nursery with the barren rubber playground described in Chapter 8 trains local women to work in the childcare field; their children can sit in the nursery whilst their mothers undergo training.)

This emphasis on parental education arises mostly in unequal societies with high levels of poverty, since inequality is justified by the assumption that the poor are inadequate rather than exploited. In those countries that have universal early education and childcare services and redistributive incomes, there is very little concern about parental education or parental involvement. The emphasis instead is on democratic participation. The curriculum for early years settings in Nordic countries, for example, is very broad and general and it is left to committees of parents and staff to flesh it out. Similarly the famous nurseries in Reggio Emilia in Italy are constructed around concepts of community and co-construction.

The above discussion, and indeed much of the book, has assumed that age-related institutions are the norm for children. Children are segregated from older children with specially trained people to educate and care for them, who do no other work whilst with the children. Like schooling, nurseries are based on the ideas of age segregation and specialized people. This enables children to learn. In this sense, nurseries are an extension of school, places devoted to children's learning.

Nurseries and kindergartens are not 'normal'. It is more normal, historically and geographically, for children to grow up in communities where life is lived publicly, rather than privately behind closed doors. There are typically many different activities being undertaken by people of all ages, and many different kinds of conversation to tune into. The children take part in some of these activities, and listen to some of the conversations. The extract with which this book began, from Flora Thompson's *Lark Rise*, illustrated such an environment. This kind of community life has more or less disappeared from modern industrialized societies, but what kinds of substitute exist? Children in nurseries and kindergartens more often than not lead narrow and safeguarded lives. Nurseries are devoted to play and learning – child development – but are divorced from work and adult conversation and interests. They can be deeply boring places for adults and children alike. There are some attempts to develop intergenerational projects, and to create spaces for generations to mix and to engage in real activities, but these are few and far between.

Good and bad practice: one system for everybody?

Most countries try to provide some guidelines for good practice. These are contained in regulatory and/or curriculum documents. Often these documents have legal status. The 1989 Spanish Education Reform Act (LOGSE), for example, included a broad curriculum that gave a framework for those working with children aged 0–3 and 3–6. In the Nordic countries, where staff are well trained and the services are well financed, there is considerable autonomy within the system. The ministry provides loose guidelines, but nurseries are expected to make up their own curriculum and set and monitor their own standards with parents. In those countries where there is a large private or non-profit sector, such as the UK or Canada, regulations are highly prescriptive, and there is an inspectoral system to make sure they are carried out. In these countries, practitioners cannot be fully trusted to act on their own. In the ex-Soviet countries and China, the curriculum was also highly prescriptive – in China it used to run to 18 volumes. But, paradoxically, staff were also well trained, and their job was to 'perform' the curriculum, to make it as interesting as possible, rather like actors interpreting a script.

Internationally the most widely known guidelines for practice and training are those compiled and distributed by the US National Association for the Education of Young Children (NAEYC). These guidelines, called *Developmentally Appropriate Practice*, have been distributed throughout the world.

They are much quoted by the World Bank and other donor organizations. *Developmentally Appropriate Practice* offers sensible advice about how to handle children and what activities to pursue with them at each age or stage of development. It cites research in child development (almost all of it from the USA) to back up the practices it advocates. It is a thoughtful and comprehensive booklet, and has been revised considerably over the past ten years to take account of its critics, especially over its sensitivity – or previous lack of it – to multicultural issues.

In the USA, early education and care provision is on an ad hoc basis through a variety of providers, mainly private. Many of these providers are likely to be untrained, and they need to make money from looking after children.[40] In this context, where educated practitioners are not the norm, and the turnover of staff and children in childcare is high, simply stated instructions, referring with authority to 'research' in child development, are a useful tool to encourage good practice and to admonish bad practice. But the authors of *Developmentally Appropriate Practice* are only concerned with micro-level interventions. They implicitly assume that good practice is context free and can be applied anywhere; and value-free, since it is based on 'scientific research'. Anybody can achieve it, in whatever kind of setting, by following the guidelines.

Developmentally Appropriate Practice is not of course value-free. It continually stresses individuality, self-assertiveness, personal choice and the availability of possessions. It is the job of the adult looking after the children to make sure that children can exercise choice between many different objects, and assert their rights over them. It takes individualistic consumer behaviour as its unwritten norm. It ignores the inequalities of society and the effects that these might produce on children. It also continually stresses the importance of adult–child affectional bonds, and downplays child–child bonds.

Other international organizations that have reviewed early education and childcare practices pay more attention to context and values. The European Union Childcare Network, a ten-year project to explore childcare across member states, produced a series of discussion booklets and a video on practice in kindergartens and nurseries. *Quality in Services for Young Children* suggests how certain questions arise from adopting certain value bases about practice including equality of access for all children. This discussion paper was followed up by a set of recommendations which stressed the role of governments in setting the necessary framework for services to develop; to provide an adequate funding base and systems for research and evaluation.

The OECD has produced useful statistics on education and economic indicators which are widely used throughout the world as benchmarks. It has recently been reviewing early education and childcare across its member states. Countries that have contributed to the review include the USA, Canada, Australia, UK, most European countries, Korea and Mexico. The reviews are carried out on a peer review basis; a small team of experts made up from contributing countries undertake the review of individual countries. These reviews are published by the OECD, and there are also international seminars held on key topics. A synthesis report *Starting Strong: Early Childhood Education and Care* summarizes the findings and makes general recommendations.[41]

The OECD report gives comparative statistics, but focuses its discussion on practice at the level of policy. Like the EU, it argues that equality of access and quality of practice are important goals for services, but that they can only be achieved by adequate public funding and by a good infrastructure of planning, evaluation and training. By these criteria, the USA performs very poorly indeed, almost bottom of the class. Nordic countries do particularly well. It is therefore ironic that the US model, which stresses individual improvement at a programme level, is so enthusiastically adopted by the World Bank and other international donors.

I began the chapter by exploring the notion of practice. What people do they always do within a context, and never in isolation. Of course, good practitioners exist, and there are some wonderful ways of encouraging and supporting the development of young children. But dull practice is not just the responsibility of dull practitioners. Practice, that is doing the same thing over and over again, makes little difference without a critical eye. This book has aimed to make people gaze carefully at how we work with young children.

Summary

This chapter gives an overview of practice across the world. In particular it contrasts the once comprehensive systems of the Soviet Union and other transitional countries, and China, with North American and European early education and care. It traces how practice grows out of political and economic conditions and traditions rather than from scientific research into child development. It suggests that, in some ways, practice in the UK, USA and other English-speaking countries is poor, although practice in these countries is also characterized by tremendous variation, in the absence of coherent and sustained government intervention.

Main messages from this chapter

1   In many countries of the North, practice is very consumption orientated, based on the premise that the more toys you buy, the more children can choose between lots of toys, the better the education. This is nonsense (except to toy manufacturers) and not based on any scientific research.

2 We have forgotten that young children are intensely physical and enjoy using their bodies. Too much practice focuses on keeping children still.

3 We underrate the pleasure that children get from each other's company and overrate the contribution of adults.

What to read next

OECD (2001) *Early Education and Care: Thematic Review of 12 Countries*. Paris: OECD. Also available at www.oecd.org.

Notes

1 She was referring to the work of the Soros Foundation, which has as its mission to introduce principles of democracy and openness in transitional countries. In each ex-communist country it runs a pre-school programme, closely modelled on Head Start in the USA.

2 According to EU childcare network and OECD thematic review

3 I have worked at intervals over a period of three years in Mongolia. Some of this work has been published by Save the Children/Department for International Development. I also worked with a Mongolian nomad, Demberel, who lived through this period of change and described how it had affected him and his family. He describes it in very favourable terms – his own life began as a goat herder on a mountainside, and he became a physicist. See Penn and Demberel 2004.

4 Bronfenbrenner 1965: 23

5 MONEE 2001

6 Penn 2004a

7 I had a long discussion with a neurologist in Kazakhstan about the rationales for these periods of rest for the brain. See Penn 2003.

8 See Penn 2004a

9 Organization of Economic Cooperation and Development – popularly known as the club of rich nations. It is currently (2004) carrying out a thematic review of early education and care across its member states. So far 17 countries have been reviewed.

10 Greenman and Stonehouse 1997

11 Penn 2002a

12 Muir 1996: 23

13 OECD 1999

14 Personal communication, Paivi Lindberg, Senior Preschool Adviser, STAKES (Ministry of Social Affairs), Finland

15   The EU Childcare Network video *Can You Feel a Colour* shows children at forest kindergartens in Denmark.

16   A recent BBC TV programme *Extreme Climates* interviewed members of the Walrus Club in Siberia. Members meet regularly to hack a hole in the ice and take a dip in the freezing lake water.

17   Penn 2004a

18   Penn 2001

19   Penn 1997: 82

20   Goldschmied and Jackson 1996: 3

21   See Penn 2000a in *Early Childhood Services*, a series of interviews with trainee nursery nurses

22   This passage is reproduced from the *Bulletin of the Sensory Awareness Foundation*, no. 14, Winter 1994, Los Angeles. The Foundation is based on the work of a Hungarian paediatrician, Emmi Pickler, and the passage is an extract from her book *Peaceful Babies, Contented Mothers*, first published in Hungarian in 1969. The work of Pickler and her associates has a wide currency, especially in Italy and the USA.

23   Yobin *et al.* 1989

24   Alderson 1999

25   Mayall *et al.* 2003

26   See Steedman 1990

27   Tobin 1995: 232

28   Toyshop brochure, quoted in Kenway and Bullen 2001: 82

29   Kline 1993

30   Seiter 1995: 11–12

31   Kenway and Bullen 2001

32   Opie and Opie 1969, quoted in Moore 1986: xiv

33   Blatchford *et al.* 1990

34   See Bishop and Curtis 2001

35   Sutton Smith 1970: 4

36   Armitage 2001: 55–6

37   Penn 2000a

38   Owen Lattimore was originally a fur trader in China who became an academic specializing in the Far East. He became Professor of Asian Studies at Leeds University. His books on nomadic life are classics.

39   See Penn 2002a for a more detailed analysis of World Bank and UNICEF literature.

40   See OECD 2000 (also summarized in OECD 2001)

41   OECD 2001

References

Abley, M. (2003) *Spoken Here: Travels among Threatened Languages*. New York: Random House.

Acheson, D. (1988) *Public Health in England*. London: HMSO.

Aggleton, P. (1990) *Health*. London: Routledge.

Ainsworth, M., Blehar, M., Waters, E. and Wall, S. (1978) *Patterns of Attachment: A Psychological Study of the Strange Situation*. New Jersey: Lawrence Erlbaum.

Alderson, P. (1993) *Children's Consent to Surgery*. Buckingham: Open University Press.

Alderson, P. (ed.) (1999) *Learning and Inclusion: The Cleves School Experience*. London: David Fulton.

Alderson, P. and Goodey, C. (1998) *Enabling Education: Experiences in Special and Ordinary Schools*. London: Tufnell Press.

Alexander, R. (2000) *Culture and Pedagogy: International Comparisons in Primary Education*. Oxford: Blackwell.

Antonovsky, A. (1987) *Unravelling the Mystery of Health: How to Manage Others and Stay Well*. New York: Wiley.

Aries, P. (1962) *Centuries of Childhood*. London: Jonathan Cape.

Armitage, M. (2001) The ins and outs of school playground play: children's use of 'play spaces', in J. Bishop and M. Curtis (eds) *Play Today in the Primary School Playground*. Buckingham: Open University Press.

Backett, K. and Alexander, H. (1991) Talking to young children about health: methods and findings, *Health Education Journal*, 50(1): 34–8.

Barker, D. (1992) *The Fetal Origins of Ill Health*. London: BMJ Publications.

Barnett, T. and Whiteside, A. (2002) *AIDS in the 21st Century: Disease and Globalization*. Hampshire: Palgrave/Macmillan.

Bauman, Z. (1995) *Life in Fragments: Essays on Postmodern Morality*. Oxford: Blackwell.

Beck, U. (1992) *Risk Society: Towards a New Modernity*. London: Sage.

Berlin, I. (1997) *The Sense of Reality: Studies in Ideas and Their History*. London: Pimlico.

Bishop, J. and Curtis, M. (eds) (2001) *Play Today in the Primary School Playground*. Buckingham: Open University Press.

Blatchford, P., Creeser, R. and Mooney, A. (1990) Playground games and playtime: the children's view, *Educational Research*, 32(3): 163–74.

Bodman, F. (1945) Aggressive play, in *Play and Mental Health*. London: New Era/New Education Fellowship.

Bogin, B. (1998) Evolutionary and biological aspects of childhood, in C. Panter-Brick (ed.) *Biosocial Perspectives on Children*. Cambridge: Cambridge University Press.

Bornstein, M. (1991) *Cultural Approaches to Parenting*. London: Lawrence Erlbaum.

Botting, B. (ed.) (1995) *The Health of Our Children*, Decennial Supplement. London: OPSC.

Bowlby (1952) *Maternal Care and Mental Health*. Geneva. World Health Organization. Later popularized as *Childcare and the Growth of Love*. London: Penguin, 1953.

Bradbury, B. and Jantti, M. (1999) *Child Poverty Across Industrialized Nations*, EPS 71. Florence: UNICEF Innocenti Centre.

Bradshaw, J. (2002) Child poverty and child outcomes, *Children and Society*, 16: 40–55.

Bredekamp, S. and Copple, C. (eds) (1997) *Developmentally Appropriate Practice in Early Childhood Programs*, 2nd edition. Washington: National Association for the Education of Young Children.

British Medical Journal (2002) *Global Voices on the Aids Catastrophe*, No. 7331 (special issue).

Bronfenbrenner, U. (1965) *Two Worlds of Childhood*. London: Penguin.

Bronfenbrenner, U. (1979) *The Ecology of Human Development: Experiments by Nature and Design*. Cambridge, MA: Harvard University Press.

Bruer, J. (1999) *The Myth of the First Three Years*. New York: The Free Press.

Bruner, J. (1960) *The Process of Education*. Cambridge, MA: Harvard University Press.

Bruner, J. (1980) *Under Five in Britain*. London: Grant McIntyre.

Bruner, J. (1982) Formats of language acquisition, *American Journal of Semiotics*, 1: 1–16.

Bruner, J. (1990) *Acts of Meaning*. Cambridge, MA: Harvard University Press.

Bruner, J. (1996) *The Culture of Education*. Cambridge, MA: Harvard University Press.

Burman, E. (1994) *Deconstructing Developmental Psychology*. London: Routledge.

Chamoiseau, P. (1999) *Childhood*. London: Granta.

Chomsky, N. (2003) *Power and Terror*. New York: Seven Stories Press.

Christensen, P. and James, A. (eds) (2000) *Research with Children: Perspectives and Practices*. London: Falmer Press.

Chugani, H.T., Phelps, M.E. and Mazziota, J.C. (1987) Positron emission tomography study of human brain function development, *Annals of Neurology*, 22: 487–97.

Clark, A. and Moss, P. (2001) *Listening to Young Children: The Mosaic Approach*. London: National Children's Bureau.

Clifford, J. and Marcus, G. (1984) *Writing Culture: The Poetics and Politics of Ethnography*. Los Angeles: University of California Press.

Cole, M. (1996) *Cultural Psychology: A Once and Future Discipline*. Cambridge, MA: The Belknap Press.

Cole, M. and Cole, S. (1996) *The Development of Children*, 3rd edition. New York: W.H. Freeman.

Cole, M. and Cole, S. (2002) *The Development of Children*, 4th edition. New York: W.H. Freeman.

Corsaro, W. (1985) *Friendship and Peer Culture in the Early Years*. New Jersey: Ablex.

Cunningham, H. (1991) *The Children of the Poor: Representations of Childhood Since the Seventeenth Century*. Oxford: Blackwell.

Davis, J., Watson, N. and Cunningham-Burley, S. (2000) Learning the lives of disabled children: Developing a reflexive approach, in P. Christensen and A. James (eds) *Research with Children: Perspectives and Practices*. London: Falmer Press.

Dawkins, R. (1976) *The Selfish Gene*. Oxford: Oxford University Press.

Dawkins, R. (1988) *The Blind Watchmaker*. London: Penguin.

Deacon, T. (1997) *The Symbolic Species: The Co-evolution of Language and the Human Brain*. London: Allen Lane.

De Lissa, L. (1945) *Education up to Seven Plus*, NSA pamphlet. London.

Dennis, C. and Gallagher, R. (2001) *The Human Genome*. Hampshire: Palgrave/Nature Publishing Group.

Department of Education (1978) *Nursery Education*, Circular 2/73. London.

Department for Education and Science (2003) *Every Child Matters*, Green Paper, 8 September 2003. Availiable at www.dfes.gov.uk

Donaldson, M. (1978) *Children's Minds*. London: Fontana.

Dudek, M. (1999) *Kindergarten Architecture*. London: Spon.

Dunn, J. (1984) *Sisters and Brothers*. Cambridge, MA: Harvard University Press.

Dunn, J. (1988) *The Beginnings of Social Understanding*. Oxford: Blackwell.

Dunn, J. (1993) *Young Children's Close Relationships*. London: Sage.

Eldering, L. and Leseman, P. (1999) *Effective Early Education*. London: Falmer Press.

European Commission Childcare Network (1994) *Quality in Services for Young Children: A Discussion Paper*, DGV/B/4. Brussels: European Commission.

European Commission Childcare Network (1996) *Quality Targets in Services for Young Children*, DGV/B/4. Brussels: European Commission.

Evans, D. and Zarate, O. (1999) *Introducing Evolutionary Psychology*. Cambridge: Icon.

Fassin, D. (2004) Public health as culture: the social construction of the childhood lead poisoning epidemic in France, *British Medical Journal*, in press.

Faulkner, W. (1964) *Short Stories*. London: Penguin.

Faulkner, W. (1965) *Uncle Willy and Other Stories*. London: Penguin.

Ferguson, S. and Fitzgerald, H. (1954) *History of the Second World War: Studies in Social Services*. London: HMSO.

Fitz-Gibbon, C. (1996) *Monitoring Education: Indicators, Quality and Effectiveness*. London: Cassell.

Gardner, D. (1956) *The Education of Young Children*. London: Methuen.

Gardner, H. (1983) *Frames of Mind: The Theory of Multiple Intelligences*. New York: Basic Books.

Gardner, H. (1993) *The Unschooled Mind*. London: Fontana.

Gathorne-Hardy, J. (1972) *The Rise and Fall of the British Nanny*. London: Hodder and Stoughton.

Geertz, C. (1973) *The Interpretation of Cultures*. London: Fontana.

George, S. and Sabelli, F. (1994) *Faith and Credit: The World Bank's Secular Empire*. London: Penguin.

Giddens, A. (1991) *Modernity and Self-identity: Self and Society in the Late Modern Age*. Cambridge: Polity Press.

Goldschmied, E. and Jackson, S. (1996) *People Under Three*. London: Routledge.

Goleman, D. (1996) *Emotional Intelligence: Why It Can Matter More than IQ*. London: Bloomsbury.

Gopnick, A., Meltzoff, A. and Kuhl, P. (1999) *How Babies Think: The Science of Childhood*. London: Weidenfeld and Nicolson.

Gould, S.J. (2000) *The Lying Stones of Marrakech*. London: Jonathan Cape.

Greenman, J. and Stonehouse, A. (1997) *Prime Times: A Handbook for Excellence in Infant and Toddler Programs*. Sydney: Longman.

Grieg, A. and Taylor, J. (1999) *Doing Research with Children*. London: Sage.

Hall, D. and Elliman, D. (2003) *Health for All Children*, 4th edition. Oxford: Oxford University Press.

Hardyment, C. (1984) *Dream Babies*. Oxford: Oxford University Press.

Hart, R. (1997) *Children's Participation: The Theory and Practice of Involving Young Children in Community Development and Environmental Care*. London: Earthscan/UNICEF.

Heath, S.B. (1983) *Ways with Words: Language, Life and Work in Communities and Classrooms*. Cambridge, MA: Harvard University Press.

Heussler, H., Polnay, L. and Katz, M. (2000) The times are they a'changing? *Children and Society*, 14: 254–66.

Highfield Junior School, Plymouth (1997) *Changing Our School: Promoting Positive Behavior*. London: Institute of Education.

HMSO (1967) *Children and Their Primary Schools: A Report of the Central Advisory Council for Education (England)* (Plowden Report). London: HMSO.

Hobsbawm, E. (1997) *On History*. London: Weidenfeld and Nicolson.

Hood, S. (2001) *The State of London's Children*. London: Office of the Children's Rights Commissioner for London.

Horrobin, D. (2003) *Not in the Genes*. Available at www.guardian.co.uk.

Huxley, A. (2000) *Brave New World*. London: Penguin.

Isaacs, S. (1929) *The Nursery Years: The Mind of the Child from Birth to Six Years*. London: Routledge.

Isaacs, S. (1930) *Intellectual Growth in Young Children*. London: Routledge.

Jahoda, G. and Lewis, I. (1987) *Acquiring Culture: Cross-cultural Studies in Child Development*. London: Academic Press.

James, A., Jenks, C. and Prout, A. (1998) *Theorizing Childhood*. Cambridge: Polity Press.

Jardine, L. (1999) *Ingenious Pursuits*. London: Little, Brown.

Jones, L. (2000) What is health?, in J. Katz, A. Peberdy and J. Douglas (eds) *Promoting Health, Knowledge and Practice*. Hampshire: Palgrave, pp. 18–36.

Jones, S. (1999) *Almost Like a Whale: The Origin of Species Updated*. London: Doubleday.

Kagan, J. (1984) *The Nature of the Child*. New York: Basic Books.

Kagan, J. (1998) *Three Seductive Ideas*. Cambridge, MA: Harvard University Press.

Kaldor, M. (1999) *New and Old Wars: Organized Violence in a Global Era*. Cambridge: Polity Press.

Kapuscinski, R. (2001) *The Shadow of the Sun: My African Life*. London: Allen Lane.

Kenway, J. and Bullen, E. (2001) *Consuming Children*. Buckingham: Open University Press.

Kessen, W. (1965) *The Child*. New York: John Wiley.

Kline, S. (1993) *Out of the Garden: Toys, TV and Children's Culture in the Age of Marketing*. London: Verso.

Kotulak, R. (1996) *Inside the Brain: Revolutionary Discoveries of How the Mind Works*. Kansas City: Andrews McMeel.

Lamming, G. (1979) *In the Castle of My Skin*. London: Longman.

Lattimore, O. (1962) *Nomads and Commissars: Mongolia Revisted*. Oxford: Oxford University Press.

Lave, J. and Wenger, E. (1992) *Situated Learning: Legitimate Peripheral Participation*. Cambridge: Cambridge University Press.

Laye, C. (1959) *The African Child: Memories of a West African Childhood*. London: Fontana.

LeDoux, J. (1998)*The Emotional Brain*. London: Weidenfeld and Nicolson.

Levine, R., Dixon, S., Levine, S., Richman, A., Leiderman, P., Keefer, C. and Brazleton, T. (1994) *Childcare and Culture: Lessons from Africa*. Cambridge: Cambridge University Press.

MacCulloch, D. (1999) *Tudor Church Militant: Edward VI and the Protestant Reformation*. London: Allen Lane.

Machel, G. (2001) *The Impact of War on Children*. London: Hurst.

MacKinnon, D. (2003) Children and work, in J. Maybin and M. Woodhead (eds) *Childhoods in Context*. Chichester: John Wiley, pp. 173–218.

Malinowski, B. (1967) *A Diary in the Strict Sense of the Term*. New York: Harcourt Brace and World Inc.

Marshall, R. (1940) *Arctic Village*. London: Penguin.

Mayall, B. (2001) Children's health in schools, in P. Foley, J. Roche and S. Tucker (eds) *Children in Society: Contemporary Theory, Policy and Practice*. Hampshire: Open University/Palgrave.

Mayall, B. (2002) *Towards a Sociology of Childhood: Thinking from Children's Lives*. Buckingham: Open University Press.

Mayall, B., Turner, H., Wiggins, M., Hood, S. and Dickinson, R. (2003) *Evaluation of the National Theatre Education Department's Drama Work in Primary Schools. Interim Report.* London: Social Science Research Unit, Institute of Education.

Mead, M. (1975) *Growing Up in New Guinea.* London: Pelican.

Meade, A. (2001) One hundred billion neurons: How do they become organized? in T. David (ed.) *Promoting Evidence Based Practice in Early Childhood Education: Research and its Implications.* London: JAI, pp. 3–26.

Mental Health Foundation (1999) *Bright Futures.* London: Mental Health Foundation.

Midgley, M. (1998) One world but a big one, in S. Rose (ed.) *From Brains to Consciousness? Essays on the New Sciences of Mind.* London: Penguin, pp. 246–70.

Miller, J. (1996) *Never Too Young: How Children Can Take Responsibility and Make Decisions. A Handbook for Early Years Workers.* London: NEYN/SCF.

Miller, J. (1999) *Young Children as Decision Makers: On Raising Children's Rights in England.* London: SCF.

MONEE (2001) *Ten Years of Transition.* Project MONEE, CEE/CIS/Baltic Republics. Regional Monitoring Report no 8. Florence: UNICEF.

Montagu, A. (1978) *Learning Non-aggression.* Oxford: Oxford University Press.

Moore, R. (1986) *Childhood Domains.* Berkeley, CA: MIG Communications.

Muir, J. (1913) *The Wilderness Journeys.* Edinburgh: Canongate. First published in 1913 as *Story of My Boyhood and Youth.*

Murray, L. and Andrews, L. (2000) *The Social Baby: Understanding Babies' Communication from Birth.* Richmond: Children's Project Publishing.

Mustard, J. Frazer (1999) *The Early Years Study.* Early Years Task Force, Government of Ontario, Canada.

Myers, R. (2000) *Thematic Studies: Early Childhood Care and Development.* World Education Forum Education for All Assessment. Paris: UNESCO.

Nabokov, V. (1967) *Speak Memory: An Autobiography Revisted.* London: Weidenfeld and Nicolson.

Newson, C. (1995) The patio projects, *Co-ordinate,* 10–11 January.

NSA (1927) *Nursery School Education. Statement of Policy.* London.

NSDN (1923) *Address to the First International Conference on Day Nurseries,* PLPES, BAECE archives.

Oakley, A. (2000) *Experiments in Knowing: Gender and Method in the Social Sciences.* Cambridge: Polity Press.

Ochs, E. and Schieffelin, B. (1984) Language acquisition and socialization, in R. Shweder and R. LeVine (eds) *Culture Theory: Essays on Mind, Self and Emotion.* Cambridge: Cambridge University Press.

O'Connor, F. (1963) *My Oedipus Complex and Other Stories.* London: Penguin.

OECD (1999) *Norway: Early Childhood Education and Care.* Country Note, 1 June. Paris: OECD. www.oecd.org

OECD (2000) *United States: Early Childhood Education and Care.* Country Note, 1 July. Paris: OECD. www.oecd.org

OECD (2001) *Starting Strong: Early Childhood Education and Care*. Paris: OECD.

Opie, P. and Opie, I. (1959) *The Lore and Language of Schoolchildren*. Oxford: Oxford University Press.

Orme, N. (2001) *Medieval Children*. New Haven, CT: Yale University Press.

Peacock, J. (1986) *The Anthropological Lens: Harsh Light, Soft Focus*. Cambridge: Cambridge University Press.

Penn, H. (1997) *Comparing Nurseries: Staff and Children in Italy, Spain and the UK*. London: Paul Chapman.

Penn, H. (1999) Children in the majority world: Is Outer Mongolia really so far away?, in S. Hood, B. Mayall and S. Oliver (eds) *Critical Issues in Social Research*. Buckingham: Open University Press, pp. 25–39.

Penn, H. (2000a) Is working with young children a good job?, in H. Penn (ed.) *Early Childhood Services: Theory, Policy and Practice*. Buckingham: Open University Press, pp. 115–130.

Penn, H. (2000b) Policy and practice in childcare and nursery education, *Journal of Social Policy*, 29(1): 37–54.

Penn, H. (2001) Culture and childhood in pastoralist communities: the example of Outer Mongolia, in L. Alanen and B. Mayall (eds) *Conceptualizing Adult–Child Relationships*. London: Falmer Press, pp. 86–98.

Penn, H. (2002a) The World Bank's view of early childhood, *Childhood*, 9(1).

Penn, H. (2002b) Maintains a good pace to lessons: inconsistencies and contextual factors affecting OFSTED inspections of nursery schools, *British Educational Research Journal*, 28(6): 879–88.

Penn, H. (2004a) *Report on Early Education in Kazakhstan*, in Education Sector Review of Kazakhstan. Manila: Asian Development Bank.

Penn, H. (2004b) Round and round the mulberry bush: private and public in the history of early education and care, in R. Aldrich (ed.) *Private and Public: Studies in the History of Knowledge and Education*. London: Woburn Press.

Penn, H. (2004c) *Unequal Childhoods*. London: Routledge.

Penn, H. with Demberel (2004) Nomadic education in Mongolia, in C. Dyer and S. Kratli (eds) *The Education of Nomadic Peoples: Issues, Provision and Prospects*. London: Berghahn Books.

Penn, H. *et al.* (2004) *What is the Impact of Out-of-home Integrated Care and Education Settings on Children aged 0–6 and their Parents?* EPPI-Centre Early Years Review Group. www.eppi.ioe.ac.uk

Piaget, J. and Inhelder, B. (1969) *The Psychology of the Child*. New York: Basic Books.

Pinker, S. (1995)*The Language Instinct*. London: Penguin.

Pinker, S. (1998) *How the Mind Works*. London: Penguin.

Plowden, B. (1977) Opening address. Children and parents: self-help and the voluntary role, in *0–5: A Changing Population. Implications for Parents, the Public and Policy Makers*. London: Voluntary Organizations Liaison Committee.

Pollock, L. (1987) *Parents and Children over Three Centuries*. London: Fourth Estate.

Porter, T. (1995) *Trust in Numbers: The Pursuit of Objectivity in Science and Public Life.* New Jersey: Princeton University Press.

Pridmore, P. and Bendelow, G. (1995) Images of health, explaining beliefs of children using the 'draw and write' technique, *Health Education Journal,* 54(4): 473–88.

Punch, S. (2001) Negotiating autonomy: childhoods in rural Bolivia, in L. Alanen and B. Mayall (eds) *Conceptualizing Adult–Child Relationships.* London: Routledge, pp. 23–36.

Rahnema, M. (ed.) with Bawtree, V. (1997) *The Post-development Reader.* London: Zed Books.

Ramey, C. and Campbell, F. (1991) Poverty, early childhood education, and academic competence: the abecedarian experiment, in A. Huston (ed.) *Children in Poverty: Child Development and Public Policy.* Cambridge: Cambridge University Press, pp. 190–221.

Rawls, J. (1999) *A Theory of Justice,* 2nd edition. Oxford: Oxford University Press.

Richards, M. (1998) The meeting of nature and nurture and the development of children; some conclusions, in C. Pantner-Brick (ed.) *Biosocial Perspectives on Children.* Cambridge: Cambridge University Press, pp. 131–58.

Ridley, M. (1999) *Genome.* London: Fourth Estate.

Riley, D. (1983) *War in the Nursery.* London: Virago.

Rogoff, B. (1990) *Apprenticeship in Thinking: Cognitive Development in a Social Context.* Oxford: Oxford University Press.

Rorty, R. (1989) *Contingency, Irony and Solidarity.* Cambridge: Cambridge University Press.

Rosaldo, R. (1993) *Culture and Truth: The Remaking of Social Analysis.* London: Routledge.

Rose, N. (1989) *Governing the Soul.* London: Routledge.

Rose, S. (ed.) (1999) *From Brains to Conciousness? Essays on the New Sciences of the Mind.* London: Penguin.

Rose, H. and Rose, S. (eds) (2000) *Alas Poor Darwin.* London: Jonathan Cape.

Rose, S. (2003) *The Making of Memory: From Molecules to Mind.* London: Vintage.

Rosemberg, F. (2000) *The Doctrine of National Security and the Brazilian Early Childhood Care and Education Programme.* Paper given at the EECERA conference, Institute of Education, London, August 2000.

Rosetti-Ferreira, M., Ramon, F. and Barriero, A. (2000) *Improving Early Child Care and Education in Developing Countries.* State of the Art lecture given at the International Congress of Psychology, Stockholm, Sweden.

Rossie, J. (1999) *Toys, Culture and Society.* Halmstad: Nordic Centre for Research on Toys and Educational Media.

Russell, B. (1926) *On Education, Especially in Early Childhood.* London: Allen and Unwin.

Said, E. (1999) *Out of Place.* London: Granta.

Scarr, S. (1992) Developmental theories for the 1990s: development and individual differences, *Child Development*, 63: 1–19.

Scarr, S. (1993) Biological and cultural diversity: the legacy of Darwin for development, *Child Development*, 64: 1333–53.

Scheper Hughes, N. (1993) *Death Without Weeping*. Los Angeles: University of California Press.

Scheper Hughes, N. (ed.) (1998) *Small Wars*. Los Angeles: University of California Press.

Schuman, J. (1998) Childhood, infant and perinatal mortality in 1996: social and biological factors in the deaths of children aged under three, *Population Trends*, 92: 5–14.

Seedhouse, D. (1986) *Health, The Foundation for Achievement*. Chichester: John Wiley.

Seiter, E. (1995) *Sold Separately: Children and Parents in Consumer Culture*. New Jersey: Rutgers University Press, pp. 11–12.

Serdula, M.K., Ivery, D., Coates, R.J., Freedman, D.S., Williamson, D.F., and Byers, T. (1993) Child obesity, *Preventative Medicine*, 22(2): 167–77.

Serpell, R. (1993) *The Significance of Schooling: Life Journeys in an African Society*. Cambridge: Cambridge University Press.

Sharman, C., Cross, W. and Vennis, D. (1995) *Observing Children: A Practical Guide, Case Studies*. London: Cassell.

Singer, I.B. (1977) *A Crown of Feathers and Other Stories*. London: Penguin.

Skinner, B. (1974) *About Behaviourism*. London: Jonathan Cape.

Steedman, C. (1982) *The Tidy House*. London: Virago.

Steedman,C. (1988) Mother made conscious: the historical development of a primary school pedagogy, in M. Woodhead and A. McGrath (eds) *Family, School and Society*. London: Hodder and Stoughton, pp. 83–95.

Steedman, C. (1990) *Childhood, Culture and Class in Britain: Margaret McMillan 1860–1931*. London: Virago.

Stephens, S. (1995) *Children and the Politics of Culture*. New Jersey: Princeton University Press.

Stiglitz, J. (2002) *Globalization and its Discontents*. London: Penguin.

Street, B. (1999) Meanings of culture in development; a case study from literacy, in F. Leach and A. Little (eds) *Education, Cultures and Economics: Dilemmas for Development*. Brighton: Falmer Press.

Sutton Smith, B. (1970) Psychology of childlore: the triviality barrier, *Western Folklore*, 29: 1–8.

Sutton Smith, B. (1986) *Toys as Culture*. New York: Gardner Press.

Sutton Smith, B. (1999) The rhetorics of adult and child play theories, in S. Reifel (ed.) *Advances in Early Education and Day Care*. London: JAI Press, pp. 149–62.

Thompson, F. (1939) *Lark Rise*. Oxford: Oxford University Press.

Titmuss, R. (1943) *Birth, Poverty and Wealth: A Study of Infant Mortality*. London: Hamish Hamilton.

Tobin, J. (1995) Post-structural research in early childhood education, in J. Hatch, (ed.) *Qualitative Research in Early Childhood Settings*. Connecticut: Praeger, pp. 223–43.

Tobin, J., Wu, D. and Davidson, D. (1989) *Preschool in Three Cultures: Japan, China and the United States*. New Haven, CT: Yale University Press.

Tucker, N. (1977) *Childhood*. London: Fontana.

Tudor Hart, B. (1938) *Toys in the Nursery*. London: Country Life.

Tudor-Hart, J. (1971) The Inverse Care Law, *Lancet*, 27 February: 405–12.

Tunstill, J., Allnock, D., Meadows, P. and McLeod, A. (2002) *Early Experiences of Implementing Sure Start – Report and Executive Summary*. London: DfES.

UNICEF (2001) *The State of the World's Children*. New York: UNICEF.

van Eyken, W. (ed.) (1973) *Education, the Child and Society: A Documentary History 1900–1973*. London: Penguin.

Vygotsky, L. (1978) *Mind in Society*. Cambridge, MA: Harvard University Press.

Wadsworth, M. and Kuh, D. (1997) Childhood influences on adult health, *Epidemiology*, 11(1): 2–20.

Watson, J. (1928) *The Psychological Care of Infant and Child*. London: Allen and Unwin.

Weikart, T. (1996) High quality preschool programs found to improve adult status, in *Childhood*, 3(1): 117–20.

Wilson, E.O. (1998) *Consilience: The Unity of Knowledge*. London: Little, Brown.

Wolf, E. (1990) *Europe and the People Without History*. London: University of California Press.

World Health Organization (1995) *Global School Health Initiative*. Available at www.who.org

World Health Organization (1997) *Promoting Health through Schools*. Report of a WHO Expert Committee on Comprehensive School Health Education and Promotion. Geneva: World Health Organization.

Young, M.E. (1998) Policy implications of early childhood development programmes, in *Nutrition, Health and Child Development*. Washington: Pan American Health Organization/World Bank, pp. 209–24.

Yudkin, S. (1967) *A Report on the Care of Pre-school Children*. London: NSCN.

Yudkin, S. and Holme, A. (1963) *Working Mothers and Their Children*. London: Michael Joseph.

Zelitzer, V. (1985) *Pricing the Priceless Child*. New York: Basic Books.

Zuckerman, M. (1993) History and developmental psychology: a dangerous liaison, in G. Elder, J. Modell and R. Parke (eds) *Children in Time and Space: Developmental and Historical Insights*. Cambridge: Cambridge University Press, pp. 230–5.

Index

Related books from Open University Press
Purchase from www.openup.co.uk or order through your local bookseller

OBSERVING HARRY
CHILD DEVELOPMENT AND LEARNING 2–5
Cath Arnold

This book is about Harry, a determined little boy, who is intrinsically motivated to explore his world from an early age. His parents and grandparents find him so fascinating that they keep a written and video diary of Harry's play from when he is 8 months to five years. The author offers theories about how children learn and applies the theories to the observations of Harry.

The book demonstrates how effectively Harry accesses each area of the curriculum through his interests. It shows how Harry develops coping strategies when the family experiences major changes. It also highlights the contribution made by Harry's parents and his early years educators to his early education. Much of what we learn about Harry's early learning can be applied to many other young children.

This book about one child's early development and learning will be of interest to all who are fascinated by how young children learn – nursery practitioners, early years teachers, parents, students and advisers.

Contents
Introduction – Background about the book and using observation to assess children's development and learning – Getting to know Harry and his family – Using theory to understand Harry's development and learning – Harry's physical development – Harry's personal, social and emotional development – Harry learns to communicate, to use language and to become literate – Harry's mathematical development – Harry's creative development – Harry gains knowledge and understanding of the world – Harry's story – reflections and making connections – References – Index.

160pp   0 335 21301 4 (Paperback)   0 335 21302 2 (Hardback)

AN INTRODUCTION TO CHILDHOOD STUDIES

Mary Jane Kehily (ed)

- What is childhood and how can it be understood and studied?
- How do our views of childhood shape the ways in which children are treated?

Educationalists and social scientists are increasingly interested in childhood as a distinct social category, and Childhood Studies is now a recognised area of research and analysis. This book brings together the key themes of Childhood Studies in a broad and accessible introduction for students and practitioners working in this field. Contributors examine childhood from historical, socio-cultural and policy perspectives. Each chapter is written by an expert who looks at a different aspect of childhood. The final chapter pulls together the ideas and themes and considers the future of childhood as a subject of study and a social category.

This key textbook is designed for students of Childhood Studies, as well as child psychology, children's literature, the sociology of youth and childhood, cultural studies, social policy and anthropology.

Contents
Section 1: Historical Approaches – The historical construction of childhood – Children's Literature: an historical approach – Innocence and experience: an historical approach to childhood and sexuality – Section Two: Socio-Cultural Approaches – The Sociology of Childhood – Developmental psychology and the construction of the child – New media, new childhoods? – Section Three: Policy Perspectives – Promoting better childhoods – Children's Rights: international policy and lived practice – Law and Children/Law and Childhood – Conclusion: The Future of Childhood?

Contributors
David Buckingham, Rachel Burr, Diana Gittins, Peter Hunt, Chris Jenks, Mary Jane Kehily, Daniel Monk, Heather Montgomery, Wendy Stainton Rogers, Valerie Walkerdine

208pp   0 335 21267 0 (Paperback)   0 335 21268 9 (Hardback)

DOING EARLY CHILDHOOD RESEARCH
THEORY AND PRACTICE
Glenda Mac Naughton, Sharne Rolfe and
Iram Siraj-Blatchford (eds)

There are a growing number of courses on early childhood education at university level. This has placed new demands on both students and staff as research is a key feature of many of these courses. Research training is an important element in both undergraduate and postgraduate degrees in early childhood education and there is a genuine need for an accessible textbook that addresses the particular research issues which are a feature of this important field.

Doing Early Childhood Research introduces the most common qualitative and quantitative methods in the early childhood context. The contributors cover a wide range of conventional and newer approaches including observation, surveys, action research, ethnography, policy analysis and poststructuralist approaches. The reader is shown step by step how to select a topic, review the literature, design their research project, analyse data and produce a report.

Throughout, the emphasis is on practical application of the methods and the text is illustrated by a wide range of examples and case studies. Each chapter includes checklists, explanations of key concepts, annotated further reading and questions for reflection.

Written by leading international early childhood researchers, this book is a standard introduction to research in the early childhood field.

Contents
Introduction – Glossary – Part 1: The nature of research – Research as a tool – The research process – Research paradigms, perspectives and methods – Doing research for the first time – Ethics in early childhood research – Part 2: Analysis and design – Design issues – Quantitative designs and statistical analysis – Qualitative designs and analysis – Equity issues in research design – Part 3: The research process in action – Surveys and questionnaires – Interviewing children – Interviewing adults – An ethnographic approach to researching young children's learning – Action research – Direct observation – Policy research – Case study – Appendices – Index.

320pp 0 335 20902 5 (Paperback)

SHAPING EARLY CHILDHOOD
LEARNERS, CURRICULUM AND CONTEXTS
Glenda Mac Naughton

This key textbook introduces students and practitioners to a wide range of different approaches to early childhood. It provides practical strategies for developing and implementing early learning experiences that promote excellence and equity for children. By examining different perspectives, the book helps early childhood practitioners to navigate their way through competing views, make informed choices, and be critically reflective in their work. In an accessible, lively and user-friendly way, it explores issues such as:

- What constitutes an appropriate early childhood curriculum
- How best to study and assess children
- Involving parents and children in early childhood learning

The book features a range of pedagogical devices to inspire early childhood workers to reflect critically on their work and the ideas underpinning it, including boxed definitions of key terms; ideas summary charts and ideas galleries; clarification exercises; case studies; further reading lists.

This essential textbook is ideal for students undertaking early childhood qualifications at degree level, Masters courses in early childhood education, and for practitioners who work with children from birth to eight in early childhood settings.

Contents
Foreword – Acknowledgements – Introduction – Part 1: Models of the learner – Reflecting on the learner – Models of the learner: Conforming to nature, conforming to culture – Models of the learner: reforming through interaction between nature and culture – Models of the learner: Transforming culture and nature – Models of the learner: Critical reflections – Part 2: Positions on the early childhood curriculum – Reflecting on the early childhood curriculum – Curriculum position: conforming to society – Curriculum position: reforming society – Curriculum position: transforming society – Curriculum positions: critical reflections – Part 3: Curriculum contexts – Reflecting on contexts – Curriculum contexts: parents and communities – Curriculum contexts: becoming an early childhood professional – Curriculum contexts: critical reflections – References – Index.

368pp 0 335 21106 2 (Paperback)